The Sun Neither Rises nor Sets

KIM LM LONGSTREET

One Printers Way
Altona, MB R0G 0B0
Canada

www.friesenpress.com

Copyright © 2023 by Kim LM Longstreet
First Edition — 2023

All rights reserved. No part of this book may be reproduced in any form on by an electronic or mechanical means, including information storage and retrieval systems, without permission in writing from FriesenPress, except by a reviewer who may quote brief passages in a review.

The events and conversations in this book have been set down to the best of the author's ability, although names and details have been omitted to protect the privacy of individuals.

Front and Back cover designs by Richard Longstreet

ISBN
978-1-03-917044-5 (Hardcover)
978-1-03-917043-8 (Paperback)
978-1-03-917045-2 (eBook)

1. POETRY, EPIC

Distributed to the trade by The Ingram Book Company

Table of Contents

Prologue — vii

Chapter One — I Am an Imperfect Being — 1

Chapter Two — On the Road to Finding My Soul — 5

Chapter Three — There is Rhyme and There is Reason — 24

Chapter Four — God. Creator. Universe. Higher Power. — 30

Chapter Five — You Have a Soul — 47

Chapter Six — Pure Intentions — 57

Chapter Seven — Happenstance — 101

Chapter Eight — To Believe or Not to Believe — 105

Chapter Nine — There Is Only Now — 109

Chapter Ten — Turned Inside Out We Are All the Same — 113

Chapter Eleven — Ask and Ye Shall Receive — 117

Chapter Twelve — You Call It Christianity; I Call It Spirituality — 122

Chapter Thirteen — Infractions, I Got 'em — 129

Chapter Fourteen — Bestselling Book of All Time — 135

Chapter Fifteen — Bricks, Mortar, Soul, Cornerstone — 142

Chapter Sixteen — Bound to a Higher Power — 146

Chapter Seventeen — Yeshua — 160

Chapter Eighteen — Fire & Brimstone — 169

Chapter Nineteen — Salvaging Your Soul — 174

Chapter Twenty — What Goes around Comes Around	177
Chapter Twenty-One — Spiritual Apprehension	183
Chapter Twenty-Two — Driven by Desire	187
Chapter Twenty-Three — Irresistible Power	192
Chapter Twenty-Four — Second Glances	198
Chapter Twenty-Five — Values Are Cliché	201
Chapter Twenty-Six — Teach, Don't Preach	206
Chapter Twenty-Seven — Natural Selection	212
Chapter Twenty-Eight — You Are Not a Superior Being	215
Chapter Twenty-Nine — You Are Never Alone	221
Chapter Thirty — Choose Compassion over Cynicism	225
Chapter Thirty-One — Relationship Musings	233
Chapter Thirty-Two — Lived Happily Ever After	241
Chapter Thirty-Three — It Is All About Me	252
Chapter Thirty-Four — Difficult to Move	255
Chapter Thirty-Five — Pay It No Mind	258
Chapter Thirty-Six — Freedom from Disturbance	271
Chapter Thirty-Seven — Do Not Take My Word for It	274
Epilogue	282
About the Author	284

Prologue

The sun is centred in the solar system; therefore, it neither rises nor sets. The observation of rising and setting of the sun is due to the rotation of the earth. The earth rotates once every 23 hours, 56 minutes, and 4.09053 seconds at a speed of 1,000 miles per hour. Gravity is the force by which a planet or other body draws objects toward its centre. The force of gravity keeps all planets in orbit around the sun.

Pause here and give that paragraph a moment of thought. Why *do* we say sunrise and sunset instead of earthrise and earthset? If your brain slipped while you were answering that question, you are now thinking about life in another way, and this book is meant for you at this time in your life.

Everything you know right now is because it was taught to you by a person, a book, or media. How often have you taken that information and questioned it for yourself? In my opinion, our greatest weakness as humans is that we are constantly seeking affirmation from others. The downfall to doing that is that we are seeking it from people who are just as broken as we are. They can only give to you what they know until they permit themselves to know more. Therein lies the challenge of life for all of us: the necessity for self-driven capacity building to change our own minds for the betterment of all beings.

There are eight billion beings on this planet hovering in our universe called the Milky Way. The number of other universes out there is humungous, and we know extraordinarily little about them. It can boggle the mind when we conjure up the existence of our tiny speck of earth in the vastness of all the universes.

It quickly puts things into perspective about how much space you use and how you should protect that space every day. This can be hard to achieve when your thoughts and other's thoughts mesh together in your head. Your inner whisper, which I call your soul, gets muffled, and a feeling of discontent grows within you day by day. Not understanding why there is discontent will inevitably lead to finding fault in yourself and others while you struggle to connect the dots.

Each of us is energy and destined to return to the source of our energy. In the meantime, while we are residing on earth, our main challenge needs to be finding our souls, in which unfathomable energy is stored. When you are combative against yourself about seeking your soul, you bring negative energy to your space on earth. When you pool yours and everyone else's negative energy, you get an earth that you are seeing today. We've made our earth this way. Imagine what the possibilities could be if we turned our attention toward finding our souls and using their energy for goodness.

The sun rises. The sun sets. No, it does not. The earth rises and the earth sets. If the magnitude of that lifelong learned falsehood does not force you to reconsider everything you know, I am not sure what will. It is no coincidence that this book *has* chosen you at this exact moment in your life. I truly hope it gives you the aha moments that have been freely given to me over the years simply because I have chosen to believe in something bigger than myself.

On my thirty-sixth birthday I was compelled, by a force that still holds me in awe, to put pen to paper and write the rhymes for this book. It took a year to finish. I knew my soul had shared something profound and that when the time was right it would be shared with other souls. For eighteen years the rhymes sat idle in my bedroom closet until my soul whispered that it was time to publish the book.

I never questioned why I was chosen to share these words in the way that they are written. My higher power told me when I was six years old to trust, and that by doing so an understanding would be shared with me one day. So I trusted. Then I wrote. And now I share.

Find your soul. Listen to what it wants. Let go of what you cannot control. Trust the process.

Chapter One — I Am an Imperfect Being

By the age of six I was afraid to do any wrong. I was a good child, but I didn't know how I belonged.

The foster home I was in was full of abuse, and to them I could do no right and was of no good use.

I felt like a slave with no hope for freedom, and I was worked every day with only more abuses to come.

It was never good enough, even my best, and at six years old, perfection came to be my conquest.

In this home is where God's presence came to me; it was at a church tucked away in some trees.

I was all by myself outside when it occurred, and there was no visual, only a voice that I heard.

A warmth came over me that I knew not to fear, and intuitively I knew it was God that had appeared.

The feeling was a warmth that held my body, and six years of pain lifted, and I no longer felt naughty.

A voice soothed away all my doubt, and I was told to have faith and I would learn what it was about.

In that moment God gave me a strength that I cherish, and I knew that without Him I would perish.

That time with God did not stop the mayhem I saw, but it did instill in me that I must follow His law.

I continued to suffer abuse from others, but deep inside I knew there was a point for all the bother.

My suffering was a way to experience life and it was important to God that I knew what is all our strife.

This gave me compassion for what others survived and an understanding of what we are all deprived.

When I was less than two, my mother left my life forever and I was discarded by an unfit father.

She had her reasons for removing herself from the mix, and she died in a plane crash when I was six.

I wish I could remember the woman who gave me birth, who was taken too soon from this earth.

My childhood was spent in foster homes, and never in all my life since have I ever felt that alone.

I suffered abuses that a child should not know, and I coped with the pain as I continued to grow.

The memories I recall from when I was a child still hold me in awe that I was able to remain so mild.

A childhood like mine is how cycles continue, and my brother is a testament to what abuse can do.

He chose the addictions to help ease away his pain, and he abused others to avoid being hurt again.

We experienced much of the same abuses in life, but I accepted mine, and his have given him rife.

It was from that church that I received my first Bible, and I have it to this day as a reminder of my survival.

Oddly enough, I received it a month after my mother died, and years later I learned that, and then I cried.

It gives me great comfort to hold the Bible in my hands and think back to the day that my life truly began.

I like to fan the pages and smell the aroma of God; His scent is unique and its nowhere else I have trod.

Before I was nine my father married two more women, but neither worked out and divorce was their end.

He is married now to wife number four, and we do not talk, as we have chosen different paths to walk.

My teenage years were when I tried to break free, keeping in mind that I must never lose me.

A boy broke my heart so bad I tried to end it all and didn't care anymore that I had yet to hear my call.

I can imagine God's hurt when I knocked on His door, but it didn't open, and I returned to learn more.

After that I was date raped by a so-called friend, and becoming a mom brought my teens to an end.

I had zero role models of good parenting; how could I give to this baby what was not given to me?

Early on I decided to raise him as I had not been, and I would be the best mom that he had ever seen.

It was terrifying being pregnant when I wasn't an adult, with no understanding of what love was about.

In my life I have lost two wonderful men; one I did not marry and the other was my only husband.

They gave me a love that I did not feel worthy of, and in my own way for them I still carry love.

My only marriage failed, lasting only a year; why was it that I could not keep anyone I loved near?

My longest love relationship was years of dysfunction and ended harshly from lack of communication.

I am now thirty-six and my son is seventeen, and the time is right to share what God has taught to me.

In my brief synopsis of my life to this point you may wonder, as I did, how God could disappoint.

No mother, no father, no relationship that worked, it is no wonder that you think I should have a quirk.

You may feel differently reading what I have to say; for unknown reasons, things go a certain way.

I am on my own and have been for many years, using the time wisely to learn, laugh, and shed tears.

I have been able to reflect on the life that God gave me, and I have written about all that I have seen.

From the time I was six I knew I had things to say, and I knew that in time I would be given that day.

God gave me a purpose for His own reasons, knowing that understanding would take many seasons.

I didn't question His intent, for He had made it clear, and I did as He asked to keep Him near.

Because of my faith God has shared His insight, and surviving was to ensure I would get it right.

Chapter Two – On the Road to Finding My Soul

My life changed on December 2, 1987, when into my life came a gift sent from heaven. Nineteen was too young to have a baby, I am sure, but who knew that my only son would help me to find a cure? His conception was not done in the right way, for karma is swift to dole out what you do and what you say. I have never believed my son to be an unwanted mistake, as he came to show me what in life is all fake.

It is almost eighteen years later, and I have something to say about the young man I have raised to cherish each day. His story begins long before the day he was born, for he was born to a mom whose soul was tattered and torn. My childhood was the exact opposite of his, and what he was able to have is all that I missed. It could have been so easy to repeat the cycle and deny my son the life to which I knew he was entitled.

What I chose to do instead was break away from the norm and try my best to let him never regret that he was born. I did not want him to suffer the atrocities done unto me, and it became my goal to never cause him any suffering. My son is a true testament that a person can change to raise a child and bring him of age. When I think back over my life and where it went, I marvel at the son that from heaven God sent. It has become clear why my son came my way, and I cherish the fact that God gave him to me that day.

His conception, a miracle, had to be fate, even though he was produced by an unwanted rape. My son's father is a man who I thought was my friend, but he showed his true colours and brought our friendship to an end. All these years later I do not hold a grudge for what he did, because even without him I raised a wonderful kid. My son has never known his father and that does make me sad, but it takes more than sperm to give you the title of Dad. Not having his father in my son's life is a regret, but I have given him instead a mom on whom he can depend.

Let us go back in time so that you can see what I mean when I say that my son was a gift sent to me. My childhood was one that leaves a lot to be desired, and I view it now simply as a tool to help others feel inspired. I was a New Year's baby, born first in a small town to two people whose own lives were not very sound. They already had a son before they decided to have me, and our family went to four where there had only been three.

Times must have been bad, but I do not remember the strife, for I was only with my family for one and half years of my life. My mother left my father before I was two. She was beaten down, sad, and did not know what else to do. Her leaving was the beginning of more turmoil to come, and I am sure it was extremely hard for her to leave her daughter and son.

As a mom I can imagine what must have been her pain to leave behind her children that she may never see again. She must have been really mixed up to do this thing, walking away from the children that into this world she did bring. I sit today and try to imagine how she must have felt that day when she removed herself from my life with nothing else to say.

Less than two years old and I did not know a thing about what her decision into my life would bring. I was faced with this same decision when I had my son. Do I try to be a mom to him even though I am so young? I had my son one month before my twentieth birthday, and my choices were to keep him or send him away. To be honest, others felt I should give him up and allow him a life where he would be given so much.

My decision was always easy when I thought about my life, and there was no way that I would let my son have that unwanted strife. When I made the decision to keep him as my own, I knew that he would have the life that I had not known.

So off went my mother without a backwards glance, leaving us with a father who did not give us a chance. My brother and I were in too many foster homes to count. Some were good homes, and some left me with doubts.

Upheaval after upheaval and no place to call home — that is the only childhood I have even known.

My abuse started young and was of every degree, and I do not remember many times when someone was not hurting me. I have seen it all, from physical, to emotional, to sexual abuse, each done unto me to make me feel of no use. To this day I grieve once in a while for that little girl who endured the life into which she was hurled. I feel sad for her and all that she lost, but I admire her for surviving at all costs.

In amongst all that my father married a second time, and we went to live with them, hoping everything would be fine. I was still very young; the exact age eludes me, and three kids of her own she brought to our extended family. What a grand thing to finally have a family so large and be in a home with two parents in charge. But family number two was not all that it seemed, and the abuse did not stop, nor did my suffering.

One bright spot was my sister whom they conceived; if nothing else, that is the one good thing they achieved. Three of us kids could say we had a father, and the other three could say they had a mother. Our family could not blend, and the end was in sight, for there was too much over which they did fight. If the parents cannot get it right, what is a child to do when they have no foundation to pull them through?

Abandoned by mom number two, what was a girl to think? Was there no end to this mayhem pushing me to the brink? My father's second wife took my sister and her kids away. What a dark spot in my life, and I've yet to forget that day. She packed all her belongings and her kids in the car, leaving my brother and I behind to carry another scar.

My father was not home when she took the kids and went, and when he came home we were cried out and spent. It was a long and tragic day for two kids so young to spend all alone, wondering what was to come. Back into foster care my father sent us. We were too much of a bother over which to make a fuss.

In five short years I had already lived a lifetime, dealing with issues that were someone else's crime. Why was it that no one cared about a little girl who was sad, lonely, and scared? By now my brother and I are on two opposite parallels. Mine was acceptance and his was living his personal hell. Quietly and meekly, I took what was doled out to me, but my brother defied everyone, refusing to show that he was weak.

I tried so hard to be good and was a people pleaser, but my brother's antics were not making our lives any easier. I would find myself involved with what he did bad, and we both suffered when it was found out to make someone mad. All we had was each other so we had to stick together; no matter what he did, he was still my brother. At one point foster care wanted to put us in separate homes, but my brother threw such a fit that they left that thought alone.

We ended up in a home that was worse than the rest, and I could never do right even if I tried my best. Punishment was swift and meant to hurt, and I received no loving words, just ones that were curt. My chore list was heavy for a small child of five: pulling weeds, picking stones, and gathering eggs to survive. Picking berries, plucking chickens, feeding slop to the pigs; my hands were never idle, and each day always brought unwanted things.

If the chores were not done to their thoughts of perfection, the punishment was a beating and more human rejection. It is a scary place to be when you can do nothing right, and your every waking moment is spent trying to avoid a fight. The burden is heavy, and the tears will not stop when your world has no bottom or top. You exist, you survive hoping tomorrow is better, but each night when you rest your pillow gets wetter.

I started school while in this home, but what a mess. I did not have any skills to show the class. No one had taken the time to teach me the basics. I could not say my ABCs, count to ten — oh man, what a fix. Just one more thing to add to my insecurities: not being as good as everyone else with their learning. Where they were book smart, my smarts were of a different sort. I had learned in five years that life can really hurt.

I could say that life was hard, and that people can be cruel and that the goal of some is to use you as a garden tool. I had learned that idle hands are the devil's playground and that I was to suffer abuse and not make a sound. I had learned that love was not for someone like me, and I was not important and should not be heard or seen.

It was in and amongst all of this that I first met God, and He came at a time when I thought I could no longer trod. Each Sunday we went to this tiny church in the trees, and this was my only bright spot at the end of my week. My burdens were lightened and a child I was able to be. For one brief hour each week it was just God and me. It was my secret that I told no one else about: the God I had seen who took away all my doubt. It was peace that I felt as God gave me a hug and told me that He had reasons for what I was to lug.

It was in this church that I received my first Bible as a reminder that it is humans that are cruel, and God is much kinder. I was six years old when the book was put into my hands, and all these years later, I hold it and remember where I have been. This Bible has been with me every step of the way as a reminder to hear God and not what humans have to say.

My brother and I stayed in this home for a couple more years until one day my brother had the beating that both of us feared. His beating was so bad that I did not recognize his face, and his spirit was shattered and that was a disgrace. Up until then I believe he did have some hope, but they beat that out of him, and he could no longer cope.

Away we went to live with my father and his third wife. Finally, we could get out from under all that strife. My father for the third time seemed to want to settle down, but neither of them were prepared for what was coming around. I was about eight and my brother was about ten, and into our lives a lot had been done by then. I was steadfast in believing what God showed me as true, and my brother was too hard for the light to shine through.

Our paths in life were determined by now. My brother despised and my faith knew no earthly bounds. Where he had no trust, I knew of a better way, and he did not believe, but I listened to what God had to say. My father did try to give us a life that was normal, but it was all fake and the façade was too formal. The abuse still occurred, and the rules were rigid. Everyone in our house was emotionally frigid.

I was tolerated as someone to put up with, and my hope for a happy family became more of a myth. I wanted humans to accept me as God had already done and for them to know that there is a better outcome. So I struggled as best as I could with what I had and my main concern in life became avoiding making others mad.

That is hard to do when they are unhappy anyway and their sole purpose in life is to ruin every good day. I tried not to believe what they said was the truth, and I had to believe that it was God that would give them reproof. I had to hold on to why God wanted me to be meek and why it was necessary to forgive and turn the other cheek. I had to see the goodness in each soul God created, for I knew someday He would give me His insight if I waited.

I had chances to not give my best and succumb to what I knew was not one of God's tests. God's tests are designed to bring good out in everyone, and He will never give you a test that diminishes one of His daughters or sons.

My father was not ready to take us in, that is true. We went to live with him in an apartment that was only meant for two. From there we moved to another apartment and then a trailer. Our family life was rocky, but our material items got better. They did try to give us things to bring our childhood back, but the toys did not fill the void, for it was love that we lacked.

I did not understand this emotion as a young child. The only love I knew was the love when I was being defiled. Turmoil and mayhem are the only life I knew, and happiness was not an emotion I held as true. My brother distrusted as well and was forever bad, and he too did not believe there was better than the life that he had. His constant antics caused each of us our own pain. His was on a path to destruction, never to return again.

Peace was unknown to him, for all he understood was wrath, and he pushed the envelope too far just to see the aftermath. A saint's patience would be tested trying to deal with him. There was no hope for recovery, and all he knew was how to sin. My father drank a lot and was rarely ever home, and when he was there his drunken mood always set the tone.

As much as I wanted his love, I stayed out of his way, for he rarely had any words of love or encouragement to say. I always felt like a burden and that hurt so much, never to be accepted by a father who was out of touch. I did my best to be a good and loving daughter, but it was not enough for him, who could not be a father. It was no better with the woman I called "Mom," for she was nowhere near ready to raise children.

Two young children dropped in your life was a true test, and I give her the credit for trying to give us the best. Her focus was on attaining many material things, and she was obsessed with our tub never having any rings. Her home had to be perfection to hide the truth: an alcoholic husband, an imperfect daughter, and a son with no couth. I tried so hard to be what she wanted me to be. A perfect daughter for the world to see. I cooked, I cleaned, I tried to do everything well, but it was just never good enough or to her very swell.

I was eleven years old when we up and moved twelve hours away. Maybe moving so far would bring a happy new day. The house we built was the first in which we had normal living. A shrine to everyone to say that we were doing some forgiving. We had come a long way from that tiny apartment to five acres of land in a house with brand-new carpet.

The façade, it continued. Everything was all fake. A beautiful house does not a happy family make. My brother was no more than thirteen when he left this place with one final beating from my father to scar his sad face. Back into foster care he went with no debate. Maybe someone else could fix what we knew was too late. Things should have gotten better, but they did not, and even without my brother there, my parents still fought.

A life-changing moment happened when I was about thirteen and I got to meet my biological mother's family. It was then that I learned that my real mom was dead and that she had died when I was six, without anything being said. Reflecting back to when I was six, I got that first Bible given to me a month after she took her seat at God's table. Could it be that the Bible was my mom in disguise? And she has been with me every day since her demise?

For the very first time in my life, I felt like I belonged, and my gramma's love began to heal where I was wronged. She loved me unconditionally and that was new. Her absolute faith in God is what pulled her through. I loved just sitting with her and being me. Never once did she ever hurt me or go out of her way to be mean. She never judged me and instead showed me how to love while guiding me to the God that I knew was above.

Never had I known such peace and contentment as in all those treasured moments that we spent. Gramma always had a hug when you arrived, and she gave you another for all that you survived. When you had to go, another hug she would bring your way. Gramma had a way to make everyone's day. It was Gramma's strength that gave me courage at the age of fifteen to leave my father's third marriage. He had done something that could only be construed as unforgiveable. I had enough and wanted to protect my soul from being degradable.

Child welfare took over and for once I did not care. I just wanted to leave and be anywhere but there. My long road to recovery began with that decision, and it was not going to be easy, but I had God in my vision. My gramma had given me a taste of what life was all about, and I trusted her and God without any doubt.

Being human, I had to keep making mistakes, as it was the only way to learn that God was not at all fake. I started to emerge from the shell I was hidden in, and a few choices I made were borderline sin. It felt good, this ability to make the choices I wanted without being pushed down, teased, and taunted. They were my choices whether they were right or wrong, and one by one I shed the burdens I had carried along.

I freed up enough space to fall in love as my first love swept down on me on the wings of a dove. It was absolute bliss that this man brought, and he showed me something other than what I had been taught. Our time together was brief, and I took it hard, and what I did then was to play my suicide card. Getting and losing this love was more than I could take, and I thought this was the ultimate hurt in all my heartbreaks.

Strange things happened to me after I took all those pills, and the amount I took should have found me to be killed. Three times I came back from the brink of death, as it was not my time and God continued to give me another breath. I do not know what I saw, but it was truly divine, with God and His angels telling me that it was not my time.

I survived that ordeal to live and breathe another day to share with others what God said in a loving way. I vowed I would not do that again and for that I have kept my word, as I had a purpose in life, and it had yet to be heard. It was shortly after that that I became pregnant. Why was one heartbreak after another into my life hell-bent?

I had just turned nineteen and was ready to try again when I made a mistake and trusted another young man. It was all in fun, this game devised to make his girlfriend jealous. How could I know that what was in his heart was malicious? Pregnant at nineteen, what a blow that was to take, all resulting from my own decisions and mistakes. I could not put the blame on anyone except myself, as it was my own decision that brought this karma about.

What should I do now, keep the baby or let it go? How could I give a baby all that I had never known? I knew I had made the right choice when they put him in my arms, and from that second to now, he has wooed me with his charms. He was cute and perfection, with all his fingers and toes and his beautiful blue eyes and adorable button nose. Looking down at him I thought my heart would burst, and I knew a love that was defiant to the worst.

By now my father was with his fourth wife, still unhappy and settling for more strife. She loved him more than he loved her, and his continued dysfunction she continued to endure. Surprisingly, my father did not demean me or call me down when I told him that a grandchild was coming around. He took to my son like it was his second chance to make amends for his negligence.

I returned to work shortly after giving birth. My baby was going to have a good life, even if that meant moving heaven and earth. My father's fourth wife took my son under her wing so I could work and ensure my son had everything. She babysat my son, and they developed a bond during those long hours that I worked and was gone.

Every spare moment I had was given to my son, and what time we had together I would always ensure was fun. I would hold him, kiss him, and tell him that I cared. I would tell him that I was there and to never be scared. We would cuddle, and I would pull him close and kiss him on the end of his cute button nose. I loved him so much and I forever told him that. He was never going to know where my love came and went.

He was showered with praise and encouragement his every waking moment and then tucked safely in at night without a worry to ferment. Allowing him to have a childhood of innocence kept away my own demons, and never on him did I vent. Right from the get-go I knew what to do right: it was to do the opposite of my own childhood plight. He received my constant love and admiration for everything he did and brought to me for my interpretation.

I would praise him profusely and tell him that he did great and for his next accomplishment I could not wait. Every holiday was celebrated in a grand way, and he had a party for each of his birthdays. He had a full tummy and never knew hunger, as I never wanted him to know that hunger can linger. Before he attended school, he was ahead of his class, for he could read, write, and even do some math.

I encouraged him to try everything at least once, and he kept busy doing things he found to be fun. His confidence was huge and he was self-assured, and there was not much that he did not or could not learn. I partook in all his school activities and sports; as his mom, I was his number-one fan, of course.

When my son was four, I got married one summer and it lasted less than a year, which was a bummer. That man was not my son's father, but he might as well have been, as he treated him like gold, and they were fast friends. We had been dating since my son was five months old, and getting married one day seem unavoidable. My ex-husband was an alcoholic that drank every day, but he never abused me or my son in any way.

His drinking became something I could not bear, and after less than a year of marriage I got out of there. It was a loss for my son and his first hurt, but to this day they are still friends and talk in spurts. I was too proud to go home, so we went on welfare, and my son continued like he did not have a care. His trust in me was big and he knew not to worry, because Mom always came through in a big hurry.

I went back to school and finished my grade twelve, and at the age of twenty-three one test would tell it all. I passed that test and enrolled in a secretarial course, which is what I wanted to be, so it did not take any force. I graduated from that and embarked on my career. Failure was not an option and something that I feared. In the meantime, my son kept on trudging along and he had no worries because he was where he belonged. Mom was still ensuring he had an untroubled home, and he could depend on the fact that he would never be alone.

A year after my divorce I fell in love all over again, and it was love at first sight when I was introduced to this man. He had his issues, but who did not have some? His biggest hang-up was trying to accept my son. For the first time my son's happiness came second as I succumbed to the love that came to beckon.

Do not get me wrong, my son did not lack anything: he was still the apple of my eye and made my heart sing.

The ways of my childhood came back to haunt me, and I tried to be something other than what I could be. Desperation to not have this third love fail pushed it away from me to no avail. I loved my son yet I went back to this relationship often, and my heart began to harden instead of to soften. I tried everything in my power to make it work, but his disregard for my son was his biggest quirk.

I hung in there for several years before I gave up. Too much had taken place, and I had had enough. Away he went into the arms of another, and I had to do damage control with my son for my weakness as a mother. That time was a definite hurt for my son, having to watch his mom be unloved by someone. If nothing else, our bond only grew much stronger as he watched his mom come from down under.

There had been no physical abuse, it was all mental, and I had to get back from where I had gone to. To be honest, I will say that it was a hurt I'd never had, and the struggle to continue almost made me go mad. I lived in a fog and conducted each day like a machine, and where I was at was the lowest I had ever been.

By now my son was a teenager at a tender age, and I could not let him down, so I kept him at centre stage. Both of us could have given into the temptations of life; all those things put in your path to deal with your strife. He could have become a kid who did not care, and I could have stayed depressed, thinking that life was not fair. Neither one of these things did either of us do, and we leaned on each other to pull us through.

My son learned wisdom from year to year as he got ready to face the world without fear. Raising my son has been my greatest accomplishment, as he knew only love and no hatred on him did I ever vent. There were some bumps along the way, but there had to be more than one for him to understand sadness and that it was not all fun.

He learned perseverance and how to keep an open mind. He learned how to have compassion even when others were not kind. He kept the innocence of his youth and still has some today. His thoughts are about mentoring children and helping them to play. He has a heart of gold that spurns him on to help others. He has his own dreams and goals that make his heart flutter.

As a teen he did not smoke, drink, or use drugs. He understood the burdens that these can make a human lug. His passion in life was to play basketball. He worked hard at it and thankfully he is tall. He was smart in school and was on track to graduate. He had known all his life that it is for that that I wait. He is funny and serious all rolled up into one. He knows when to be real and when to have fun.

He has God in his life, and he was baptized at ten. He knows from me that he was heaven-sent. He would give you anything, including the shirt off his back. He wants everyone to have what he did not lack. He has a soft spot for the animals of Mother Nature. He has the compassion to never hurt a living creature. He has wisdom that astounds those that are old. He has taken to heart all that his mom has told. He has a soul that others want to be around. He is wise beyond his years because his foundation is sound.

He respects all humans, no matter who they are. He understands not to judge what got them that far. He sees good in everyone and accepts their bad. He can put himself in their shoes to see why they are sad. He knows that no one is perfect and everyone makes mistakes. He gets that some people give and others just take. He has been my one and only child and given me little grief. He has been the highlight of my life in a time that now seems too brief.

He has been the one constant in my life that I could depend on. He has always remained when everyone else was gone. He has seen me at my worst and seen me at my best. He understood my own peace and unrest. He has written his own things on the great Mom that I have been. He has told me several times that he is glad I am his kin.

I may never fully understand why my son was given to me, but I am grateful for all that he has given me to see. He's been a treasure since he was laid into my waiting arms, and today he is a wonderful man with many of his own charms. I do believe that my son is an angel sent from heaven in disguise, for he came to me so soon after I had planned my demise. Do I run from him, or do I decide to give him my best? This gift was sent from heaven as one of

God's given tests. Do I trust what I had known from the age of six? That God had the answers and only He has the fix?

By now you have gathered that I hold my son in high regard, and I see him as God's reward for a life that was so hard. What I taught to my son that was not taught to me was to have self worth and be anything you want to be.

I gave him the freedom to make his own decisions and to have dreams, goals, and to follow his visions. I kept my own childhood to the forefront of my mind as a reminder of how I felt when others could be unkind. I never wanted my son to fear having me around, and it was important that he knew my love had no bounds. A punishment for him was to sit and have a time-out. Never was he punished with an object or a backhanded clout.

An explanation was always given to help him understand that doing wrong will always receive someone's reprimand. He learned early on that life is built around our choices and to always listen for guidance from his inner voices. One voice urges you toward good and the other toward bad, and listening to one or the other will make you happy or sad.

He was taught that in everything there is always a lesson. The right decisions bring you peace and the wrong ones leave you guessing. The golden rule in life is something that he always knew: do unto others as you would have them do unto you. He knew that to forgive is what sets you free, and he was the kid on the playground that would turn the other cheek.

I taught him that in life, karma comes with no sound and that good and bad deeds are what brings karma around. He gets that no human can define who you really are, and he has learned that believing in yourself is what will take you far. He knows to take nothing for granted that comes to him each day, and he understands that it's divinity that makes things go a certain way.

Everything my son knows is what God has taught to me about having faith in a God that you have yet to meet. In times of trouble, he knows that it is God that can pull you through and it is to Him that you must turn when you are not sure what to do. He knows that everything happens for a reason, no matter what, and he understands that every lesson brings something to be taught. He is secure enough not to hold much to what others think. His inner wisdom always shows him what is the missing link. He knows that children are influenced, and he sets a good example. His patience for children is strong and of this trait he is ample.

There is nothing on this earth more precious than a child. They are a miracle to be loved and never to be defiled. You start out with a baby that depends completely on you, and before you know it, they are an adult doing what they can to pull through. You only have one chance to influence a human this way, and doing it right ensures that they will listen to what you have to say.

I think the key to parenting is to always have respect and know that it is always what your child wants and not what you expect. Trying to force a square peg into a round hole spells disaster, and accepting that your child is human makes the wisdom come faster. When you can see your child as someone with their own soul, you will be less likely to give them burdens to hold.

What we need to understand is that our children are borrowed, and they are here one day only to go off and live their life tomorrow. Some stay until they are ready to leave, and others cannot wait to go, but it is inevitable that they will leave and live with what they know.

Many conversations I have had with my son to prepare us for this: the day he will go and each other we will surely miss. Understanding that my son would be an adult one day ensured that I carefully chose the words I wanted to say. I knew that my influence in his life was strong, and I had to be an example of what was right and was wrong.

I knew that he would carry his childhood for a lifetime. How could I give him eighteen years that were also mine? We would both carry the memories of how he was raised, and I wanted no memories of disrespect, just memories of praise.

My son wrote an English essay in his seventeenth year, and it still chokes me up and to my eye brings a tear. The essay was all about someone that he respected a lot. The words were about me and everything that he had been taught. It was in that moment that I knew I had done all right to have my son write what was truly his own insight. It was clear to me that we had been a good team, both of us influenced by someone that cannot be seen.

Today I understand where my life went, and I get why God gave me a son that was heaven-sent. I had zero skills to be a parent and of that I was scared, but my son came to me to help me to be prepared. He came to me as one of God's many life tests, and I know now that he is what has finally given my soul some rest.

Being a parent is the hardest thing that anyone will ever do, as none of us have the exact formula and none of us have a clue. There is no special book telling you how your child will turn out, and for that reason as parents we are filled with self-doubt. We worry and fret that we are not doing it right, and we do not look inside of ourselves for our divine insight.

What I know today I knew back when I was six, which is to never give someone a hurt that only they could fix. Once you have hurt someone you can never take it back, and you leave them searching for something that they lack. As a small child I knew there was a better way, and I knew I had to listen and not disregard what God had to say.

As an adult I knew I could take on the victim role, and it would have been easy to shut down and not hear my soul. I could have continued the cycle of abuse with my son and excused it away as what to me was done. He could have lived a life of which I had only known, and I could have excused it away as a love not grown.

Instead, I made a choice to do everything in my power to ensure my son knew he was loved every hour. My power was not earthly, as it came from someone divine. I was guided by an urgency to not be cruel but to be kind. No human alive gave me lessons to raise my child. I did what I knew would make his childhood mild.

You may wonder why it is that I write all these words. I write them so that every child can be seen and heard. In every child I see a fresh page for them to write their life story with the freedom to live without what made me sorry. I see in every child a wisdom beyond their years, for it is every child that hears what God whispers in their ears. It is children that God will reveal Himself to, and a child is never afraid when God tells them what to do.

Children are innocent because God makes them that way, and it is us that take away the innocence with what we do and say. We are the ones that instruct our children not to believe when we do the opposite of what God gives them to see. Our own insecurities are what we unknowingly teach them by reliving a childhood that is not now, but back then.

We try to mould our children into what they cannot be, for God has shown them a life path that is unknown to you or me. An unhappy child is one that is forced to ignore their fate to please a parent that will not give them a break. Pushing a child to do what their heart does not desire diminishes their spirit, and to them you will become a liar.

You see, a child's destiny does not belong in your hands. When you can accept that as truth is when you will understand. A child knows before you do what will become of them, and to force it another way will only cause you mayhem. Your child has your genes and some of your traits, but that is where it ends and their own future waits.

God has already written what He wants your child to be, and getting them there ends when they are eighteen, for you and me. You have one chance to give a child eighteen wonderful years, and after that it is up to them to overcome what they fear. When they become an adult, you must accept that your job is done, and you can choose to be proud or ashamed of who your child has become.

It is too late by then to change anything that you did; they are who they are whether you approve of it. You cannot reteach anything that they have been taught, and you have had eighteen years where you accept that or not. Right or wrong, a child's path is chosen by the time they are a teen, and it is up to you by then to have shown them a love they will forever see.

That love is the love that they will have for themselves, and it is a love that they can carry on their life shelf. Teaching a child to love themselves can be a grueling task if you yourself are fake and hiding behind a mask. If you are not true to yourself, what will your child learn? What will they teach their own children when it is their turn?

Allowing your child to see that you are human and you also make mistakes gives them the foundation they need to be real and not fake. Letting them see that Mom and Dad are not perfection will help them to accept what in the mirror is their reflection. You will receive more respect from your child when you are real because it allows them to open up and allows them to feel.

I have always been open with my son and we talk a lot, and without knowing it, through those talks we are both being taught. When you accept your child as a person and not a burden to carry, you will give them a peace in their heart even when life gets scary.

My son is an only child, because truly I only wanted one. Strangely enough, I did not want a daughter, but I wanted a son. I was thrilled when my doctor said it was a boy. One more reason to accept him; I think was God's ploy. Being an only child certainly has its ups and downs, having no brother or sister with which to play around. My son has expressed that he wished I had had another, someone that he could call his sister or brother.

By saying this he does not make me feel bad, and he knows that it was my decision and not his to be had. I admire people who have decided to have more than one child, because raising one to adulthood was anything but mild. I do not regret my decision, as I know it was the right one, and the proof of that is shown on the man I call my son.

My son is living proof that life is all about choices and what can be achieved when you hear your inner voices. He is a testament to the fact that the cycle of abuse can end when you embrace your child and see them as a Godsend. When people tell me that I am lucky to have such a great son, I tell them that anyone can do what I have done.

I never take the credit as my own for who he is, and by not including God in his upbringing I would be remiss. God has been with me since the day I was born, and He is not to blame for the humans that made my soul torn. He gives everyone the choices to do the right thing, and it was humans, not God, who had no love to bring.

God's love is endless for those of us who believe, and it is only God's love that will help you to achieve. Had I chosen to follow what others did, I know I would have a very mixed-up kid. If I would have taken the path of "poor, pitiful me," my son would have had a life I never wanted him to see. But I chose to see the signs and hear what God had to say, and by doing that I avoided the dark side that beckons each day.

It amazes me the wisdom that God has shared. He has shown me so much and not much has He spared. I do not question His choice in confiding in me, and I marvel that He is with me for all eternity. It is a privilege for me to be in His good grace, and being with Him is better than being any place. The seven wonders of the world do not compare to Him. His kingdom is boundary-less, and it has no restrictive rim.

Every day is a miracle designed by Him while you slept, and what you do with that day from Him will be remembered and kept. Did you make the most of it and put your best foot forward? Or did you shun life and decide you have the right to be a coward? Do you allow humans to define who you are each day? Or do you take the time to hear what God has to say?

It is not an easy task to keep God in your sight when humans want to bring you down to their own delight. What makes it easier is to see them for who they are, as people who are also carrying around their own scar. We have no right to judge what it is that we do not know, and it is not our place to pick apart what made someone else grow.

Each human has a story that is theirs to carry, and to forget that is what makes life scary. Why is it that we want to bring each other down? Why do we deceive with a smile and enjoy someone's frown? What is being accomplished by hurting each other this way, except to give each other's souls scars to carry each day?

God is quite clear with His thoughts on this matter. He is the one that pays back and brings His karma to shatter. God is insistent that what you give out you get back, and the proof of that can be found in all that you lack. I am not talking about all the material things that you hold so dear. I am talking about the soul to which you have not been sincere. It is your soul that God grades, not the things you own. We as humans do not see the value of a soul that is unknown.

I know of what I speak. I have known it since I was a child. God's payback can be painfully hard, or it can be blissfully mild. No one is safe from God keeping things on an even score. Good or bad karma, which of these do you want more? It saddens God to see how we knowingly treat each other, and this is done because it is with our own soul that we do not bother.

It is impossible to hurt others when you acknowledge your soul, and by understanding this, loving others will become your goal. Your soul is where God is housed inside you and me. Recognizing that will give you the life you want to see. It is to a child that God will reveal who He is, and He will show them the soul that as adults we miss.

Some of us will remember what God showed us that day, and others cannot pinpoint the time or remember what God had to say. What I remember is a love so pure and it was as soft as silk. A love that folded you in and assured you that you had no guilt. There was no vision; I cannot tell you what God looks like, but His presence was a warmth you cannot see with your eyes. I could feel Him when He engulfed me in His embrace, and I could hear Him talk without ever having to see His face.

His exact words elude me, but they were always assuring. I was never scared when He spoke; there was never any fearing. I felt a peace that lifted me up and took away my doubt. A peace until now I could never talk about. As a child I knew that no adults would believe what I had to say, but God and I both know what took place on those Sundays.

I am content knowing that I am doing as God said, for He is behind all these words you have just read. I have no formal training on how to author a book. My writing comes from my soul, of which I have taken a second look. I have one more thing to share before ending this chapter. A moment so pure that it tells me that only God matters.

My son was ten years old when he was baptized. We both took classes to help us understand a religion that we did not recognize. He was baptized at Easter, and it was a grand affair. All the parishioners, my friends, and close family were there. When the ceremony was done and my son sat down next to me, he said with assurance, "I just felt Jesus go into me." I never doubted him for a second, because I already knew. My son is a testament to what God had shown me as true.

Chapter Three — There is Rhyme and There is Reason

What God has taught me …

is that as humans we make mistakes and He forgives them if your faith is not fake.

is that He is the keeper of my soul and only He has the power to keep my soul full.

is that patience will bring results and to go against God's wisdom is to Him an insult.

is that everyone has free will and to force others to change will leave you feeling ill.

is that children need love, and demeaning a child brings the wrath of God from above.

is that all sins are punished in time and He will make amends for your hidden crime.

is that all humans are truly weak and to not always judge the words that they speak.

is that all humans are equal and He does not honour how we elevate certain people.

is that everyone has something to teach and not only those we deem to preach.

is that there's goodness in everyone and it is wrong to judge what can be undone.

is that He is in control of all things and it is futile to want more than what He brings.

is that life is not fair and He must keep the balance of what goes on down here.

is that I truly matter to Him, as does everyone that He wants to see not sin.

is that peace is an attainable place and to accept that we are one race.

is that we are to love Him more than anything else to help us to love others and ourselves.

is that we all have the answer to life and it is buried beneath our need to cause strife.

is that I can change, and everyone can do the same, no matter their age.

is that forgiveness will set you free and to forgive others as they have forgiven me.

is that being wealthy is a test; He will judge those who do not share with the rest.

is that only His opinion counts, and in the end, it is He who tallies the accounts.

is that to parent we must be a child and to love another you must always be mild.

is that each day is a new chance to accept that your soul deserves a second glance.

is that He is watching all that I do, and He misses nothing I do to pull myself through.

is that perfection cannot be achieved and you will fail if that is what you perceive.

is that faith is not reserved for one day, and you must revere Him daily in some way.

is that He speaks to us through signs, and we are to read between the lines.

is that to doubt Him is a slow death, and a disbelieving soul will hurt to its last breath.

is that a prayer is a conversation with a chance to learn what is God's motivation.

is that I cannot have all that I want, and He gives more to me than wealth can flaunt.

is that nothing is as it appears to be; today is not tomorrow or the past you have seen.

is that I take nothing for granted: the air, the water, and the food that is planted.

is that a soul can survive and endure, and it knows that God is its only saving cure.

is that life must keep going forward, and life is short and only borrowed.

is that pain is experience turned inside out and the ache is how we overcome doubt.

is that respect is something we earn, and peace will come when it is this fact we learn.

is that children have all the insight and it is taken away by adults who are not right.

is that nothing is a coincidence, and life is designed with reward and consequence.

is that selfishness is a death trap and those that do this think Satan gets a bad rap.

is that beauty is not seen on people but seen in whoever keeps their cup half full.

is that hell is here on earth and a place for souls to stay who do not know their worth.

is that it is never too late to make amends, and doing this will benefit you in the end.

is that everyone has a purpose, and not seeking that makes your discontent worsen.

is that humans do not mean to be cruel but treated hurtfully they will act a fool.

is that not everyone will like you, but God's love will always pull you through.

is that war is not the solution and there is no justification for murdering a population.

is that friends are a valuable gift who expect nothing from giving your soul a lift.

is that to control others is futile, and life is meant to help others to go the extra mile.

is that I must put myself in another's shoes, and by doing this I will have nothing to lose.

is that when you genuinely believe, all things will come to you in ways you cannot perceive.

is that we do not choose who we love, and they come to teach us lessons from above.

is that humans want to be validated and we should give them the love they have awaited.

is that greed is the root of all evil, and a soul's worth is more than commodities we deal.

is that we cannot choose our families, and they must make amends for treating you unfairly.

is that credit is given where it is due; endure what you must, but God always brings it back to you.

is that everyone wants to be deep, and His wisdom is there for all of us to sow and then reap.

is that your biggest pain will subside, and denial of that pain puts you on a long and lonely ride.

is that gossipers do not have a life and there is no justification for causing someone undue strife.

is that there is so much to learn and receiving life's knowledge is something that we must earn.

is that there is always an explanation and eventually you will receive it with no expectation.

is that we each have a talent to share and we are to find our talent and use it to make others stare.

is that His and our times are not the same and His plans do not include our human mind games.

is that we waste time worrying and the outcome of any situation will not be rectified by our hurrying.

is that I am my only friend, and we must be able to love the one with whom so much time we spend.

is that to love means to sacrifice. One cannot run out of love, as God gives enough to suffice.

is that we are born to die, and your first breath is the same as the last one you give with a sigh.

is that greatness is not wasted on the vain, and everyone can help others without thought of gain.

is that in life there should be no regrets, and rectifying discontent will always be your best bet.

is that we judge others from our fear. You must realize that what you want least you will draw near.

is that others will treat you as you want and there is no sweeter sound then their traits that you flaunt.

is that faith takes on many forms, and time is wasted thinking you're right and others should conform.

is that there is no substitute for having faith, for God won't let you down when on Him you wait.

is that by working together we can change, but thinking of ourselves as family is too strange.

is that I have so much more to say about what God shared with me at least once a day.

Chapter Four — God. Creator. Universe. Higher Power.

An atheist was seated next to a dusty old cowboy on an airplane, and he turned to him and said, "Do you want to talk? Flights go quicker if you strike up a conversation with your fellow passenger."

The old cowboy, who had just started to read his book, replied to the total stranger, "What would you want to talk about?"

"Oh, I don't know," said the atheist. "How about why there is no God, or no heaven or hell, or no life after death?" He smiled smugly.

"Okay," the cowboy said. "Those could be interesting topics, but let me ask you a question first. A horse, a cow, and a deer all eat the same stuff — grass. Yet a deer excretes little pellets, while a cow turns out a flat patty, but a horse produces clumps. Why do you suppose that is?"

The atheist, visibly surprised by the cowboy's intelligence, thought about it and said, "Hmmm, I have no idea."

To which the cowboy replied, "Do you really feel qualified to discuss God, heaven and hell, or life after death when you don't know crap?" Author unknown

I had great apprehension when I started to write this rhyme. Who am I to write about our greatest gift of all time? I am not a scholar and I have not studied every book. Why has God given me words for people to take a second look? I do not have fame nor riches or anything to my credit. What can I say to help others to finally get it?

I am a believer, and that is all that God needs, but where does all this wisdom come from to plant the seeds? I have had many tribulations that allow me His insight. When will I write the piece that finally gets it right? I am a sinner who is unworthy of God's love. Why did He choose me to share what I know is above?

God is many things to some and nothing at all to others. There are those who believe and some that could not be bothered. Some of us believe that loving God is way too hard, while others accept His way as what is written on their card. Believers and nonbelievers live together each day, both wanting to change the other with what they have to say.

Many emotions are shared by these two distinct groups as they adamantly try to give each other their truth. They want validation that it is okay to believe what they wish, and it is important to both that they do not appear selfish. There can be no winners when both minds are closed, and it is impossible to be convinced when you are indisposed.

Many books I have read to help me find the answers to life. Each book quotes scripture and all its strife. Although the verses are powerful, they are only words unless your soul is allowed to be heard. The whisper of your soul is where you are to be led, and the whisper cannot be found in any book that you have read.

We want to believe that somewhere it's written clear what it takes to find meaning in the soul that you hold near. No book has ever been written, except the Bible, that will lead you to your soul and all that it is liable. Author after author has struggled to find the right words to say, but each book leaves us longing and from our convictions we do not sway.

I too am one of those authors who wants to say the right thing to help you to love God and all that He must bring. On this topic I get speechless about a love so divine, and I cannot seem to describe it and no words can I find. What I have learned is that people do not want to read scripture. What they want is to know how they fit in the bigger picture.

God is very aware that learning from scripture can be hard, but He gave us scripture to learn and to not disregard. God authored an entire book dedicated to following His way, and many have interpreted it to be what they want it to say. Some get so wrapped up in it that they forget they are human, and they lose perspective and become rigid and unmoving.

No person on earth can follow God's words to perfection, and thinking you can sets you up for human rejection. We must make mistakes, for that is how we learn, and it is through our mistakes that God's wisdom we earn. God takes many forms. He is not all that you believe Him to be. He takes on the image that your humanness wants to see.

What you think He is is not what others can see too, and your relationship with God is how your faith pulls you through. The starting block for every soul is to simply have faith. It is to believe without a doubt and to no longer wait. No two persons will believe in God the same way, for each of us has our own story in which He will have His say.

God designed us to be unique for reasons of His own, but all of us have the power to figure out the unknown. We all want to know what our purpose is in life as we breed discontent and cause our own strife. We are looking for worldly confirmation that we are doing it right, and we turn to others for their approval and ignore God's insight. People turn to one another to get a pat on the back yet leave feeling like there is still something that they lack.

What is lacking is the will to search out their soul, because they are wanting others to help them to reach their final goal. The journey to finding your soul can only be done by you, and your soul is God that is pulling you through. Finding your soul is to take away that restless feeling, that feeling of confusion that overshadows your healing.

Everyone's purpose in life is the same thing, and that is to find your soul and learn what it must bring. That is the battle that we fight with ourselves every day, to listen to the whisper of our soul and what it has to say. On your soul is written the answers to your life, but you have buried those answers under all your strife. Your answers are your own to find because no one else knows your soul that God has clearly defined.

The search for answers cannot be found outside you. Your soul holds the answers for all that you are to do. *It cannot be that simple,* you think as you read this and then continue to search for the soul that you miss. Acknowledging your soul is to accept God as true, and by doing this you allow God to help you to be you. Our discontentment with life is because we try to be what we are not. We must go inside of ourself and unlearn what we have been taught.

Someone has shaped us to be what they think we should be when meanwhile they are battling a soul that they cannot see. What someone has taught you does not necessarily make it right. Ask yourself what it is that causes your insides to fight. What is the turmoil that pushes you to search for more? Finding that is the key to finding where your soul is sore.

Just maybe us humans have it all wrong, trying to force what we believe where it does not belong. What if it is true and we have a soul inside and all this time we have been letting our humanness decide? What if God made it easy to find the answer? Could it be that simple to have it written on our character?

I know as you read this that you are looking for a point. You are wanting me to say words to have you and your soul join. What you must understand is that on your soul it is written, and you are to find your soul and with it become smitten.

What I have learned in life is my own truth and that what I know has been backed up by God's proof. He has never left me to flounder without His guidance, and it is I who have chosen to think that I didn't have abundance. I thought I knew it all and had life figured out. I had all the answers, and I carried all the clout.

What a revelation to realize that I was wrong to think for one second that I had it right all along. How foolish I felt when I received God's reprimand, which was given from love to help me to understand. God is in everyone; He is not reserved for the righteous. Your soul is where God lives and why we are so curious. We search and search for the meaning of our life each day, and we ignore what it is that our soul has to say.

We want to believe that it has to be more profound than that to find the answers to our life and what we lack. As humans we live to impress each other with what we own, and we forget to impress ourselves by embracing the unknown. Our greatest accomplishments in life cannot be measured by wealth. There is no price on a soul and how you gain its spiritual health.

Your soul was given to you freely, and to God it is priceless. He values all souls and on them is His permanent address. Once you understand that God is inside your body, you begin to have purpose and it's Him you want to embody. You will transform and see things through God's eyes, and it will become much harder to believe in human lies. You will learn to hear the whisper of your blessed soul, and finding its purpose becomes yours and God's common goal. Without realizing it, you get the purpose you seek, and it started by admitting where you are weak.

So how do you find your soul when you do not know where to start? It is all about re-evaluating and taking what you've known apart. You must open your mind to grasp the truth, and you must be willing to accept God's loving reproof. It begins with releasing control in order to build faith. God has the control, and that should never be up for debate.

He is the only one who can see what lies further down the road, and your regrets in life are from not listening to what He told. To hear your soul is a guarantee for more blessings to come your way. Ignorance will no longer be an excuse not to hear what the whisper has to say.

Have you ever had a fear so urgent that you felt lost? Has the feeling been one to do something great at all costs? Did you embrace the feeling, or did you run from it? Were you able to hear your whisper even a little bit? We are constantly receiving messages from God to our souls, and each message is designed to bring us closer to His fold. How you deal with God's teaching is a true test of faith. He, not us, has all the time in the world to wait.

I knew incredibly young that I was destined to do something. God had forewarned me that He had much for me to bring. Never did I imagine that He would use me to write so much. Everything I write is done through my hand and God's touch. My own soul has been whispering to me my whole life, and the truths I have had to overcome have cut like a knife.

I know now that God was grooming me to speak His words, and to do that I had to suffer and hurt. As a child I could not grasp the atrocities done unto me, but today as an adult I understand that human weakness is what I needed to see. All the abuses I had to endure, with resignation on my part, are now acceptances by me that God was there from the start.

My encounter with God makes some a skeptic, but what I learned from God that day has made my life less hectic. It was a Sunday and off to church we had to go. I was in a foster home suffering abuses that I should not know.

Church was the only place where I truly felt safe. It was a reprieve from the daily abuses I had to face. Outside of this church is where God revealed Himself to me. I felt a voice and no image did I see.

I felt, more than I heard, what the voice had to say. It was a conversation with God that I remember to this day. There was a calmness and peace like I have never felt since, and I was told that there was a reason, and I was of significance. I was told not to worry and that God would always be there. I was told that God would make right what I knew was unfair.

This encounter took only seconds, but I remember it well, and only recently have I chosen to open up and tell. I do not share this to make others fear my intent. I share this to help others to see in themselves where God came and went. We've all had our moment with God yet act like we did not. We fear human rejection so we deny what should never be forgot.

I know what I felt when I was a child, and today I can understand why my childhood was not mild. What some can take a lifetime to learn I saw as a child, and much wisdom did I earn. It was impossible for me to divert my faith, and at times it was hard to be patient and wait.

What I was feeling was an unreachable itch that was used to dig deep inside myself for the visions to match. Somewhere inside I knew I had the answers I desired, but it was God's time, not mine, that would make them transpire. His timetable is His; patience will reveal the way, and faith is how you get to hear what He has to say.

You must be able to blindly have faith that God is right to receive His blessings, wisdom, and insight. You must accept that everything in your life is designed. It is important to give up control and to be resigned. God cannot work through you if you struggle and fight; God cannot assist you if you think that you have all the might.

It is only when you let your humanness be released that God can reveal your purpose that He wants to teach. If you depend on worldly things to see you through, then God has no space in your soul to show you what to do. If you are consumed with finding answers on your own, you will be unable to find what your soul has always known.

We each hold the answer to life and do not realize that. All the answers you desire can be found where you have sat. You take the answers with you wherever you go. Your answers are your own and for no one else to know. No one can tell you what only your soul has to say, and it is up to you to hear with each new day. Fear deters us from accepting that which is our fate, and we insist that humans know and on them we wait.

To ignore your whisper is to feel restlessness so intense that you fear your sanity and continue with the pretense. You think that if you succumb to it you will surely go mad, so you push it away and continue to be sad. That urgency you feel is God speaking to your soul. He is wanting you to listen and to rest from what you toil.

We call it unhappiness when we do not feel right inside, but to God it's a wake-up call for you to finally decide. Discontent with oneself can only be resolved through God. It is He who will be the one to give you an approving nod. We have come to believe not to trust that which we cannot see, and God is included in that category because humans are naïve.

God is all around us, and you encounter Him every day. Look in the mirror if you do not understand what I say. You are a miracle that God created with care, and you are who you are even if you think it is unfair. What you must accept is that God does not make mistakes, and it's us as humans that choose to be all that is fake. We are the ones that discourage each other's true intent, for we fear that our own chances have came and went.

God has the final say of when your time is up. He is the only one that decides when you have had enough. God gave you your soul and He can also take it away. He gives you many opportunities to hear what it has to say. You yourself must decide that change needs to happen, and when the change occurs is when your soul approves with clapping.

You will know in yourself that you have chosen the right path. It is a feeling like you can manage all the aftermath. Acceptance will replace apprehension in all that you do, and you will begin to depend on yourself to help pull you through. God has never let me down, but my humanness has when I have tried to override God for what I thought I should amass.

My humanness wanted earthly things to show I was doing it right, and God only ever wanted me to freely have His insight. I have had my own battles with God to my own detriment, and God answered all my triumphs with His own comment. When I followed my humanness is when I took a hard slam, and I learned along the way that it is God who defines who I am.

Selfishness is the key to why humans have a hard go. Those who are selfish think there is nothing else to know. They believe they have the answers and have nothing to share. Truly those who are selfish are the ones who think life is unfair. You must be selfless to see your own soul, for what is written there is an acceptance of the unknown.

It is not God's intent for us to know every outcome. Knowing all the answers would take away all the fun. Each day of your life should be seen as a surprise. Each moment is a chance for God to reward you with a prize. Your greatest achievements in life do not have a price tag, and they do not impress your soul that you may have allowed to sag. Your greatest accomplishment in life must be finding yourself. Who you are is not written in a book on anyone's shelf.

Your life story is written on your soul for you to read each day, and only you hold the answers to what your soul has to say. I cannot tell you your answers; they are your own to find. All I can tell you is that to yourself you must be kind. Get to know who you are and accept what you learn. You hold the answers to the peace that you want to earn.

No one knows you inside and out as God already does, and only He knows what will come to you from above. He will not hurt you; you will do that yourself when you defy, but God will point out where you have chosen to lie. It is in that moment that you can choose to accept or fight. God will never force you to agree and accept His insight. All He can do is give you the chance to succumb to His way, but you must be the one to determine which way you will sway.

God never gives up and your chances are never-ending. It is God's life mission to wear down what you are defending. If you hurt, you hurt because you choose to be, and if you are angry, your anger is what you choose to see. If you are impatient, you rush to forget your pain, and if you are boastful, you loudly about yourself proclaim. If you are judgmental, you judge others for who you are, and if you are unforgiving, you grudgingly nurture your scars.

If you are confident, you override what others feel, and if you are happy, you harbour it for no one else to steal. If you are loved, you doubt and search for more to fulfill, and if you are accepted, you think there must be more still. If you are blessed, you worry that it will be taken away, and if you are successful, you fear that it will be gone some day.

Our humanness allows us to breed confusion and discontent even when we should feel honoured for where God came and went. We cannot resolve ourselves to the fact that God is in charge, and into our own life we allow our humanness to barge. It is the fear of the unknown that makes us feel desperate, and we worry that life is slipping away before we get it. Have you considered that what you seek is close and your guide is God, who is already in the know? God tests us all the time for us to take notice of Him. He is there to reward honorable deeds and to punish all sins.

Life seems to go well when we meet the needs of others, and life seems to go downhill when we get consumed with our bother. It is through others that we truly learn our mistakes. God uses us to show each other where we are fake. It is up to you to overcome what God has shown as truth and understand that it is God, not humans, who is giving you reproof.

We resent other humans for pointing out our error when really it's God trying to make all the rules fair. We would rather begrudge those who we think hurt us. What we forget is that there is a lesson in all the fuss. It is a true test of your faith to look at the other side and view each human as a place where God resides. By doing this you feel compassion instead of resentment, because you understand that it's God pointing out your discontentment.

Humans are tools that God uses to fix and repair. All humans have a mission and God's wisdom to share. As you do not want to be denounced, give others the same respect. One of God's lessons could come from someone that you do not expect. View every soul as having a reason to be in your life. Doing this will eliminate much of your undue strife.

Every soul has a purpose, and it deserves your attention, and all souls have a mission that has God's full intention. Never doubt for one second that your life is for naught. God's purpose for you is to share what you have been taught. It may be something big or something you think is small, but remember that what you know can prevent someone's fall.

Do not allow your humanness to let you think others are weak, for God has given all souls the power to have something to speak. You may not agree and slough off what they have to say, but the wisdom of their words will come back to you one day. That was their mission to open your eyes to see. Could be that they wanted your own soul to be set free.

Our biggest fear in life is to be told that we are wrong. To be told this makes us feel as if we do not belong. The question is: why does it matter what humans think of you? Their opinion is of little importance in what your soul must do. You know you have it right when you have listened to your soul, but as humans we try to divert each other from that goal.

We worry that someone is ahead and leaving us behind, so we try to match what their soul has already defined. Therein lies the problem of why so many souls wander, because our humanness disavows God's words given to us to ponder. We search and search for something to help us make sense but overlook the fact that the answers are not over the fence.

All the answers you seek are right under your nose, and they are hidden behind the door you have chosen to close. Behind it is something that can scare us half to death. It is the question: why am I here to take another breath? We ask the question without really wanting the answer, because we know the truth will mean changing what matters.

We would rather deny that we hold our destiny so near and prefer to live with our haunts and the things we fear. Take it from me that it is much easier to fess up and accept that God knows all, and you do not know much. When God is allowed in your life, a huge burden is lifted and you begin to see His plan and where you are gifted.

What seemed important before will start to take a back seat, and suddenly you will see more in the people that you meet. Everyone will become like a messenger from God, and you will value their soul and where it too has trod. Their status in life is no longer how you define them, and you can see their soul when your own you have finally met.

It is impossible not to have empathy when you know the truth that it is God, not humans, who get to give reproof. The sympathy you feel when you see that a soul is lost must be used to help that soul at all costs. It is not for you to fix, but you can be an example. God will do the work for you to give a soul a sample. To appear like you know all and they know nothing is to take away from the soul what God must bring.

Through your soul is how God connects to each of us, and no other soul will trust in you if you are kicking up a fuss. All souls that find the answers have an urgency to share, and by doing so some other souls may get a big scare. It is not good to overwhelm others with what your soul has. Remember, it took you a long time for the wisdom to amass.

All humans resist when change has come around. Change is the only way to show us where we are not sound. Those that refuse change need to be managed with compassion, for those are the souls that must find their own passion. Anyone who thinks they have all that they need to know are the ones who desperately seek the answers that are unknown.

The journey of each soul never ends on this earth. All souls are leading back to the one that gave them birth. It is a lifelong journey to learn what you are here to do, and the challenge is to depend on God to pull you through. Bottom line: that is what we fear each day: the trust to have faith and hope in what God has to say. Our humanness gives us impatience when we do not see results, and we take the easy way out and our soul takes the assault.

I have lived with that doubt that God does not know best, and I have also lived with a soul that has had much unrest. As with everyone, I too struggled with the fear of losing control, and it was imperative to me that I always be in the know. What I failed to see is that none of us has it right and there is no substitute for God's insight.

God's insight is gradual, and you will not receive it all at once, and our impatience is what will not allow us to take another chance. We want relief so badly that we get frustrated easily, and we get angry at God for giving what we think is too measly. You must be willing to earn what God must share, and it is important to not give up when you think He is being unfair.

To get the answers you seek, you must trust that He knows best. The distrust you feel is what is giving your soul its unrest. Without you realizing it, God will work wonders for you each day, for He knows what your soul seeks when to Him you pray. I know of what I speak, for I too have been in your shoes. I have distrusted God and ignored what my soul already knew.

My own journey to God was not an easy path to take, because I was raised to believe that I had to be fake. The abuses and dysfunctions that I suffered as a child made my road to adulthood anything but mild. My mistakes were many and I did try to learn, but my fumbling soul knew there was something else I had to earn. I sought relief for my agitated soul in worldly things, but what I was searching for nothing on earth could ever bring.

Finally, I dragged myself and my limping soul to church, and then and only then did I end my human search. I gave up control and turned my soul back over to God, and I learned the error of my ways and the path I was supposed to trod. To this very day I am held in awe at God's infinite power, at how He doles out mercy when you are in your darkest hour.

It amazes me that He never lets me go without, and He delivers if I believe without a doubt. My riches in life are not things that others can see. My wealth is the wisdom that God has shared with me. The price I had to pay for the peace that I know was to trust that God would show me where to go. For this I did not have to exchange human currency, for God gave me His wisdom and insight so freely.

For reasons unknown to me, He gave me these words to write, and all that I have written comes from God's insight. His words are delivered through me for humans to understand, and I believe that to not share them will be my reprimand. Many hours I have spent putting words to paper wondering what the result of the wisdom will be that I cater.

I think of those who will shun the words I have to say, and it is for those souls that I will pray. I cannot judge the doubters, for I was once one of them as I too tried to keep my soul quiet and locked up in a pen. My only concern now is my soul and to do as it says, for I know that God will be there when humans start to razz.

Humanness will try to have me doubt what God has written, but I now understand humans, and it is with God that I am smitten. No human has been able to match the wisdom that God has shared, and with God on my side, I have no reason to be scared. I do not have to defend the words I was prompted to write. From God's lips to my hand, He has shared His insight.

It is not the battle of words that God wants to incur. It is for each of us find our soul and allow it to be heard. We must understand the doubters and why they are here. It is them, not God, who have us living in fear. God is not to be feared, but He is to be held in high regard. Putting Him first is what we humans find so hard. We are given human rules that God does not apply. You must follow God's way if you want His reply.

We cower away from God's rules thinking they are too hard, and we revere the humans' way and hold it in high regard. God has two rules that make the rest of His rules make sense. They are to love God first, then love yourself and others next. When you have put God first, your answers become clear. Loving your soul and others' souls will bring God near.

Hate, disdain, and judgment have no place in God's world, and those who feel these things will always topple their hurdle. It is impossible to be God-like when you choose to deceive, and honesty with yourself is what you first must achieve. Can you hold your head up knowing you caused no one pain? Are you able to say you did not hurt another for personal gain?

There is always payback for the times we ignored God, and we must receive all karma for the path we chose to trod. Both good and bad deeds will receive God's payback, for God ensures that each soul has what He knows it lacks. There is no rhyme or reason for when God brings His karma down. It is when you least expect it that God's karma comes around. No one is safe from karma and what it must bring, and your karma can make you sad or make you want to sing.

Avoiding karma is impossible because it is both good and bad. What you must consider is: what kind of karma did you have? Are you in disarray, thinking that life has no direction, or are you content knowing that it is all done by God's perfection? A hard pill for us to swallow is to accept what is our fate, and we struggle to be right and allow ourselves to be up for debate.

Instead of accepting the truth, we fight for what we believe, and, in the meantime, we ignore our soul and what it must achieve. Therein lies the answer to what every soul must seek: the ability to accept our soul and where it is weak. Recognition of this gives you the strength you desire, and acknowledging that you are not alone will take you that much higher.

Our humanness gives us limits, but God's way is wide open, and there is no end to His mercy for that with which we are coping. He has an endless supply of wisdom to share with you and is willing to interject when you do not know what to do. Your frustrations with life are due to your disregard of this, and your contentment will come when you accept that which you have missed.

It is not God's wish for any soul to ever go without, and we humans must begin to understand what He is all about. The mayhem that we see each day has not been done by God, but it is the karma that He has doled out for the paths we have chosen to trod. God must keep the scales balanced to serve His own purpose, for each time we disregard a soul we make karma worsen.

God is keeping score, because in the end it is up to Him. Only He can judge where a soul has been. God's way is not complicated and is pretty cut and dried. Have you listened to your soul and tried? You cannot command from God, as it is He that owns you. He will command, and it is up to you to hear and do. To plead ignorance when you know what you hear is to cause God to give to you what you fear.

Honesty with God is needed to ensure you are on the right track, and to take that away will leave you to hold the slack. God does not play games, because all souls need Him too, but if you are not ready for Him then He will leave you to pull through. God knows true sincerity, and it is on this that He waits. It is naïve to think that God is not in charge of your fate.

Your relationship with God cannot be built around lies, and to find your answers you must cut human ties. There is no human who can give you what God must share. No human can give your soul God's unending care. God's power is not to be feared; it is to be held in high regard. He is the only one to pull you through when it gets too hard.

Each day when I open my eyes, I marvel that I can. How do I sleep each night, only to rise again? Why does He continue to give us a new day? What a loving God we have to give chances for our doubts to sway. Nothing compares to the peace that God has given to me. It is a comfort to know that God is caring for what I cannot see.

If I keep my focus on God and what He wants, I know that He will take care of what my nemesis flaunts. To retaliate on my own takes away from Gods' plans, and He has shown me enough times that only He understands. I endure what humans dish out and I defy them, because to succumb to their ways will bring me karma again.

Temptation comes each day to deter my faith's path, but I ignore temptation to avoid God's aftermath. I choose not to defy God because I know His power is immense, and for that reason I live freely and avoid what makes others tense. The stresses of life do not bother me because He will provide, and I have faith that I will receive what I need to survive.

I have been given so much, and God continues to give me more. I do not question His provisions and ask Him, "What for"? It is not lost on me that people wonder about my sanity. I know I am the odd one out in a society that runs on vanity. Having the best of everything is the least of my worries. Pleasing God before anything takes away the need to be sorry.

We are in awe of those who have millions to spend, and to be truthful is to wish that we could be one of them. Even for just one day so you could experience the other side. That one opportunity to feel important in a limousine ride. Why do we think that these selected ones have what it takes? Do we not realize that God is using them to show us what is fake?

All the riches in the world do not impress God at all, and if you want to impress God, try saving a soul from a fall. God has His own accounting system in which no money trades hands, and your debits and credits are based on how you treat humans. Have you valued God higher than you think your value is worth? God cannot value in heaven that which we feel is worthy on earth.

In God's eyes all souls are equal no matter what you may think, and it is our soul that will determine if we rise or if we sink. Our priority system is out of order when we have souls that are lost, but we insist on amassing earthly riches at any cost. Millions of dollars are spent to fight wars each day. What right do we have to murder a soul that did not have a say?

We are fighting a losing battle to try and gain control. Have we not figured out that humanness is not the way to go? You cannot force change and you will always lose if you try. Change will only come when to our human ways we will die. Our society has become numb so that we can cope, and we go along with the masses and have lost the will to hope. No one has the answers to reverse what we have done, so we ignore our souls and each other we shun.

There is a way out, and all souls know the truth: that we can save each other if we would just accept God's reproof. The time has come for us to shift into a different gear. Now is the time that for our souls we must fear. Each day that we waste disregarding what is our fate is another day closer to our God who patiently waits. His clock is ticking, and He has given us many chances, and our time is coming to face what we did not give second glances.

We do not have time to waste, and it is to our souls we need to listen. God is speaking quite clearly about what we are missing. It is imperative that we finally get our priorities straight. Embrace your soul today and do not stop or hesitate. Accept your fate and take your place in His plan. Now is the time to step up and do all that you can.

All the souls on earth must unite and become one. It may sound impossible, but I know it can be done. It is simplicity at its best, the answer to this feat, and that is to cherish all souls whether or not you ever meet. To say a simple prayer each day is to let God know you are on board. Please, God, save all souls and no longer let us hoard. Our humanness will question how these words can do anything, but our souls will not question the peace that these words will bring.

To pray for all souls puts your soul in the pack, and praying for all souls will show you what your soul lacks. All souls praying in harmony is like music to God's ears, and He will deliver the answers to still our fears. As you read this, it is possible that you are doubting what I write, and I am sure you have questions about all this insight.

The very fact that you question should be your start, and God is giving you another opportunity to finally do your part. Take a moment to reflect on what God and I have to say. Accepting your soul will be the start of a new way. Embrace it wholeheartedly and release your human doubt, for God does have all the answers and only He can show your soul what it is all about.

Chapter Five — You Have a Soul

The human body is an absolute work of art; each of us has all the same parts.

Your brain and your heart both keep you alive; lose one or the other and you would die.

Your brain and your heart work quietly each day as a team to help you move and store what you say.

Each one of them has an important job and at one time or another has caused each of us to sob.

You can have a broken heart or a mental breakdown and blame each one when our soul isn't sound.

Do you think with your head or with your heart? How are you supposed to tell the two of them apart?

We have all been advised to follow one or the other when we have tribulations and all of life's bother.

Reliance on the battle of the brain and the heart is what keeps our soul from taking part.

No textbook diagram shows a picture of a soul because we are not exactly sure where it would go.

Does your soul live in your heart or in your head? Where exactly inside does the soul make its bed?

Your soul lives in you, from your head to your toes, and it is with you wherever you go.

Your soul some of us have called our personality; it is the person you think makes up your reality.

Your soul is what is giving you life, and without it your brain and heart would have no might.

Not having a soul would make your body a machine, each part perfection and each part so clean.

Thank goodness each one of us is given a soul to know, experience, and to live and to grow.

Your soul was created with you in mind, and the body that came with it is its shelter for a brief time.

Your body is the temple in which your soul lives; your soul is the temple from which God will give.

Your existence on earth was never by chance, and the soul you have was given more than a glance.

It was designed with a divine purpose in mind, and it is this purpose that we each must find.

That is why you were given a brain and a heart, for no other reason than to give you your start.

When these two things can no longer go on living, your soul returns to the one who did the giving.

We scoff at this thing that we call a soul because we cannot explain its ultimate goal.

It is easier to think that our body is all biological because the thought of a soul is not logical.

It is easier to believe that when you are dead you are done instead of believing in God and His son.

We would much rather plod along in our life and not listen to our soul's divine insight.

We struggle with feelings felt in the brain and heart and forget that the soul is another body part.

The Sun Neither Rises nor Sets

Your soul uses the brain and heart as its tools to show you that neither the heart nor brain rules.

Your soul is your heart and brain's discontent; it is the side of us in which our entire life is spent.

Your soul is that whisper that you hear deep inside of where your brain and heart both must reside.

It is that whisper that we choose to ignore as we saunter through life thinking there is no more.

The mechanics of the body are astounding, it is true, but it is only a body without the soul that is you.

The soul whispers a calling to you and me, but it is with our heart and brain that we choose to see.

Our brain and heart denounces the calling, yet neither can explain why you keep on falling.

Our brain and heart seem to jockey for first position to help you make all your life's many decisions.

Neither of them will ever win in that long race, because it is your soul that has all of God's good grace.

Accepting what your soul says as the truth will open the doors to what you are really supposed to do.

Believing in your soul is believing in God without doubt; doing this will show you what life's all about.

Accepting that to which you have been called will not make you perfect, for you are a human after all.

What you choose to do with the whisper will be a battle of the heart and brain to have the last word.

Following what it is that your soul has to say is difficult because the heart and brain get in the way.

We think these two organs have all the clout and dismiss a soul using another's self-doubt.

Your soul is exactly the way God wants it to be; that is why He gave one to both you and me.

It is your soul that holds God's tests of all time; your soul is the free will that He gave you to climb.

Believing in your soul and what it has to offer will show you that you are your life's best author.

Understanding that your soul is a God-given gift will give your sagging hopes a much-needed lift.

When you believe that your soul is worthy, the battle of the brain and heart will be less of a flurry.

Trusting in the whisper of what your soul has to say will help you to cherish and embrace each day.

It takes commitment from you to give up the control of all in your life that you cannot begin to know.

You must realize that the control belongs elsewhere, and what you control is to hear the whisper.

Our lives are spent rushing through each day, and we push aside what it is that our soul has to say.

We are driven by our brain and our heart, each of them delaying what we know we should start.

Our heart leads us in all the matters of love, and our brain tracks whether they are the one.

The heart is for love, and the brain is for hate, and your soul is the peace on which we each wait.

When these three things are in alignment is the time that your soul is ready for refinement.

It is then that your soul will dictate to you exactly what it is that your soul is supposed to do.

Some hear the whisper and decide it is not for them and let their heart and brain battle again.

It is inevitable, though, once you hear the whisper, to silence the yearning that feels like a twister.

It feels like you have forgotten something and you cannot recall it no matter how hard you think.

It nags and goes around and around your insides and when it will stop is only for you to decide.

It is up to you to discern the whisper you hear and to embrace it with love and without any fear.

Your soul is not there to steer you wrong; it is there to guide you in life as you mosey along.

Signs are put in our path each day, a visual from God when we can't hear what our soul has to say.

We ignore the signs, deny the whispering, and then heave a sad sigh about what our life must bring.

Everyone has a soul, no matter the body's condition; all bodies have a whisper to which to listen.

We feel pity for those with half an arm. We think God has let their soul come to some harm.

Their purpose cannot be heard by you or me; what they teach is that all is not what it seems.

They are chosen by God with the utmost care, not for you to pity and certainly not for you to stare.

Their purpose in life is known only to them, and it may be that their purpose is to help you to begin.

To pity someone and think their body has less is one of God's many soul-searching tests.

Feeling sorry for someone who cannot function completely is wrong because you are what you see.

What our outer body displays as imperfection is what each of our souls sees as its own recognition.

Your doubt about souls is kept inside of you, tucked away so others can't see that you have one too.

Our focus seems to be to find our soul's own faults, to deny its perfection that we continue to doubt.

You are given free will because God wanted it that way to help you hear what the whisper has to say.

God molded your soul to be exactly as He wants, and He gave it a whisper from which He taunts.

Your soul is the cornerstone of your heart and brain, and when they stop it is your soul that remains.

What happens to a soul when your body is a corpse; well, it must go back to God, of course.

Religions say that the righteous are saved, but in heaven there is room for the souls that God made.

How God decides if your soul lives for eternity is dependent on how you manage the hell that you see.

Hell is on earth, and it is what you live every day; heaven is where a soul must make its way.

Hell is why we ignore the whisper of our soul; heaven is your purpose and your soul's ultimate goal.

God keeps each soul until His judgment day, and that is the moment that He will have His final say.

His teachings in the Bible are made clear, and your soul knows them all and keeps them near.

Whether or not you listen to what your soul has to say, your destiny is decided when God has His way.

Into your soul God breathed His precious life and gave it the will to choose wrong from right.

The battle of your brain, heart, and your soul is to get back to God and know that it met its goal.

The Sun Neither Rises nor Sets

Your calling from God is in each of us, and your soul knows that hearing it is a must.

The discontent you may feel comes from your soul when you ignore its whisper and continue to toil.

The frustration of your soul is a thing called free will, which blocks what your soul whispers still.

What would be the point if God made it that easy for all of us to hear the whisper that keeps teasing?

You would be born and dead in the same day if your soul heard God's calling before it got underway.

No matter the amount of time you spend on this earth, your soul has a purpose that needs to be heard.

Your life could be long, or it could be short; only God knows how much time your soul has to work.

The Lord giveth and the Lord taketh away, and it is He, not your soul, who has the final say.

Questioning why He takes a soul when He wants pushes you away from your soul and what it flaunts.

It is not your concern to question what only He knows, for by doing this, your soul will cease to grow.

A soul's purpose would be meaningless if it knew everything; God's infinite wisdom controls all things.

No sense can be made of His ultimate plan, and it is up to His souls to do what they can.

Two rules are ingrained into each soul; love God first and each other second are from what we recoil.

How can I love a God that I cannot even see? Overcoming that doubt will be your soul's victory.

How can I love everyone when no one seems to care? Loving others is why your soul is there.

It is your soul's whisper that speaks volumes to you, and tapping into it is what you need to do.

A soul's calling is available across the board, and it is to be shared and not for you to hoard.

God does not rank callings as better than the rest; having you fulfill your calling is your soul's test.

Your calling is something you think you cannot do; your calling is something you think is not you.

That is the way it is supposed to be, the battle of your heart, brain, and soul to help you see.

We don't take the time to sit and discern, and the whisper we have we regard without concern.

We just want to get through each day and hope the next one will bring what we want our way.

So each day we go through our routine, pushing aside what we don't think will set us free.

We take each other for granted and stifle our soul with what we think our heart and brain know.

Inside each of us is a wisdom so profound and can be received when we hear a whispering sound.

What you do with the grace shared with you is up to your free will to think carefully through.

Reading a self-help book from cover to cover will not tell you what your soul needs to discover.

You will put the book down thinking it's too hard and return to what you think is written on your card.

You stay with what it is you think you know and decide to put up with the yearning of your soul.

Self-help books teach you about yourself; they cannot teach you to hear the whisper that you shelf.

Believing in God and your soul's true intent are yours to discover through your own discontent.

How to hear the calling that your soul beckons you to will be by accepting His rules as true.

Love God first and then love everyone else; that includes loving your soul as you love yourself.

Your choices made from ignorance are because you did not give your soul a second glance.

You ignored your soul and what it knows best and used your free will to follow along with the rest.

Your soul absolutely knows wrong from right; God has given it that much of His divine insight.

It is into that insight that He planted the seed that makes us accountable for every good or bad deed.

You know in your soul when you made the mistake of snubbing life and choosing instead to be fake.

Your soul is given to you to live and to learn, and your soul could care less how much money you earn.

You trip your soul up with the choices you make, but it keeps trying no matter how long it takes.

All souls are equipped with self-doubt to teach that it's not an easy road to learn what God is all about.

How uneventful our lives would truly be without free will guiding us to choices A or B.

Believing that your soul has a mission is the starting point to what only your soul can envision.

Accepting the mission of what your soul knows as true will be a hard thing your soul must go through.

Following through with the mission is a hard test, and not doing so will give your soul unrest.

By believing, accepting, and following through, your soul will find peace in all that you do.

When you add up the peace each soul has found, a whisper will be heard worldwide that is profound.

Our differences will cease to exist, because we know that good conquers the evil we could not resist.

The next time someone tells you to follow your head or your heart, call on your soul to play out its part.

For your body is where your soul must reside, and inside of your soul is where God must decide.

Chapter Six – Pure Intentions

I have tried to pinpoint the exact time my mission came clear, for it was around about that time that my soul drew near. There must be many moments from which I could choose, the times that I questioned and asked, "What do I have to lose?" My journey to God was thwarted with many bumps along the way, and there were many times that I ignored what God had to say.

I would not be human if I said that I did not have doubt when I realized that God was going to share what it was all about. *"Why me, Lord?"* I would ask. *"There is nothing I must share. Leave me alone, Lord, for I have accepted what was unfair. Do not use me, Lord, for no one is going to listen to me. Stop with the whispering, Lord, for I have had enough to see."*

Oh, how I struggled and fought to ignore God's calling, and I did not want to own up to where I knew I was falling. I thought I had it right to sit back and be quiet. To never speak again about my life and to hide it. Of course, God had a different plan, as I have learned is His way. What He has in His mind no human can sway.

Many times I chose to see me as doing my best, but for some reason my life seemed to have upheaval and unrest. I did not want to be noticed, so I kept my mouth shut. The last thing I wanted was for others to think I was nuts. I have always been philosophical and able to dig deep, my mind always working overtime even when I sleep.

I questioned my normalcy as humans see that to be, and it came to me quickly that I was further ahead than they can see. Maybe I am the crazy one to think that God speaks through me. What if it's my own ramblings that

I give to others to read? It would be simpler to think that it's not God that beckons, but my found soul will not let me believe that for a second.

The only explanation I have for all the things that I write is that God has given me the words to share His insight. I have no writing abilities, and I have not been widely published, and what I have written only a few have read with little bias. I heard my calling every day to write just the right thing, and after what I have written I know there is more to bring.

I cannot help but feel that God has something else for me to share, but for me to find out depends on making souls aware. I have written many lines that rhyme for I am not sure what. Am I truly a messenger for what God wants taught? How is it possible that what I say could really matter? I am only a human with a soul that can shatter.

Isn't it enough, Lord, that I believe in you without any doubt? Why would you put me in a position to have my faith tossed about? It is futile to question God's wisdom, I have learned that. He has His reasons for why you are exactly where you are at. I have resigned myself to rest humbly in God's arms, knowing what He has waiting for me is not going to cause me any harm.

To falter and doubt what God has yet to reveal will not change the course of my fate that is already sealed. I am truly in awe when I read the lines of my rhymes, and I meekly thank God for choosing me each time. I am so unworthy of God's wisdom, and I know this, and why He has chosen me is not for me to second guess. What it comes down to is an acceptance of one's soul. On each soul is written a mission and is each human's goal.

Grasping that early on will make your journey worthwhile and ignoring that will leave you wanting and in denial. I was born to write in a style that is all my own, and there must be a reason that I write in a way that is unknown. I have tried to write the same way that other authors do, but the words do not flow, and the message will not come through.

My writings are in no way written to belittle or preach. Each thing that I have written is God wanting to teach. I am simply a means for God to use to show a different way. I cannot judge others; God will have His judgment day. My intimate relationship with God from others will bring disdain, and I understand humans are here to cause pain.

Everything I have written will come under scrutiny, and I have accepted what others will have to say about me. There are those who will fear the lines that they read, for they will see in themselves what it is they need. I know I will be called a liar and unstable, but that is okay because I know my place at God's table. People will want to debate the words that I have said, and they will denounce me as not being right in my head.

I am aware of the resistance that humans feel. We are all afraid to take ownership and to be real. We go along with the masses to avoid doing what is right. It is simpler to deny the truth, and our fate we fight. I certainly do not have all the answers, that is for sure; if I did then we would all have the spiritual cure.

What God allows me to know, I have put to paper. The words are given to help us now and to cherish later. All that is written is to benefit our souls and their mission. To embrace God's teachings is what your soul is wishing. If I allow my humanness to override what I know is true, then I know I would be unable to deliver these words to you.

My faith in God keeps me secure, and on Him I focus. I know that He will be there to help me overcome the fuss. Many human facts will be given to me to consider, brought to me by discontented souls that have chosen to be bitter. They come to cast doubt and sway me from the truth, and to succumb to their distrust will bring to me God's reproof.

I am not here to defend what I write, because I cannot. Truly I tell you that it is on God whom you must vent. I am but a messenger, and it is God that knows all. What I am doing is following along with my call. God is giving you an opportunity to stop with all the lies. What He wants is for all our souls to be given a try. There is more to life, and we have the answers to what we fear. Take it from me: His intention is pure, and your soul knows what is needed to bring it near.

I felt my calling all my life, but I had no clue it would be sharing wisdom in rhymes.

I never dreamed that all my suffering and abuse would ever come to any beneficial use.

All the tribulations that I had to endure are now just a distant blur.

They no longer have a hold on me, and they have helped me to be the person you see.

I have never held a grudge against anyone for anything to me that they may have done.

Even at a very naïve and early age I never succumbed to the feel-sorry-for-me rage.

As an adult I can put myself in their shoes and understand what they chose to do.

I have forgiven them even if they do not know, which has given me room for myself to grow.

My friends and family think I'm deep, and they say I am strong even when I am weak.

They marvel at my philosophies about life, whether they think them to be wrong or to be right.

They aren't surprised that my thoughts are on paper; they've heard them sooner or later.

Twenty-four years ago, at the age of thirty, I turned to God in a moment of hurting.

Up until then I was not a devout Catholic, and I wanted to believe that I was making it.

I lived my life not hurting anyone, and I thought that was all that needed to be done.

I guess you could say that I was a pushover, never wanting to see a living thing suffer.

Concerned with someone else's pain and never hurting others for my personal gain.

I am still that person, but I know so much more, for today I know how to let my soul soar.

I would not trade the peace that I have inside, even if God took away my only child.

The Sun Neither Rises nor Sets

The pain of losing my son would no doubt be great, but God's infinite wisdom I do not debate.

I know that His reasons always come clear if your soul is left open and you are willing to hear.

I see God's presence in every day of my life, and it is all mixed up with the love and the strife.

I take everything as a blessing, which helps me to see what keeps most people guessing.

My insight has come directly from God, and I call it truth, but you may consider it odd.

I will not excuse a single thing that I write; all of it written non-stop over many days and nights.

When I celebrated my thirty-sixth birthday, God's gift to me was His wisdom that filled many pages.

When you read, keep your soul open so that you can understand how I have been coping.

I do not profess to know everything, except that the rhymes are written to make you think.

I did not graduate high school and I have no degrees, but I do have a diploma to be a secretary.

Only one other book have I ever written, and me and one other knows what is in it.

I know it was written to show me that I could, even if I do not think that it is really that good.

It was written several years ago to prepare me for what I could not begin to know.

In life everything happens for a reason, as a life is designed just like every season.

There is a purpose behind everything, and I watch for what God is going to bring.

His messages to me He does not have to shout, for I believe in Him without any doubt.

My soul has been tested since I was a child, and from those tests these rhymes are compiled.

He was put into my hands at the age of six, when a Bible I received was added to the mix.

The same Bible sits today on my shelf, and I am now able to understand what it is all about.

I received it a month after my mother died, and I did not know her then, so no tears did I cry.

I was thirteen when I was told of her demise, and my life was torn open and I saw the disguise.

A whole new world was opened to me when I got to meet my mom's family.

My gramma was the pinnacle of faith, and I know today that it was on her that my soul did wait.

I loved that she believed without a doubt, and from her I learned what faith was all about.

I cherish our time together and our many talks we had about my mother.

My gramma taught me faith by her example, and her love was sweet and more than ample.

Gramma lived and breathed for God every day, and I hung on to every word that she had to say.

Her teachings that life could be endured were the words that my soul had always heard.

My first Bible and my time with my gramma taught me what I needed to know about karma.

I know she would be pleased with what I wrote, and I will end her introduction on that note.

To fret and worry is all for naught; you should be forever thankful for all you got.

Begging, pleading, and crying will not help, only onto deaf ears these things will melt.

Only when you have purged them away will your worries be forgotten for a day.

As hard as it is to believe sometimes, what has happened to you has all been designed.

You do not have a say, you cannot change a thing, it is your choices that good or bad bring.

Having faith can be a challenging thing to do when you are bogged down and feeling blue.

From experience these words I do speak because my own faith at times has been weak.

But in the end, when all is said and done, I have to admit that gaining faith was fun.

Fun because I learned and I grew, and my haphazard faith saw me through.

Why do you wait for the next shoe to drop, another test of your faith, another catastrophe to stop?

Why is the only time we look heavenward when all else has failed and our pleas go unheard?

Why is it then God's time to react when we give up control and want to give it back?

Why do we not leave it where it belongs and stop thinking that He is the one who is wrong?

Oh, if only these words I would always heed, never would I find myself in need.

Blessings and miracles, they are so bountiful; why do I question that they aren't so plentiful?

How can I get my message across that a life with no God is a disheartening loss?

You can't believe what you cannot see, but you believe in the air that you breathe.

It cannot be touched, nor can it be seen, but it is vital and something that we all need.

God is like the air that is around all of us, and faith and belief in Him is a must.

Me, my life at times has been misery, all the abuses in the world have been done unto me.

Whippings, beatings, assaults of all kinds are the scars that I carry in my mind.

How can a child survive all these things? Can it be by believing that life has good things to bring?

My mother abandoned me so young, and she died in a plane crash before her song was done.

My father feels he did the best he could, but his decisions were selfish and not very good.

However, those are not for me to judge, he will answer to those to the power above.

I cannot say that my life has been a total loss, for I have many more bridges yet to cross.

Each I will meet with my head held high, knowing that God is watching from far in the sky.

He is not only there but in all that you see: the birds, the sun, the stars, and the trees.

He did not have a hand in these things you say, but you can't explain the four seasons away.

How did these things come about, the grass, the tulips, the snowflake, and the doubt?

The Sun Neither Rises nor Sets

These things to make you think, like the mountains, the animals, the water you drink.

Yes, science tries to explain it away, but questions remain without answers ... too many to say.

Yes, there is an upside, but there is also a down to all those things that make us frown.

Murder, disease, famine, wars are done by the human race, and God sees them as a disgrace.

You do not have a say, you cannot change a thing; it is your choices that good or bad bring.

He does not create all the bad that you see; He gives you the opportunity to not let them be.

His love, His forgiveness, His faith is great, and He sits by and patiently waits.

He longs for our awakening to the fact that we are the answer for what we lack.

You say, "Oh, I can't do anything, just little ol' me." But united we can accomplish anything.

"Get your head out of the clouds, come down to earth; what you speak of has no worth."

How can togetherness not be a better way, when so far all that we have done has gone astray?

Who says the world must be the way that it is: torn, tattered, and losing its grip.

It is salvageable, that which has gone awry, but not in one day, and we will all have to try.

The mindsets, the one-track thinking, the caught-in-a-trap are reasons that things look black.

What are the answers to what can be done? Is it as simple as loving ourselves and everyone?

Of course, it all must start from within, by taking stock of who we are and what we must give.

A little or a lot is not what it is about: opening our hearts and minds will give us some clout.

"Well, I give and I give," you say unto me, "my money I can give to only things that I see."

Your money is not the answer, my friend, because your money cannot help you at the end.

God's soul carries both your and my name, and He tracks how we are playing life's game.

The game of life that He gave to us so freely to follow the rules and play so cleanly.

But we change the rules to suit our needs, and it's our souls that we displease.

We as humans have made so many rules, and all it has done to us is make us want to duel.

His rules are so much simpler to follow, and He has two that can make everything mellow.

One is to love Him above all things, two is to love each other and everything.

Love can be interesting in so many ways; loving nights is different that loving days.

Think about all the things that you love, each a blessing that could have been a "might of."

Might have gone a different way, you see, but your choices, good or bad, made it be.

Think of your life as an unfinished quilt and each patch is a choice upon which your life is built.

Some patches are sewn on tight and secure, while others are left undone from fear.

Dealing with what a patch represented was maybe a wrong that wasn't repented.

So what is the worst that can happen if you repent on that patch and make it fasten?

The worst is the restlessness that you feel inside: the itch, the ache, which cannot be denied.

Owning up to your unfinished patch is a freeing moment that nothing can match.

Finishing that patch on your quilt releases you from the sadness, anger, and guilt.

How can we be free from these emotions? Simple: by forgiving ourselves for all the commotion.

If you caused someone to be in pain, forgive yourself and they will do the same.

If you were caused pain by someone else, forgive them and then forgive yourself.

"It's not that simple," you cynics shout as you pull your tattered quilt up to hide your doubt.

So what is it that you suggest for completing your quilt, which is your soul's conquest?

"I don't know," you say as you shrug your shoulder and get another year older.

"It is too hard to fix mistakes; there have been too many, and they are done, for goodness' sake."

Okay, that much I can say is true, but can't you understand that they are what makes you blue?

The burden of carrying all of that around will eventually topple you down to the ground.

Then when you are down and feeling out, only then do you cry out and at God you shout.

Releasing burdens is not at all easy, but it must be done sincerely, not haphazardly.

God can see into a heart and knows if you are true about what you want to depart.

If you ask for forgiveness and you know it is not true, only disappointment will come unto you.

If you believe with all your heart and might, only then will He lift the veil and give you insight.

It is not fair to ask for forgiveness with a weak heart; that is the insincerity that keeps us apart.

That does not stop God from loving you, though, as He waits for you to believe and know.

He will never turn away those who are sincere, and He continues to hold the rest very dear.

He will not give up on you no matter what you do, but to be with Him you must be true.

"So what do I get from this undying devotion to this God you speak of with such emotion?"

"Will He make me rich or keep me poor? Will He make me happy or keep me sore?"

"Can He make all of my wishes come true? Will everything I ask for always come through?"

Depends on what you feel is important; are you asking for you, or for another's comfort?

It is not all about you, you must know that; it is about the homeless child eating your trash.

"Harsh," you say, "that's really gross," and then you deny the image and eat your toast.

We are emotional beings, you and I, and we do not want to hurt others or make them cry.

But we do so, whether we mean to or not, by turning a blind eye and acting like it is all forgot.

People think they have it so bad, yet they have everything someone wishes they had.

We want more, and we keep searching high and low, when really the answer we want is close.

Under your nose, which protrudes from your face, are the wanted answers in the right place.

It is always with you; you take it everywhere you go. What I speak of is your longed-for soul.

Without it you are nothing but skin and bone, and God gave it to you to nurture and own.

It is something that you received for free, and it is there from day one and will last for eternity.

No two souls are ever the same; each one is unique and has its own name.

Your soul is your essence, and it is only for you, and it is God's plan that you keep it true.

"Why am I here?" That is always the question. "What exactly am I supposed to accomplish?"

"I don't see significance for my time on this earth; what was the reason that I was given birth?"

Not to be flippant, but I will quote a cliché: we are here for a reason, but it is not for us to say.

WHY is an acronym spelt backwards, you see: **Y**our **H**oly **W**ill is what makes it all be.

It is not for us to question His way; it is only up to us to make the best of each day.

He has a plan and that is why He gave you a quilt; it is yours alone to complete to the hilt.

At everyone else's quilts we are always looking, judging, poking fun at, and always resenting.

She is so good because her quilt is so neat; look at his, what a mess, what a deadbeat.

Yes, we do it and do not even try to deny the truth that we judge others to get us through.

She is fat, he is short, she is selfish, he is poor; these things don't matter at heaven's door.

God does not say any of these things. What He asks is, "What to this world did you bring?

"Did you love me first and all else second? Did you put others above your own reckon?

"You didn't, and for that I am sorry; many years I gave you, and you spent them in worry.

"You had but two small rules to keep, and compared to your own, mine are not too steep."

Each of us will have our judgment day; God does the judging, and it is not for humans to say.

Let me assure you that it is never too late to make the most of your life if you do not hesitate.

Good deeds done without thought of return by you will bring you joy and get you through.

Here is the secret to honorable deeds and tasks: doing them gives return without ask.

Someday, someway, you get in return what you so selflessly gave without thought of earn.

We don't always take the time to consider how an unselfish act softens a heart that is bitter.

Could be your heart or theirs; it's amazing what happens when you show that you care.

The moment is here and then it is gone, and we realize that moment is for what we long.

That feeling of love so fresh, and without even knowing it we have passed God's test.

He gives us these chances when we least expect, and it is up to us to watch for the next.

If you see someone in need and keep going by, God says a prayer for you and lets out a sigh.

He never gives up; He keeps cluttering our path with choices that bring us either good or bad.

Do unto others as you want them to do to you: we learn this rule before we are in grade two.

Why do we insist our children do this thing, and as adults out the window this rule we fling?

Could it truly be as simple as that? Share your toys, your dolls, your glove, and bat?

Please do not tell me that this teaching is in vain and that we discard it to cause each other pain.

We marvel at the innocence of youth; we do not want them to grow up and learn the truth.

But grow up they do and life they embrace, and we hope that God gives them grace.

Here is a question I get asked a lot: Why does a child die before they are a tot?

This is a hard one to understand and explain, especially to those affected by such great pain.

You say it yourself when you ask the question WHY: Your Holy Will is what makes us cry.

His purpose in taking away someone so young should not be viewed as a song unsung.

Remember, as hard as it is to believe sometimes, your life does have a design.

You do not have a say, you cannot change a thing, it is your choices that good or bad bring.

Good things happen to bad people, and bad things happen to those who attend a steeple.

"That is what I am talking about," you say with a smirk. "Trusting in God does not work."

"Even by believing in Him bad things will happen, so why don't you just stop your yapping?"

You must believe that it goes much deeper, that having faith makes the ante much steeper.

The deeper the faith, the harder the tests that separate the believers from the rest.

Blindly trusting that His way is right makes all the worries of the world take flight.

Once you let that control go you begin to see things that you did not know.

If you try and dictate your fate, it will be that much longer on His grace that you will wait.

Giving up control does not mean you let up; many challenges will come to overflow your cup.

How you meet those challenges is a test to ensure that you are doing your best.

"It sounds like a lot of work, it sounds too hard, it's much easier to hold all of the cards."

I have been trying to tell you this all along, that thinking you have the control is wrong.

While you resist, He will watch over you, but until you stop resisting, there is nothing He can do.

Think about it like this, if you will, an example to help your denying become still.

Take a caterpillar becoming a cocoon; opened too soon, the butterfly will ruin.

It evolves over time and before breaking free it will struggle just fine.

By not knowing the ways of nature you helped the butterfly, thinking you were doing it a favour.

Taking control of something that you do not understand takes away what could have been.

Your life is like the evolution of a butterfly, and you go from crawling to flying high in the sky.

If you will allow what will be to be, in the end you too will be set free.

There is nothing you can do to stop what is coming, so you might as well stop running.

Turn and face whatever is coming your way and believe that He will get you through the day.

You are still thinking, *Who is she to write this by herself, without a degree on her bookshelf?*

"She has nothing to prove the words she writes; who is she to tell us what is wrong or right?"

God chooses His authors with the utmost care, and He will speak through those who dare.

Daring to believe without hesitation or cause that the only way to salvation is without pause.

Only those who can manage the ridicule and strife will speak out the words that cut like a knife.

The trials and tribulations I have had to endure have all added up to this rhyme and its cure.

My childhood saw much pain and abuse, and as a teenager I was made to feel I was of no use.

I tried to end my life at that time, but the forces foresaw my life's holy rhyme.

Pushed back I was from the brink of death, only to become with child and give it breath.

A young teen mother so I became. *Egads! Now what? My life will surely never be the same.*

Then it started, my real first test; do I treat him as I was, or do I give him my best?

They say that you become what you are taught. That's hogwash; what I was taught I am not.

I am not an alcoholic nor an abuser, you see, but for the grace of God there could easily go me.

I refuse to believe that it is right to hurt others, like the life lessons given to me and my brother.

As my abusers sought to discipline me, their look was one that I never wanted my son to see.

The feeling of terror I had to the tips of my toes is not what someone I love should know.

As I endured each slap, punch, and kick, I knew there was no way on another I could inflict.

The humiliation and shame are immense when someone is trying to make your soul diminish.

During that time I got my first Bible when I was six, and I have forever treasured this special gift.

I have the very same Bible to this day, given to me a month after my mother passed away.

I think there must be some significance from above to have this steady reminder of God's love.

I remember looking at the pictures so clear; they were colourful, so alive, and full of my tears.

Not really understanding what I had in my hands, I knew it was to be a faithful friend.

I took it with me to the foster homes, never leaving it behind no matter where I had to go.

The Sun Neither Rises nor Sets

This Bible today is still in very good shape, no rips or tears and no need for any tape.

I have cared for this book with all my heart, and it is where my faith and belief got their start.

Even as a small child I always knew that hope and faith would get me through.

Years later I think back on those times when the abuse I suffered had no reason or rhyme.

Seeing myself so small and full of fright yet still surrounded by a protective light.

It was like they tried to beat the goodness out of me, but He wouldn't allow me to admit defeat.

Meekly the lashings I would endure, never hitting back and just allowing the hurt.

"Wow," you say, "what was your crime?" There wasn't any; they just slapped me on a dime.

Back then foster home abuse was hush hush, and no one cared why these children were mush.

Until the day my brother was beat beyond recognition; only then did they make an admission.

My father married four separate times, and these women weren't mothers of any kind.

Only one of them ever taught me a single thing, and that was to be insecure about everything.

You are fat, you are dumb, you are not the perfect kid; of you I wish I were rid.

How mean and unfair we humans can be to lash out at someone we know is weaker than thee.

Who gave you permission to do such a thing, and unto another only unhappiness you can bring?

When did we decide that degrading someone was fine? Why has our respect for each other declined?

Why are there homeless people and children starving? Is it really God disregarding?

You see a person begging on the street, but your eyes you avert; you don't want them to meet.

"Excuse me, can you spare some change?" and you brush by thinking they are deranged.

Maybe you were just given a test; God wanted to see what was your best.

Myself, no loose change would I offer to give, and instead I would give them God's wish.

To the nearest eatery I would take them for warmth, comfort, and some food.

Maybe it is only the money they want, and "For what will you need it?" would be my response.

Sometimes they share or they do not, and I say, "Offering to feed you is what I got."

Many mouths I have fed this way, and I know I did give it my best on that day.

As long as you don't see it then it's not true. It is okay if it happens to others, but not to you.

Is there no way that we can help all souls? Should freeing them be each of our goals?

Our priorities are way out of whack; people are paid millions while others lack.

How do you put a price on a human life? Paying them enough to make them feel right?

If I do not have a God-given talent, is it fair to judge me as less gallant?

If I can't do what millionaires can do, does that make me unworthy to touch their shoe?

What about the millions spent on destruction? Couldn't the monies be used for construction?

The Sun Neither Rises nor Sets

Building homes for, and educating, our homeless are solutions for those under this stress.

Offering a hand up is what we are here for, and it is what we need to do to settle the score.

Billions we spend on fast food and junk yet brush off the beggar as a helpless drunk.

"They're not my problem," you say. My friend, you and I create the problem every day.

We do this by letting the earth rise and set and know we did not give our best.

"I'm busy, I'm stressed, I have issues of my own, I don't have space for everyone," you groan.

"I did not get them in the position they are in. They did that through their own stupid sin."

Maybe so, you could have a point there, but right, wrong, or indifferent, is it really fair?

It is not yours or my place to pass judgment on other human beings' choices or decisions.

Just as you have your own of these to make, you do not want others to judge your mistakes.

Another atrocity that happens every day is the abuse on an animal that has no say.

What must go through a human's mind to treat a helpless animal so unkind?

The horror stories we hear about these crimes make us blind with rage at times.

Our people, our animals, our earth is suffering, and we wait for each other to do the recovering.

So where do we start, where do we begin? It is all right there; you just start from within.

You need to get your priorities straight by accepting that none of your possessions can you take.

All they really are is a shrine unto yourself, and no one else cares what you have on your shelf.

You want others to think you have it all, but your house of cards is getting ready to fall.

All those things that you hold in high regard will not be at your funeral to be admired.

It will just be you in a big pine box with everyone whispering yet no one talks.

Tears they may shed about your demise, but are they real tears or just a disguise?

What are the people whispering as they sit there? "He was a good, kind man and always fair."

"She was spiteful and hated to be kissed; he was honest, and his spirit will be missed."

That is when it counts, and the mark you left on others will give God no doubt.

"Why should I care what people say? It is too late by then and will not matter anyway."

Yes, by then it is too late, that is for sure, but if you start now, life can be endured.

It is overwhelming to think what needs changing; you are not the only person who is raging.

Okay, so let us take if from the top once again: change must come from you and from within.

You must take stock of your emotional inventory and all that stuff that makes up your life story.

Do not trivialize it or keep it locked up inside but use it to your advantage and visualize.

The Sun Neither Rises nor Sets

See yourself as the good person that you are, as someone with immense potential to go so far.

Nothing is beyond your limit, and you need to believe that starting this very minute.

Forget all that negativity you have heard; it is for the best if you just forget every word.

Holding on to sadness and wallowing in self pity is a waste when we need to create unity.

We want to be heard and validated, but it is not another human for which we have waited.

There is no human that deeply cares about your hangups or your scares.

They listen and give some comfort, but when you are gone they move to another.

Your problems are the least of their worries, and you must be careful who hears your stories.

Unloading your grievances onto them will not give you closure or confidence.

They cannot make your situation any better, so why do you continue to be such a fretter?

You must stop worrying about things you can't control, and there are a lot of them, as you know.

You cannot control people even if you try, for that is a losing battle that will only make you cry.

They are who they are, and it is not for you to say how they get through their day.

You should appreciate them for who they are and not nag, belittle them, and push them too far.

When you continue to do these things, you make them want to leave the scene.

They begin to think, *I am not worthy, maybe it's time to find someone who will accept me.*

So, subtly at first, around they will look, and suddenly one day they are off the hook.

They find that someone to make them happy and leave behind the nagger who is crying sadly.

What could have been different? Try next time to not change the person you have been sent.

Besides, when we force people to change it is really ourselves that are in so much pain.

We see in them things about ourself and want them to stop so we can continue to indulge.

If only each of us would clean off our own step before looking at our neighbour's mess.

Our society would not have its many problems if we would take responsibility for our actions.

It is so easy to point over the picket fences and notice your neighbour's differences.

But when you look back into your own home you see the same deal and your frustrations grow.

Your issues are the same whether you are rich or poor; it is about the mess behind each door.

Human needs are the same no matter who you are, and denying that will not get you far.

Love, respect, acceptance, happiness, and peace are the things we each really need.

Hate, disdain, rejection, sadness, and upheaval are the things that are promoted by evil.

You have two sides of the coin to choose from; one represents dark, and one represents sun.

Some prefer darkness over the sun, and it is from that sort of people that you must run.

We cannot mock their way, for it is only to God they will have to answer on judgment day.

As you go through each layer that makes up you, keep only the things that are real and true.

Do not dwell on what others may think, as they do not matter in the whole scheme of things.

Let them judge if that is what they want, and remember it is their own sadness that they flaunt.

Embrace your strengths no matter how small they seem; each one is a blessing and will fill a need.

Your weaknesses are good things too, and strengthening them will only strengthen you.

Your experiences there must be many; draw on them and do not leave out any.

Some are good, some are bad, some have been happy, and some have been sad.

But they have all been given to you to try out, to assess your faith, to evaluate your doubt.

We are never given more than we can handle, and for some of us our climb is a steeper angle.

Why is it that some never get any lucky breaks, and some seem to get all the take?

We think they must be doing something right to sit so arrogant in God's generous sight.

Or is it simply that those with more than the rest are the ones being given God's greatest test?

In His wisdom He is giving them a chance to use what they have for the betterment of man.

Those of us just struggling to get by, He has no doubts about how we feel inside.

Our hardships He gives to us as a reminder that if He gives you a blessing you will be kinder.

If you have struggled, you are a fortunate one to be able to appreciate what will come.

Count your blessings that you are not one of them who must keep guessing.

When you have more than you know what to do with it becomes obscured that it is a gift.

It becomes a mantra: "What else do I need? I already have everything, so why am I so unhappy?"

It's nice to not have a worry in the world, but even when having everything there is always a hurdle.

We judge our lives by looking at others, some above and below us, and some that are neither.

We are relieved that we are not below ourself and green with envy of what we glorify.

We act like this is something that we do not do; what fickle creatures we are, me and you.

Our time on this earth can be done in a blink, but we have all the time in the world, we think.

Our days they are spent with our nose to the grind, and the meaning of life we are trying to find.

It eludes us at our every step, never quite within reach, way out there in the depth.

It is right there on the tip of your tongue; the more you think about it, the more it will not come.

So you put up with this longing inside and hang on for dear life on its roller-coaster ride.

Things are good and then they're bad, but it all adds up to experiences that you never had.

Experiences like falling in love; each time was better than the last, each time was the one.

Until the right one came along, and you believed that with this love nothing could go wrong.

Sometimes that love will make it through, but other times it is not good, and we bring it to ruin.

We keep going from one love to the next and wonder why our relationships are hexed.

The reason is not your fault nor is it theirs; it is because like attracts like, they go in pairs.

"What's this?" you say. "I don't understand; I thought you said everything was designed."

It is, but it is about those choices too, the ones that will bring good or bad to you.

The choices we make are not the wisest, and somehow we knew that but denied it.

Unlike when a choice we make is good, when given the options we did what we should.

Who you are at a certain time in your life is also the one you will seek, wrong or right.

Think about when you felt lost and insecure; was it someone of the same that you drew near?

When you were feeling confident and secure, was it someone of the same that you drew near?

Is it true what is said, that opposites attract, or is that an illusion on which we all act?

We only know what we think we know until we gain more experience and let our minds grow.

We settle on what we think we are, thinking this is all there is and there is nothing more.

As hard as it is to believe sometimes, what has happened to you has all been designed.

You do not have a say, you cannot change a thing; it is your choices that good or bad bring.

You have read these lines a few times before; are they making sense, or should I say more?

You were born, raised, and given life, and your choices since have given you peace or strife.

You were given a chance to choose one or two: follow the head or the heart, what will you do?

We need to make the wrong choices sometimes to help next time to remember our crime.

We don't want to make the same mistakes against ourselves, our families, or our friend.

Not to mention those that we hold in disdain or the ones that we never want to see again.

A child has no choice about what is done unto them, because they didn't choose their parent.

For their youth they cannot take the fault, but functioning as an adult is what it is all about.

Your childhood may have been unkind, but that doesn't give you the right to hurt humankind.

Those who tried to take away your worth cannot be judged here on this earth.

They may act like they have done no wrong, but they better make amends before too long.

It goes back to that quilt with your patches; each one is yours, and no one else's does it match.

Think about getting your own quilt repaired and fixing those patches of which you are scared.

In life we have this thing called karma; it is a word that ensures you peace or harm.

If you intentionally hurt another human being, the same unto you, you will be seeing.

If you intentionally do good to another, this too will be given back to you one way or another.

Don't you see the relationship between these things that your choices in life good or bad bring?

Are you getting the picture, is it becoming clear, that your lot in life is from what you hold dear?

If you choose to hold grudges and be angry, your life will be darkness and full of misery.

If you choose to let what you cannot control go, a peace in your heart is what you will know.

We want to see those that hurt us feel the same, so we fester a grudge and let it remain.

Not realizing that by choosing to let it go is when the power you believe in will make it just so.

Once you release all that built-up pain, your heart will find solitude once again.

Holding on to it only makes life harder; you must get rid of it and start doing better.

Own up to the things that you have done wrong and stop singing someone else's sad song.

Do not carry around others' weight of deceit, for your own wrongs are what you need to defeat.

Being honest with yourself gets this chore done, and toward your quilt of life you must run.

Look at it and see where the patches are fixed because your choices made it fit.

I am not trivializing your hardships in life; perhaps we've even experienced some of the same strife.

My woes in life are no different than yours, but I choose not to let them bother me anymore.

I can never change what was done unto me, but how I deal with it now is important, you see.

I could have become that which I was taught, but I only kept the good, and the bad I am not.

I never said once that I wanted to be that way, to belittle another to make my day.

I look at the person who caused me such pain and wonder why they are full of such rage.

What happened to cause them to break and think it is okay for another's dignity to take?

Truly for them I do feel sorry, but their retribution can't be my worry.

Sometimes I wanted to wish them pain, but in doing so, karma would find its way back to me again.

So I put my trust and faith where it belongs, into the hands of the one that fixes all wrongs.

All I can do as I go through each day is try my best to follow His way.

With patience He will see me through, and if He gives me a challenge, overcome it I must do.

Putting your faith in Him does not stop you from living, but it allows you to keep on giving.

Into our worlds we get wrapped up so tight that we lose sight of what is wrong and right.

The Sun Neither Rises nor Sets

You are not alone in doing this, for I am just as at fault of following along to be one of the cult.

Ignorance, it has many followers, an excuse we use that comes in many colours.

It is what holds us back from our fullest potential and diminishes our physical and our mental.

Turning a blind eye is easier, it seems, than achieving all our hopes and dreams.

Getting by in life is hard enough without facing the choices that are tough.

What can we do about hunger, homelessness, murders, wars, extinction, and diseases?

These things were not here until we came, us humans with our many mind games.

We have turned it into a complicated mess from which none of us can find any rest.

It is our world whether we like it or not, and it is up to us to change what was previously taught.

It is time to learn that disregarding each other is what is making each of us suffer.

Each of us has a role to play, and the time has come for each of us to have our say.

Your opinions you may think matter not, and being of this mindset must stop.

You and I have been put here for a purpose, so let us get it right, unlike those before us.

Those who may have tried but too soon gave up, half full or half empty, what was their cup?

Going it alone the troubles of the world can't be solved, for this to work we need to be involved.

Don't wait on the sidelines for others to take care of it; that is the reason for the mess we're in.

We don't speak out because we think no one will care, and we fear the "who are they to dare."

What others think of you does not matter, and worrying about that adds to your mind's clutter.

The one you fret about is no different than you, a different cover, but just as insecure as you.

All of us, we look different on the outside, but our mechanics are the same on the inside.

Inside of you is where it counts the most, for that is where you house your soul.

It is truly the one and only thing that you own, and all the rest of what you have is on borrow.

Your soul, not your material things, can get you what no money can bring.

On your soul there can never be a price, and it cannot be sold by the slice.

It was given to you as an act of love from the one that you do or do not worship above.

You are not an accident or an afterthought; you are exactly as He wanted, like it or not.

Your outer self He gave you in His own wisdom, and your inner self is yours to deal with.

We judge each other from the outside, and God judges you by what is on the inside.

What is more important, do you think, your loving heart or your marble sink?

Is it your preference to keep up with the Joneses or to appreciate the fragrance of God's roses?

Are you happy with all your material things, or will the next one true happiness bring?

What is the difference between a want and a need? A car is a want, and a need is to breathe.

The car you could easily live without, but death comes with no air, and of that there is no doubt.

So the important things we take for granted, like the air we breathe and all our senses.

We are so very lucky to have them; imagine not seeing, touching, or hearing again.

All of these were given to you, with some others to make use of before they are gone in a flutter.

To those whom we think God has given the least, they are there to show others how to teach.

The answers to life cannot be found in a riddle; they are not profound and are quite little.

What you seek can be answered very easily when you take off the blinders and start to see.

Stop acting, stop faking, and just be you, and you will find that that is what others want too.

Do not think you are above or beneath anyone, for your souls are all equal in the long run.

The façade that you put on for the world to see is not fooling God, others, yourself, or me.

You are no better than others with your fancy title that we humans regard as so vital.

They are used by us to keep order, but it is wrong to think that one is better than another.

Give respect where it is due, but remember on the inside everyone is the same as me and you.

Do not get lost in things that need to change, for our choices in life are what good or bad bring.

Things are what they are because we let them be so, because we are weak and let faith go.

We stand and shake our heads in despair, thinking this world is going nowhere.

We hear the same things repeated over again and wonder if peace will bring the misery to an end.

Little do we know that it is all within grasp, but it seems like such a daunting task.

We are a society of "it's always been done this way" and balk at the first sign of any change.

We get comfortable even though it's not good, unwilling to change even when we should.

That is us, creatures of habit, and when opportunity comes, we refuse to grab it.

Why do we sit back and do nothing when we know it is our choices that good or bad bring?

When you are old enough to make decisions is the time to be responsible for your visions.

What was done unto you through your life at times does not the rest of your life define.

You can make the choice to wallow in it or decide that into your life it does not fit.

Anyone who hurt you when you had no choice will answer to God in their own voice.

Of their deeds He has kept careful track, and thanks to karma everyone gets paid back.

It is not up to you to decide their fate; God will let you know, just be forgiving and wait.

It is crucial when our children are young to teach them to love and to have a clean tongue.

The words that we say unto their little ears are what they will believe over the years.

The Sun Neither Rises nor Sets

Teach them love, peace, and how to have fun, and show them the way to get things done.

Never hurt or abuse them with malicious intent, even if that is the way your own life went.

Help them understand the unkind things in life and the things that cause upheaval and strife.

Teach them that these things are not okay so that they may do it a better way.

Raising productive adults is all our obligation, and it starts at home all the way to graduation.

Just because they are not a child of your own does not mean you won't affect how they grow.

You may encounter them one day and wouldn't it be nice to have something fruitful to say?

Do not treat them like they are not very smart, for how you act could give them their start.

So always treat them with the utmost care, and they too will learn to treat others just as fair.

Of the billions of people on this earth only a select few will enter your world.

We lose track of all those that we meet, even though each one in our life played a feat.

Some meetings were brief or by chance, and some are done through a stranger's glance.

In and amongst meeting all these strangers, only a handful or so do we regard tenderly.

We open our hearts to what was at first a stranger, never doubting them or seeing any danger.

Some of them will have our best interest at heart, and some were up to no good from the start.

We must always be ready to make our choices and listen very closely to our inner voices.

Ignoring those is what gets us into trouble and leaves us with our emotional rubble.

Each of us has overridden our gut instinct, knowing full well we were making a mistake.

Naively thinking we knew what was for the best, we forged ahead and ended up making a mess.

Your sixth sense will never steer you wrong, and it has been with you all along.

It is that feeling inside you that gives you pause and makes you hum and haw about a cause.

As you truthfully weigh out the pros and cons, go along with the one for which the list is long.

Our lives are full of split decisions, with regret and grief as the outcome that we met.

We must do those some of the time to learn the lesson of once-burnt, twice shy.

Our choices we make that are good or bad should be thanked to God for a second chance.

Do the right thing on the second go-around and make your choice with both feet on the ground.

Did you know that you are your best friend and there will be no other but yourself in the end?

It is you in the mirror that you must like the best, and finding who that is, is another of life's tests.

If you are unhappy with who you see, how is someone else supposed to be happy with thee?

You can be content and feel well by understanding what I have been trying to tell.

The Sun Neither Rises nor Sets

Release all your pent-up rage and let love and forgiveness fill the space.

Negative emotions consume too much energy, and letting them go makes you feel carefree.

Keep the errors for which you are responsible and send back any for which you are not accountable.

Carrying around an offender's burden could be a lot of the reason that you are hurting.

You have too many of your own sins to forgive, so do these first and then really start to live.

Selflessness is a good state of mind, and to be selfish is to not use it to help humankind.

When you stop with all the head games and stuff, you will realize that you do have enough.

It is not always about the all-mighty dollar or whether you're filthy rich or blue-collar.

Our needs they are the same, yours and mine, but how we tune into those is the test of all time.

Giving what we can to our fellow man brings it back to ourselves once again.

You may think that you have nothing to give, but you have what it takes for you to live.

You have your heart, mind, and soul, and helping others to find theirs should be your goal.

It's not always done by giving money, but instead giving of yourself, which will not cost a penny.

There are those times when money is a need and those with an abundance should take heed.

Money is not for you to keep, and it is onto others happiness that you should reap.

Do not think that I am trying to tell you to give it all away; keep some for another day.

If your bounty is such you do not know what to do with it, build a safe haven for our homeless.

Stock a plane and fly it overseas and give peace of mind to those children in need.

There are many groups trying to bring misery to an end, and to them our money we constantly send.

We could be one step away from rescuing our human race by pooling donations in one place.

Each group has their own agenda in mind, and their overall goal is to be generous and kind.

Imagine each group with the same intent pooling their resources under one tent.

The money could be put to better use and go where it is supposed to and not left loose.

No one person gets credit for saving the world. Togetherness is the only way, or haven't you heard?

Alone you can accomplish nothing, but working together as one we can accomplish anything.

It sounds so simple yet we make it hard with this drive of ours to draw the winning card.

We cannot take the credit, the glory is not ours to keep, the ante right now is too steep.

When we can change our way of thinking, more wisdom our way we'll keep bringing.

What society has decided to do is to put a monetary value on me and you.

God shakes His head in dismay at how we can judge another human this way.

The Sun Neither Rises nor Sets

Plenty in your life you may think you own, but no one can tell that by your headstone.

Your mark you must leave on the earth some way, and it can't be what a tombstone can say.

Your name it can be etched in cement, and it has to be there because of what you meant.

Your name, some dates, and a little verse are all that will mark what you cannot reverse.

Your deeds on this earth can be big or small, and who knows them is not important at all.

Only time will tell what good you have done when only love, not hate, does the world overrun.

It takes you and I to both make the choice to help those less fortunate to have a voice.

Less fortunate does not mean that you are poor; it applies to all of us whose souls cannot soar.

Many go through life this way, searching for what they do not understand is faith.

When a soul has faith, it has purpose, and along comes the answers that have alluded us.

You see, when you stop thinking only of yourself you begin to realize what really needs help.

You will think to yourself, *I am truly blessed, and I know I can make believers out of the rest.*

Never boast to others that your faith is ample, but teach them that by your own example.

This is done by being meek, and if you are mocked, just turn the other cheek.

Never judge them for what they do or say, and eventually they will begin to see it your way.

You are not meant to save everyone; you are to do God's tests that into your life will come.

It is up to you to watch for these things and make the choices that good or bad will bring.

To a task each one of us will be called, and it could be big, or it could be small.

We must listen for what God is trying to teach and puts right there within your reach.

A world of peace is His greatest wish, and by loving one another, this we can accomplish.

Treat others as you would your family and you will find that loving will come easily.

Those strangers that you see on the street, acknowledge them, and let your souls meet.

Sometimes a smile is all that it takes to assure another that we are not all fake.

When we allow another to see our inside, they won't feel alone on life's roller-coaster ride.

We each want to know that we are not alone but distrust the faith that we had all along.

Your faith is where you will find the answer to all your questions raised in anger.

Realizing that your life is out of control and turning it back over to God is the only way to go.

When you stop playing that which is His role, you will find the peace that is needed in your soul.

He gives us many things to think about so that we will believe and have no doubt.

Many miracles happen every day: a birth, a new life, is one of those ways.

Each of us, that is how we got our start, in a protective womb from which we must part.

The Sun Neither Rises nor Sets

It took two strangers' souls to meet to give a life to you and me.

The fact that they did is a miracle of its own; a chance meeting that gave you a life to grow.

But was it by chance or was it by fate that a certain day in history is your birthdate?

As hard as it is to believe sometimes, what has happened to you has all been designed.

You do not have a say, you cannot change a thing; it is your choices that good or bad bring.

We are each here for our own reasons, and learning our purpose comes with each season.

Some of us, we may think that we know it all, but you won't until you have answered His call.

Do you take the time to listen each day to hear Him tell you how to do it His way?

You must take time to listen hard, because His answer can't be found on a business card.

Believing in Him is your one true test, and it is what is going to help you to do your best.

If you do not believe a thing that I have to say, look in the mirror and explain your birthday.

Give me your thoughts on what needs to be done, and none of them will I ever shun.

Who you are is not for me to judge; all I can do is guide you past what it is you begrudge.

You see, I believe that God has spoken through me to help me fill my own destiny.

By writing the words that fill these pages, He is saying plainly what He has been teaching for ages.

Do not think for a second that I am a "chosen one," because we are all equal under His sun.

Through some He must spread His word, and He will not stop at me until He has been heard.

Others have been teaching what God's trying to say, and you hear it spoken at least once a day.

Whether you hear it like this or in disguise, it's God speaking to you before your demise.

Do not go to your death with regrets and instead embrace now to make a difference.

I am not naïve, and I am well aware that what I have written to some is going to scare.

They will mock me and pick the words apart and try to convince me of how we got our start.

As I said, I cannot judge what they say, and I truly wish them well on judgment day.

All I can do is write what I am told and know it is a choice I made before I grew old.

I could have attempted to ignore my calling and left it to others to do the asking.

But you see, I looked at what is on my inside, and I listened to my soul's sad sigh.

I picked up a pen and began to write that which God has given me as insight.

I am not anything spectacular, as I have given you to see; we are the same, you and me.

I am not any better than the rest, and like you I am very much trying to do my best.

Unfamiliar words we hear spoken each day, and some of them we keep or will never say.

But "God" is a word that is said in joy and delight and can be said when we have had a fright.

"Oh my God" I am sure is something that you have heard; why do we all know of these words?

God is one of the words that we toss about whether we are a believer or have our doubts.

It is a word in our lifetime that we each will say whether we choose or not to pray.

Why does this word invoke controversy, and wars are fought over this word in countries?

God is what you profess Him to be; His image is different to both you and me.

Perceive your God to be whatever you want to see as long as in something you do believe.

Our God that we know and understand teaches the same thing to bring peace unto man.

The God that we each hold in revere wants us to love and hold each other dear.

The teaching comes no matter what you think, along with the choices that good or bad bring.

Your beliefs count, do not get me wrong; I am not here to take away what you heard all along.

I do not want to duke it out with you in a ring, I just want you to see what your choices will bring.

This applies to everything in your life: the good, the bad, the happy, and the strife.

Treat each moment in your life with respect, and in return that is what you will get.

Treating your life like it does not matter is actually what is making you sadder.

Your beating heart and each breath taken are two choices you have no say in making.

Doing these comes to us naturally and so should our choices to help others come as easily.

Make loving others a part of your day before your heart stops and your breath goes away.

My friend, for your journey I wish you well as you ponder these words I was prompted to tell.

Remember, it is hard to believe sometimes that what is happening to you is designed.

You do not have a say, you cannot change a thing; it is your choices that good or bad bring.

Chapter Seven — Happenstance

Is fate truly about being in the right or wrong place at the right or wrong time? Does fate have anything to do with the teachings that I rhyme? Are all the coincidences of your day simply there by chance? Can it be that we are not giving fate a second glance?

Write about fate, a good friend suggested to me. God's view about faith is what she needed to see. Fate is not chance, nor coincidence, nor a miracle, but what we think is extraordinary is what is already in God's oracle. Your life and its significance are all a part of God's plan, and you will have to play your role whether you think you cannot or can.

What we consider to be fate is a secret that God holds, and when His time is right is when His secret will unfold. All the proper things will be put into their exact place and then, and only then, will you be a witness to God's grace. A second either way and fate would not be allowed to occur, and you must have at least one story like this that you can concur.

To understand fate, you must be open to its awesomeness, and you must dig real deep to discover how it can or cannot affect your happiness. God designed your soul to intertwine with others, and without effort on your part you are made privy to their bothers.

If you review your life and what has come your way, it will not take you long to figure out what God has to say. It is a humbling experience to realize God's loving power and how He can place happenings to ensure our crowning hour. Nothing happens by chance; it is all done by God's design, and how you react to His plan determines if you have seen His signs.

Some take for granted the good bestowed upon them and do not see the significance of where God has been. They genuinely believe that they are getting what they deserve, but what they do not know is what God has left in His reserve.

It is naïve of us to take credit for our daily life, and it is even more naïve to blame someone for our strife. God gives us opportunities every day to embrace our fate; to ignore His signs is to leave yourself in constant wait. Each day God points you in the right direction, but instead we are expecting a sign that shows His perfection.

We are waiting on God's voice to speak directly to us, and we miss the signs as we kick up a fuss. What we humans desire is not always what God wants, but we succumb to our humanness and what it taunts. Our humanness roars and God speaks in a whisper, and listening to the roar will make you none the wiser. Our humanness distracts us, and God is overlooked, and then we trash God because we think we have been rucked.

What we may consider to be fate is what we least expect. It comes as a surprise to us, and we cannot determine what is next. So we say it must be fate and just leave it at that, not considering for real what is behind the facts. We should never take lightly the goings on in our day, for every moment is God whispering with something to say. If you choose to hear God, His rewards you will reap, but to ignore Him is a sure way to diminish the soul that you keep.

In my life there have been many circumstances that I cherish, and good, bad, or indifferent they have allowed my soul not to perish. Fifty-five years on this earth and I have endured so much, never certain when I will feel God's beckoning touch. I knew incredibly young that God had a purpose for my life, and it all came down to me and how I dealt with the strife.

The temptation to ignore God was prominent in my mind. Why should I follow a God that I believed could be unkind? If I truly had a mission, why wasn't I living like a queen, and what good could come out of the abuses that I have seen?

I consider Jesus when I use an example of fate. God had His plan for Jesus that was not up for debate. Jesus preached freely and His demise was God's intent. All was in order and Jesus's fate was heaven sent. Our own lives are like this and only God knows the outcome. God doles out our fate and we will all have some.

Your life will affect the lives of others, and the significance of you is to keep God's plan in order. What you may consider to be trivial is much larger. God uses you as a tool in this world for barter. We are each a stepping stone used to pull someone up. Who that is you don't need to know, and it was not done by luck.

To view all humans as someone who is working for God will reveal to you the path that has been designed for you to trod. It makes no difference if there are those that doubt fate. God's plan must happen, and on no human can He wait. God has souls to save, and He is depending on us to help. The fate of you affects everyone and not just yourself.

It is not good enough for God that you live an uneventful life. It is important to Him that our happiness equals our strife. This is where karma fits into how fate must roll out. Karma and fate are woven together, and of that I have no doubt. Good karma, bad karma, both have come with a price. Karma and fate determine if you have been playing nice.

God already knows how He wants your life to proceed, but free will brings karma and eventually fate to intercede. Many, many chances are given to us to get on track, but our humanness cannot grasp what it is that we lack.

Souls are not random; each soul is of value, and we all have a purpose, no matter if you think it is minuscule. Right now, this second, you are exactly as God needs you to be. Your very existence has been designed to allow others to see. No matter what your opinion is of your life and where it is at, God has already determined how you will deal with that.

Every aspect of your life has a reason that it must happen, and acceptance of God will help you to hear where He is tapping. It may appear that you do not have a say in all of this, but your say comes when you acknowledge to God what you have missed. It is all about asking for guidance to do your part in the plan. It is to say that you cannot but that God can.

Fate is not accidental; it comes around as it is supposed to. You cannot stop fate, as God has too much to do. Struggling against God will not deter Him from pursuing your soul. Having all souls return to Him is God's common goal.

All of us will have a time that fate took place. There must be some moment that you know you were graced or disgraced. If you take the time to consider how your life is working out, I am sure you can peg a moment when you felt God's clout.

Whether or not you agree, God always does the right thing. He does this because He is the only one to know what your life is to bring. What you think is something that you want to be is determined by God, who has the bigger picture to see. What you think are successes and failures are done by God's hand, and acknowledging that fate is at work will help you to understand.

Fate is a complicated thing that depends solely on details, and many facets must be in place for God's plan to not fail. A boost for you may mean a step back for someone, and a step back for you may mean that a boost is yet to come. God uses our souls to guide us in the right direction. God's plan for your life is in His eye's perfection.

We are lured away from our fate by what humans display. We want to believe that other humans have figured out the way. Your way is your own and God designed it to be so, and it is futile to fight against what God already knows. To be honest with yourself is when you know you are doing right, and to be dishonest with yourself is when against God you fight.

We each carry a feeling inside that determines our contentment, and when we are not doing what we are supposed to we feel resentment. What must be understood is that the ache you feel is God. He is waiting for your acknowledgement and to give Him the go-ahead nod.

When you cease struggling against your fate as it is designed, God will give you all the tools to help your soul to be refined. You are never in control as much as you want to believe you are. Your fate is pre-determined, and it is already written in the stars.

Chapter Eight – To Believe or Not to Believe

All of us have felt doubt, and it is how we avoid pain. It is a feeling like we must not be used for personal gain. We assess a situation carefully to ensure it is right, and sometimes we do not do this and get an unexpected fight. We doubt human intent as a way to survive, and it is our doubt as humans that we think keeps us alive.

We have become a society that judges motives that are unclear, and our suspicions about others are built around fear. We have all been hurt or have hurt someone from time to time. Each of us has had an opportunity to be cruel or to be kind.

It is because of doubt that we hold God at arm's length. We are too busy doubting humans and using all our strength. We doubt the unknown therefore we question what we cannot see. Doubt is the emotion that takes away our glee.

I never doubted that there is a God, but what I had to learn was trust. I knew early on that ridding myself of doubt was a must. It was hard to go that extra step and give up control, and I had to overcome many obstacles to let the control go. It was at my lowest point and in my darkest hour that God shone His light into the place that I cowered.

I remember it well, the agony that had me by the throat and choking the living life out me and filling me with doubt. There was no way out, and I was out of hope when I finally cried out to God that I could no longer cope. I knew I was lost, and my soul was nowhere around, but what I did not know was that at that moment my soul was found.

I look back now and see myself in the throes of spiritual agony, and I am glad I wised up before it was too lengthy. The second I embraced God and accepted the truth, I knew there was no turning back from receiving His reproof. As humans we balk at anyone telling us what to do, and we do not want other people pointing the way to go through. We treat God no different and choose to ignore His insight, for as humans it is important that we are always right.

It came as a surprise to me that all humans are weak and the facades we put on are so that we do not appear meek. The airs we display to appear strong are our humanness, and it is at God that we scoff. What a revelation to realize that all humans are the same and the outer exterior does not the insides ever change.

Every single person is equal in God's eyes, and it is we humans that dictate the fate of our lives. We have planted the seeds to who we think are worthy or not, and it is us that believe the lies that have been taught. To acknowledge we are wrong is where doubt comes in. To think another way would mean to question where we have been. Can it be as simple as to trust that God knows best? Has the time come to accept that we are failing God's test?

Our denial of God's plan for what we are to do is at the root of what we ignore and refuse to use. People call me deep because my thoughts are in a different place. What people do not realize is that I have been given God's grace. They doubt my intentions because theirs are not always pure, and my absolute faith in God is what makes people unsure.

My outlook on life is simply that what will be, will be. I focus on God and try to do what He tells me. There is significance for everything that happens in my day, and no matter how small it is, I know that God must have His say. When I want to question God, I remind myself that I am human, and only then will God reveal to me what it is that I am consuming.

My intimacy with God did not happen all at once, and I earned His wisdom ounce by ounce. I accept that I am weak, and God has made me strong. God has given me the wisdom to see where I belong. I am who I am and that can never be changed. Accepting this allowed me to have from God that from what I was estranged. When I stopped battling myself because I was lost is when God gave me His wisdom that had no cost.

God gives freely the peace that I carry with me each day, and what God has taught me no human can take away. All my material things are nothing except inanimate objects, and each one was given to me by God to fill a human need. I realize that God gives to me only what I need to survive, but the richest things in my life are what I do to keep my soul alive.

What others hold in high regard I denounce as fake. A huge bank account does not a happy soul make. Our humanness believes that riches are the only way out, and we surround ourselves with them to cover our doubt. We believe that redemption comes from human approval, and if we try hard enough then they will not notice our upheaval.

All humans have doubt, and our world is proof of that. Look around yourself and take a moment to see where we are at. Children are starving and there is no money to feed. Oddly, millions of dollars are spent to satisfy our greed. For some reason we think we are owed what we get, and we can accept that children starving is not our regret.

We allow homelessness and view it as not our problem and spend millions of dollars destroying other humans. What a misguided society we have that condones war by destroying unknown souls and thinking we deserve more. How is it possible that we think that this is all right, to belittle other souls and keep them up at night?

Do we think we are lucky that we are not them and continue to ignore the suffering of our children? Our human doubt is the reason we disregard, and we do not want to accept that life can be that hard. We make it complicated to ensure our victory, but God's way is not hard, and we doubt His simplicity. We have truly become a society numbed by discontent, and we have lost sight of God and where our souls came and went.

Doubt runs rampant and we distrust just to get by, and we have left it up to each other to live and to try. We have come to the point where we do not want to take our turn, unless of course we know that there is some earthly return. What is in it for me if I give a little of myself to others? And we think this as we cause someone else more bother.

"It's all about me and getting what I think I deserve. Thankfully, there are others who have been put here to serve." "I have nothing to give so therefore why should I try?" Don't we all have something to give before it's time to die?

Our doubt holds us back from trusting in God's plan, which depends solely on humans believing that they can. Our humanness, not God, causes us to live in distrust, and to change what is wrong means releasing doubt is a must. Doubt is an emotion that has come to rule the world, and we choose the easy road and ignore what we have hurled.

We think it will fix itself if we just give it time, and what we have not accepted is that now we must climb. There is a shift taking place that we should no longer ignore, and it is time to release all souls and allow them to soar. Our agenda is no longer ours, and God is giving us the signs. Those that doubt this need to accept and to God to resign.

If what I write causes you fear deep in your soul, then I suggest very strongly that finding God becomes your goal. The very fact that somewhere inside yourself you question if I am right should tell you that it's time to seek out God's insight. You cannot be saved if you doubt what your soul knows. Start today and release the doubt that within you continues to flow.

Work toward finding the answers that your soul speaks and remember that doubt is what has made all souls weak. Embrace God and hear what He must teach you, and never doubt for a second that He will pull you through. Believe that God knows best and allow Him to guide. The time has come for you to stop doubting and for you to decide.

Chapter Nine — There Is Only Now

What is around the next corner, we want to know, and some of us so badly that off to psychics we go.

We dole out money to appease our curiosity, wanting to know our future but not any atrocity.

Mostly the psychic will say what we want to hear, but sometimes they say things that put us in fear.

Their words are broad and never have an exact date and are said to make you sit back and wait.

I wonder what would happen if I saw three psychics a day; would they have the same thing to say?

If I wanted to know beyond a doubt, why wouldn't I get three opinions to give me some clout?

If your future is so clear it can be learned in an hour, why do we not leave it at that and let it flower?

Why do we have to pay money time after time to hear from someone what our life will define?

Is what the psychic says written in stone or will it have changed the next time you go?

Seeing a psychic seems to give us some hope, and we trust what they say so we are able to cope.

You are told just about anything that the future could bring, and you can interpret it to mean anything.

We are amazed when what they say comes true and wonder if the rest of it will come through.

Oh well, you think, *I'll go get my next fill; maybe my future changed, only they can tell.*

So off we go to see them with money in our pocket, thinking they will be the light in our life's socket.

It is true, and it is our human nature that we tend to believe something if it is written on paper.

That is the beauty of this thing called free will that allows us to fret or to be still.

You have the choice to let what will be to be and know that trust and faith are given to us for free.

If what a psychic says is all true, why should they take your money from you?

Don't you think if they knew what your life had to offer, that they would share it and not line their coffer?

Why should you pay to hear what they have to say when it could be said different the very next day?

We are driven to receive this constant reassurance and believe that knowing our future will comfort us.

We are told things to look forward to and then bypass on the life that was given to us to do.

Thinking you know what your future will bring puts the blinders on so that you miss the real thing.

Basing your life around what you pay to hear pushes what is important to the rear.

Believing that someone holds your life's answers will consume your life like a deadly cancer.

The Sun Neither Rises nor Sets

You lose track of where reality starts and ends, and you lose yourself when on them you depend.

It is a vicious cycle to go round and round trying to get the answers to make your soul sound.

Take a step back and take a look at what has already been written in your life's book.

Why do you fret and have unrest? Why are you thinking that other humans know you best?

What you truly seek is already on your inside and it cannot be bought to help you to decide.

How your life will proceed is a complete mystery, and no amount of money paid will reveal it to thee.

You choose to pay a psychic to say words, instead of choosing for free to hear what your soul heard.

Understanding that your future you do not need to know will replace doubt for faith to grow.

Faith, hope, and trust are given for free, and it does not cost you a penny in God to believe.

If He wanted you to know what your future held, do you not think He Himself onto you would tell?

If He wanted you to know then you would not be guessing about in life where you keep messing.

If you knew everything that was to happen to you, the truth would not help you to get through.

We do not want to know the bad, just the good; we want to hear the could and not the should.

Your life is not made to be that cut and dried that you can pay someone to help you to decide.

Paying someone to tell you their truth can be found in your self without any reproof.

Discerning what matters most to you cannot be bought; it's yours free in your soul to be taught.

We want a quick fix to this life that we find so hard and think the answer is written on some card.

How you view your life is entirely up to you, and what you get out of it is the path that you choose.

In life there is always a right and a wrong, and it is your choices in life to which you belong.

It is not for anyone to say what your future will bring; it's your choices that will define everything.

Chapter Ten — Turned Inside Out
We Are All the Same

It fascinates me, these facades we put on for the rest. The images we portray to show that we are at our best. We try so hard to impress that we forget who we are and reality becomes blurred, and our vision will not go far. It is too hard to be ourselves, so we easily conform, and we become each other, and our own soul is never worn.

If someone is different, we mark them as trouble, and at all costs we try not to let them prick our bubble. What fascinates me even more is what we perceive, as we act indifferent when we see others achieve. Meanwhile our insides are wishing that person would fall just to show us and others that they do not have it all.

That is the reality of the world that we have created. We pleasure ourselves by seeing others become deflated. What a sad situation to want to cause pain and to bring others down for our own personal gain. We do it every day and act like we are not doing wrong, yet all of us know the game and decide to play along. It is almost humorous to watch this game play out; the one where we act like we do not know what it is about.

We dance around the issues and make up our own rules and are in denial that we are looking like fools. God watches our humanness with a smile on His face, and He is truly amused when we try to put someone in their place. Our reality is not His and He lets the game go on, but playing chess against God leaves you being the pawn.

God has His own rules, which we choose to ignore, and He is many moves ahead and knows what is in store. If you doubt that for a second just look around. God is setting us up without you hearing a sound. If you are living in the reality manufactured by man, you are doing what you want and not what you can. Who are "they" and who does this choosing? Following their path or yours will determine if you are winning or losing.

God's reality gets no input from any living being. His reality is reserved for when He knows you are seeing. He allows you in when He sees that your soul is sincere. It is then that you will get a glimpse of what He holds near. You will not follow others once God has shown you His way, and you will become a living reality of His way each day.

He knows you will be an outcast for believing in Him, but it is not your worry for how others will sin. God's reality is not a place for those with doubt; if this is you, you know what I am talking about. We fear when someone suggests that there is another way, because then it is all for naught what we think, do, or say.

Our reality would shatter if we agreed that we are wrong and that what we have been living was a lie all along. Just maybe we have not been right to think that our reality is not designed by God's insight. Could the way humans think be the way out, to not believe in God and be filled with self-doubt? Are we really that naïve to not see the truth when God has given us so much of His proof?

If you do not think that the dawn of a day is proof enough, then you are locked into a reality that is too tough. To be accepting of each new day and what it can bring is the starting block to understanding everything. To have the earth rise each day without fail is a miracle against which everything else should pale.

Each earthrise is God's way to give us a chance to give His reality more than a glance. God will not force you to see what you refuse, and coming to Him unwillingly will make you of no use. It must be your own moment when you finally see that what you are living is human and not God's reality.

God's way is exact, and it does no good to question Him, for your faith has to be blind for Him to let you in. Human reality is to control, and God's is to set you free. God has no limitations on what He wants you to be. We limit ourselves because we follow what is normal and our lives become rigid, stiff, and too formal. We are afraid to step out of line for fear of rejection, and our reality becomes dependent on human perfection.

Humans have not mastered perfection and they never will. God created perfection and He is the only one to have it still. The beauty of a flower was designed by His mastermind. He created thousands, and it is impossible to know all kinds. Each flower is unique, and its beauty is to be adored, and God gave them to us freely to never hoard.

Your soul is like one of those flowers that God made. It is unique and from its beauty God did not dissuade. He admires each soul that He gave a life to lead, and each soul has a mission to live and to be freed. Our humanness will deny that we do have a soul, because the criteria is too hard to reach God's common goal.

God wants all eyes to be turned in His direction, but we avert our eyes for fear of human detection. Trusting in God allows you to see humans for what they are. We are bodies with a soul whose purpose will carry us far. Some souls are up to no good and others truly do care. Some souls cannot find their way, and some are already there.

It is good to listen to someone who has found their soul, for their soul will teach yours what it wants to know. Our struggles begin when we doubt our soul's intent, and our peace comes when our soul is content. How does one go about finding the peace of which I speak? It is by first admitting that you are weak. Strength comes when weaknesses are recognized, and true peace comes to a soul when there are no more lies.

Baring your soul to God will bring you His protection, and He will guide your steps with His own interjections. I know of what I speak, for it is my soul that I have found, and God has shared with me an insight that is profound. There is a peace in my soul in which I know God lives, and the more I accept His reality the more that He gives.

It is not material items that I want God to give to me. What I want is His wisdom that He gives away for free. His insight is not gained by receiving an hourly wage, and wisdom will not come if you must always be centre stage.

The peace of which I speak is earned by having trust, and giving up control of your reality is a must.

God cannot work His wonders when your vision is blurred. You first must recognize what it is that you need cured. If you think you are okay, then God will leave you alone. He does not force anyone to see what they must own. Where humans force us to change, God takes His own time, because God, not humans, knows the mountain you must climb.

Some humans try to play God, but they fail miserably, and what they forgot is that we are not all the same reality. All souls are made different and no two see things the same. What one finds disconcerting, another will use for personal gain. In life there is black, there is white, and there is also gray, and it is in that gray area that God wants you to hear what He has to say.

You may see black, you may see white, and the gray you may choose to ignore, but acknowledging the gray will help you to see what is in store. Combine black and white and you will always get gray, and it is in this combination that God wants us to stay. Black and white are cut and dry to make sense, but mix the two together and the wisdom is heaven-sent.

God's reality is the freedom to be the soul that you want. Human reality forces us to ignore the soul that taunts. The reality you choose will decide the destiny of your soul, but God's reality and human reality do not have the same goal. The question you must ask is: Do I want peace, or do I want strife? Accepting the answer to that question will change the reality of your life.

Chapter Eleven — Ask and Ye Shall Receive

Prayer is something you can do every day; call it what you will, think of it in your own way.

How you do it is not by others to be questioned; why you do it is what needs to be accepted.

Praying is not supposed to be a ceremony where you think what you are doing is sanctimony.

A prayer does not hold more validity because you do it down on your knees.

A prayer is not judged by how you hold your hands; it is done by what you ask for your fellow man.

All prayers go from your lips to God's ears; every single prayer is one that He will hear.

A wish is a prayer turned inside out and said by those of us filled with self-doubt.

To where are you sending this wish anyway? Is not a wish really a way to pray?

We wish things could be a certain way, and we wish for something at least once a day.

A wish is really a sort of doubters' test, to see if ours will be heard above the rest.

I wish for this, and I wish for that, we say while waiting for our life to react.

"I wish that I could win the lottery because I deserve it more than anybody."

"I wish that I could find true love because everyone else seems to have someone."

"I wish that I could have more material things because what I have in my life unhappiness brings."

"I wish that I could change the way that I look because that alone will get me off the hook."

"I wish that I had a different personality because people keep judging the one that they see."

If given three wishes, what would you wish for? Each time they are different, each time we want more.

When are we going to stop our wishing and realize in life you get back what you are dishing?

Life is filled with so many metaphors to help us understand what we are here for.

We say them, we wish them, and we do not pray, believing that life's metaphors will show the way.

Praying is straightforward, and its intent is clear; it is done to keep our faith near.

Praying will not give you everything that you want, especially if it is a miracle you want God to flaunt.

God hears every said prayer and answers them with what He considers to be fair.

So many prayers you say unto Him, and you forget where they stop and where they begin.

We pray for so many material things and forget to pray to continue to believe.

We want proof that our prayers are heard and scoff at God when we think He has not heard a word.

"There is no God because I didn't win the lottery; the promotion I got at work isn't enough, you see."

"There is no God because He has my loved ones dying; my friend had a baby after years of trying."

"There is no God because the world is filled with evil; look at me still being loving in all this upheaval."

"There is no God because my team didn't win the game; but they do have next year to try again."

"There is no God because He took my lover away; guess what, I just met my soulmate the other day."

"There is no God because bad things happen to me; in amongst them are a few blessings I see."

An answered prayer is not announced by a trumpet; it happens when you are least expecting it.

It will not necessarily come in the form that you asked, and realizing that is one of life's hardest tasks.

Every prayer that you say will not always be, because into the future you cannot see.

You do not know what is in store behind life's opening and closing doors.

Faith is always the underlying key, and with it will come your own understanding.

A prayer is always answered, believe that is true, for a prayer is God's metaphor given back to you.

When you pray to God, do you pray in jest? Is your prayer real or are you giving Him a test?

Is your prayer filled with so many conditions that your praying becomes nothing other than wishing?

Praying to God for an instant reaction seems silly even to us while we are asking.

He will not let your team score the winning run just because you pray so hard for it to come.

Your team's fate was decided before that day; no amount of praying will make it go another way.

Praying instead to accept the outcome will make winning or losing easier in the long run.

Praying is all about your needs and wants, and differentiating between the two is the hardest part.

"I want to win the lottery to pay debts — I need your wisdom, God, to show me how to pay my rent."

"I want a new car because this one has a broken trunk — I'll take any car, God, that to you isn't junk."

"I want a new love because this one isn't right — I need God to show me why this person is in my life."

"I want a new job where the money is better — I need God's assurance when I get the rejection letter."

"I want other people to change the person they are — I need God to show me that I've gone too far."

"I want things in life to always go my way — I need God's strength to get me through another day."

"I want all the answers because I have to know — I need to trust in God to let His will be so."

"I want that job promotion above everyone else — I need God's love when it goes to someone else."

Praying indiscriminately about this or that will set you up for disappointment before you even ask.

Send a prayer to God and then leave it alone; He does not need a reminder of what you bemoan.

He heard you once, twice, or a thousand times, and the amount you pray will not change His mind.

How you say the prayer can have influence — are you praying for someone else or your own wishing?

The Sun Neither Rises nor Sets

Are you praying for what you spiritually lack or are you praying to get a long-lost love back?

Are you praying for Him to give someone strength or are you telling Him your own wants at length?

Are you praying for comfort for someone who is dying or is your wish list for what you keep trying?

While you pray are you wishing well in your life or are you asking God to cause someone else strife?

When you pray, do you end it with "if it is your will" or do you say "I know that I'm right still"?

When you pray do you want an instant result, and when you do not get it do you allow yourself to sulk?

Prayer is not reserved for a certain time or place; a prayer should be said when He shows His grace.

Do not thank Him with no thought; praise Him profusely for whatever He brought.

Do not say to Him, "This isn't what I wanted"; one day you will understand the prayer that He granted.

God's plan for your life you may not understand. He can't reveal it to you even if your prayer is grand.

Only He knows when the moments are right and will answer your prayers with His insight.

Chapter Twelve — You Call It Christianity; I Call It Spirituality

I have heard many scenarios about what makes a good Christian. In all of them I understand that on a higher power you must depend. I do not dispute that and agree that something bigger than us calls the shots. What I question is: What are spirituality's shoulds and should nots?

God gave ten rules that have been construed in many ways. Each rule we use to determine who is or is not following His say. Love God; do not worship idols; do not swear; honour the Sabbath; respect your parents. Do not kill; do not cheat; do not steal; do not lie; and do not ever covet.

What is your ratio when you grade yourself on these? Are you ten out of ten or are you a human just like me? God gives us rules to teach us right from wrong. He gave them so we know on which side we belong. No human is perfection, and rules we are bound to break, and recognizing a broken rule will determine which road you take.

As with any parent, God needs to have His rules in place. He uses the rules as a means for us to stay in His good grace. We throw around so easily the title of who is most like Christ. We call them "good" Christians and see them as Christ-like. They must have an in, so we hang on to their every word, and we want them to say something that we have not already heard.

After a while what they say becomes tiresome and a bore, and we realize that being a good Christian is more like a chore. You seem to have to be this or that for God to accept you, and your frustration mounts when you think that you will not do. "Forget it. I cannot get it right," you say as you give up hope and turn to something else to help you to cope.

Having spirituality is much easier than you think. Finding your soul is what will pull you back from the brink. We are told constantly what God is expecting from us, but what is left out is that finding your soul is a must. Intellectually you can grasp what Christianity must teach, and you nod your head knowingly when you hear someone preach.

They affirm to you that believing in God is the way to go, yet you feel like there is something else for you to know. What leaves us unfulfilled are the rules that humans design, and we think that what they say is how we are defined. We are taught that we are not worthy to be in God's presence and that we are sinners who should never partake in God's essence.

God is supposedly reserved for those who are holier than you and I, and this is the misconception that has God letting out a sigh. Each and every one of us is to have an intimate relationship with God. Your relationship is your own and where no one else will trod. You are more than worthy to receive God's unending grace, and a relationship with Him is what puts your soul into place.

Your journey back to God must begin by loving Him. I am talking about a love where no other human has been. A love so deep that without it you would surely perish. A commitment so strong that it is only God that you cherish. The world does not need to know that God is your everything, and you do not have to display what to you God brings.

It is not necessary to convince humans that God exists, but what we must do is help them to find the souls that they resist. Finding your soul will allow God to do the work for you. To be a good Christian means to pull another soul through. Each human has a soul that is a piece of God. Searching out that soul and accepting it gets God's loving nod.

Do you see what I am saying to you as I write this? I am telling you what we as humans continue to miss. God's rules are to keep order, but our souls are His concern. For God to be whole again all souls to Him must return. It is our duty to save souls by being Christ-like, and we can only do this by keeping our own souls in sight. It is imperative that we stop thinking of each other as a sinner and start today by helping each other's soul to become a winner.

Saving a soul does not have to be a showy exhibition to one another. It is all about picking up a soul and brushing off its bother. A kind word or good deed can help a soul that is down, and doing this for one another will never bring from God a frown. When your intent is to do good, you make God's job easier, and it is God that you must impress and stop being a people-pleaser.

We want human affirmation that we are doing all right, but God will tell you that Himself through His insight. God is not to be feared as we have all been taught. You should only fear Him when it is Him you have not sought. Our opportunities to seek God's love are endless each day, and every time comes with a chance to give our soul a say.

Christianity comes in many forms and is built around a church, and we turn to our fellow parishioners when we are in a lurch. We seek human advice to quench a thirst that will not stop when really we should be seeking God's overflowing cup. Being a Christian does not require you to be a saint. Every single person has done something for their soul to be stained.

As much as we want to believe that there are those that do not sin, only God can determine what it is they carry within. Believe me, I am not perfect and do not profess to be, yet I know that God loves me and has a purpose for me. He gave me a talent that I never used except to journal, and now I have written many rhymes from my internal.

I am not a clergy, and I do visit my church from time to time, and for reasons unknown to me God has asked me to rhyme. I have the basics to know that I am a good Christian and my faith in God has made His rhyming my mission. I do not go out of my way to hurt others for my own gain, and I have this ability to want to help everyone who is in pain.

My compassion is for humans and all animals too, and I have been called to ensure that we all pull through. My kindness knows no bounds, and I give all that I can. Never would I deny my help to pull up another human. I have a knack to forgive that astounds my family and friends, and they cannot understand that not to forgive would be my end. I put myself in someone else's place, and by doing this I am able to see where God has graced.

I do not hold grudges for they breed negative energy, and I can only help others if my soul gets to live positively. I choose to see the good in people, especially when they are mad, and what I must ask myself is what has made them so sad. I will not judge others, for I have not lived their life, and it is not for me to say how they have dealt with their strife.

If I offend someone with the honesty that I speak, I understand that I have just shown to them where they are weak. I cannot apologize for speaking for what I know is right, and I always attempt to speak through God's insight.

To understand my views is to see my life when I was a child. What I had to endure was tough and anything but mild. When I was one and a half years of age my mom left my father for good, and I was put into foster care to be raised as best as they could. My father married again when I was around the age of three. I went to live with them, but their marriage was not meant to be.

Back to foster care I went to endure more unwanted abuse, and by age five I felt worn out and like I was of no use. At age eight I had seen more than any child should see: mental, physical, and sexual abuses had come to find me. Around this time, I went back to my father again. He was onto wife number three and wanted to make amends.

It is one thing to have strangers abuse you, but it hurts worse when done by family, and marriage number three was heading for failure, not surprisingly. By now I was a teenager and had left home to escape the carnage, but wouldn't you know it, I went back home for my father's fourth marriage.

At age nineteen I decided I'd had enough and attempted suicide. I wanted so badly to get off life's roller-coaster ride. Obviously I failed or you would not be reading all of this. A few months after that I found out that I was having my only kid. I was nineteen when my son was born. What was I going to do? I had absolutely no parenting skills to help pull me through.

That was many years ago, and now my son is a young man, and His life has been the exact opposite of mine because I chose to be a Christian. All that had been done to me my son was not to know, and I decided early on that into a productive citizen he would grow. In the process of raising my son I also raised myself. I forgave those who hurt me and stored it away on my life's shelf.

I came to realize that all my experiences had a purpose and that was to gain the compassion to see what is making humans worsen. I praise God for my ability to see both sides of the fence, and I marvel at God's power that always comes to my defence.

My compassion for all humans is the same across the board, and I do not judge anyone for what it is that their soul hoards. As with any emotion, my own emotions can run deep, but I must remind myself that God has all souls to keep. I understand that God has given me many gifts to share, and they all centre around a childhood that did not seem very fair.

To endure all of that and still embrace God was my test, and my road to spirituality has been what God knows is best. God's greatest examples of Himself are not those that we consider holy, and a soul must endure all aspects of life to understand this fully. To be able to put yourself in someone else's shoes is God's mission, and the ability to do this, is the compassion that we are missing.

A "good" Christian is not someone who is locked into judgment. God's need for all Christians is to search deeper for a commitment. You may think you are committed to God by attending church on Sunday, but has that allowed you to view humans in a different way? Do you leave church on Sunday knowing that your mission is secure, or do you attend Sunday service thinking that that is the cure?

Have you decided that you are saved because a church you support? Do you realize that it is yourself that God wants you to sort? We are all sinners whether we attend a church or not. God wants you to listen to your soul that wants to be taught. All the preachy words in the world mean little to a lost soul, and helping someone to find their soul is each of our spiritual goal.

To do this does not mean that you preach from a book. It is all about the life experiences that you did not give a second look. God gave us His teachings not to bring other souls down. It was never His intent for us to choose on whom we frown. That is not our place, and we must get over that. A Christian should not live in pretense, only in fact.

No soul is simply saved because we deem them as worthy. Only God can determine which souls are clean or dirty. As humans we can never fully know another's inside. It is only God that sees all and only He can decide. What you may think are safe from human eyes are not; God is tracking carefully what is your every thought.

My mom was Catholic, so I was baptized into this faith, and my son chose on his own to follow this way. Both of us believe in God and of that there is no doubt. What we have learned about our faith is that God holds all the clout. We require religion as a means with which to understand God, and after that it is all about you and the spirituality you choose to trod.

Religion is God's way of ensuring that our eyes are kept on Him. What we seem to forget is that religion is only where we begin. It is not enough to believe and to just let life take its course. A Christian's job is never done, but it is always better after the worst. Each day that God gives me is a chance for me to grow. It is an opportunity to open someone's eyes to what they do not know.

As I do this, I too am being taught God's holy will. I look for ways to show God's love and to others it instill. Have I doubted God from time to time? Well, yes, I have had to; how else is He to give me the wisdom I need to pull through? I have questioned God on occasion for a situation in my life, and sooner or later He showed me what caused all the strife.

It is through my conversations with God that I can see, and in those times, I am able to understand His intent for me. God is my greatest supporter, and I am so glad that He is in my corner. I have yet to see anything that matches His unending power, and following His way is for me not to cower. Nothing on this earth is mightier than the love God must give. Your life has no meaning unless you accept God's love to live.

My entire spirituality rests solely with a God that never sleeps. He is our saving grace, and every soul is what He wants to keep. Our greatest excuse is that we cannot believe in what we cannot see. I ask you then quite honestly: Why do you believe in the air that you breathe? Our air is the living breath of God that you inhale without thought. The air that keeps you alive is from a God that you may have not sought.

From God's lips to your own mouth He sends your lifeline, and to not accept that as fact is a long-standing human crime. You are kept alive with air that is free, and without it your life would end, and of that I am sure you can agree. So if you can accept that invisible air is important to you, why is it that you deny God and His ability to pull you through?

Once you accept God's existence, the next step is to let go. We must be willing to trust God and give Him control. His plan is His own, and He is willing to share your part, but it takes you to have faith in Him to give you your start. Then it is all about the patience that we humans have in short supply. It is through our patience that spirituality shows us what to try.

This process is a journey and does not happen overnight. God spoon feeds you slowly so that you can grasp His insight. If you are in tune with God, you will not miss His every sign and will trust that what takes place in your day is done by God's design. Nothing happens by accident and it's all part of His plan, and accepting this as truth is the only way that you can understand. When you have all this in place it is time to live beautifully, for you have found your soul, which is needed to love another soul unconditionally.

Chapter Thirteen — Infractions, I Got'em

Our society interprets sin as not following God's laws, and we have come to think that God's commandments have too many flaws. We see them as much too hard and diminish their intent, and instead we busily try to think of our own laws to invent. That is the greatest sin that each of us owns: to try and redo what God gave to us to know.

It is astounding to me how we can say God is not right and we do this when we keep His commandments out of sight. To read God's commandments is to read between the lines. God's commandments are meant to dissuade us from our biggest crime. All the commandments that God wrote are simple to do. Not one of them is unattainable, and they should be no problem for me and you.

Ten commandments we have been given and each one makes perfect sense, and to adhere to each one will ensure that you are in God's presence.

Commandment number one is for us to always keep God first, and by doing this the rest of the commandments will be easy to rehearse. Remembering that God must be loved before any other thing puts into perspective all the wonders that He must bring. Keeping your focus on God allows Him to reward your faith. In time all good things do come to those who can wait.

Many wars have been fought over God's commandment number two. He has asked us not to worship other idols to pull through. Think very carefully about all the religions that our world has. Each one is for a different culture to gather and have mass. God has been given many names and each one is correct; no matter the religion, it is a God that each must respect. Take away the dynamics of any religion and you will see God there. He is the driving force that keeps all religions fair.

How many times have you said "Oh my God" when you feel? Doing this is why commandment number three must be taken for real. God's name is not supposed to be used to give punch to your words, and using His name in vain is not something He wants heard. We do not even realize the insult we give to God when we use His name like it's dirt on which we trod. Its offensive to God when we use Jesus Christ as a swear. His son deserves better, as any parent out there knows to be fair.

Everyone has an opinion for what commandment number four has to say. This one teaches us to take a day to sit and pray. God asked us not to work on this day for many reasons, and it is only one day in amongst all your seasons. God's intent was for us to take some time to remember Him and all that He has done for us to have the world we live in. Whether you worship in church or at home in a chair, giving worship to God for one day a week does not seem too unfair.

Unfortunately, we did not get to choose our parents; God did that for us, and commandment five teaches us to obey them without any fuss. Our society has evolved to a point where that seems futile, but God gave us this commandment because we are each His child. If we cannot obey our parents, how are we to obey God? That is the underlying message on this commandment that we trod. Right or wrong, our parents deserve to be treated as such, because God gave them to you and about that you cannot do much.

Have you wished someone dead when you were really hurt? Commandment six teaches us not to be so angrily curt. God does not want us to kill or to even wish this on anyone. To kill another human being is where the world has come undone. Under no circumstances is it right to take another life. War is just an excuse to kill others with a gun or knife. There is no justification for ending a life before its time. Sadly, this happens often, and it is to the point where some can justify it as not a crime.

Temptation is the root behind God's commandment number seven. Somehow, we have lost the true meaning of what is heaven. Our society has accepted that sex is okay with anyone. By doing this we have defiled the soul of someone's daughter or son. The purity of sex has become tainted by committing adultery. We have become a society that does not respect marriage as sanctity. It seems to be okay to give into the tempter called sex, and by doing this we have a society without respect.

To take what is not yours makes commandment eight seem simple, but there are people who can justify what they see as being ample. "They have so much and therefore what I take will not be missed. I will take what I cannot afford and take it off my long list." Was there ever a time that you kept change that was miscounted? Even that is considered stealing when you are aware of the total that was amounted. Stealing is taking what you know is not rightfully yours. God gives you what you need, and stealing closes His door.

There have been many times when we think to lie is all right, but commandment number nine is what keeps some up at night. God teaches us not to lie, because it is a game that you will lose. All lies eventually catch up if that is what you choose. One lie leads to another and soon you forget the truth, and when a lie is found out you are left open to reproof. God wants us to be honest and pure with our words. To change the truth slightly is a lie waiting to be heard.

Every day we can find ourselves breaking commandment number ten by wishing that we were someone else every now and then. Our lives are not what we want so we covet what is another's, and this only breeds jealousy to add to all our many bothers. God gives us what He knows will fill our every need. It is our constant discontent with life that pushes us toward greed. To think we know better than God is our biggest downfall. If you would look at your own self, you would see that you have it all.

Those are our commandments that God lovingly made, but time has diminished them and made their true meaning fade. We have taken His commandments and made their intent minute. By doing this, we are in a great dispute. God's commandments were made to make adults play nice. Even adults need to listen to God's wisdom and advice.

We teach our children morals, which are really the commandments. Then our children grow up and see that adults are not doing it. It is no wonder our society is rapidly heading for demise, all because we overlook ten laws that were given by one who is wise. To disobey God has repercussions that must be taken as serious. Look around yourself and see what I mean if you are curious.

God punishes all sins in a way that is meant to teach. God cannot abide by anyone who cannot practise what He must preach. Our world is truly in shambles, and we did that on our own. God gave us fair warning when He gave us His commandments to be known. If each person were to adhere to what He had to say, our world would be given back to us before the next day.

We have made the choice to ignore God's wisdom and insight, and it will not be long before He comes back to make it right. We have proven to Him that we are not worthy to live down here when truly it is simple to keep His ten commandments near.

Our greatest sin against God is not loving Him more than anything else. By doing this we cannot love others, nor can we love ourself. God is in every soul that He gave to behold, and nurturing that soul is following the commandments that He foretold.

In God's eyes it is never too late to have your sins forgiven. He will always be there to show you what it means to be living. We are consumed with what I know God cannot abide by. Our society continues to give up and not want to try. It is our disregard for one another that has God wanting action, and to ignore your soul is counted as your biggest infraction.

If your own soul is meaningless then others will count as such. Too many souls wander each day yearning for God's touch. Sadly, they do not realize that it is God they are looking for. They believe they will be content by taking and receiving more. Each day that comes and goes is God giving us a test. We are to use each day to show that we are doing our best. Disregarding another soul is a shortcut to your own demise, and doing this allows Satan to help you stay in your disguise.

It is our need to be fake that allows sin to run rampant, and the way to be real is written on every commandment. We are only humans, after all, and we forget that, but for some reason we think that we know where it is all at. The answers we seek have not been revealed to anyone, and to think they have is from where we have come undone.

The Sun Neither Rises nor Sets

There are people on this earth who are starting to get it right, and we watch them perform miracles through the day and night. These people are trying to inspire us to think of others. They want us to see that others have a much greater bother. That is not to say that your own troubles do not matter, but don't you agree that compared to some, you have it better?

It is that understanding that will make the world unite, because doing for others will make the commandments all right. You see, when you are thinking of others you will have no time to sin, and eventually you will connect with your soul within. God's commandments are written for us to stop being selfish, and thinking of others before ourselves is His greatest wish.

Our world has become a place where to hurt others is accepted. We have become numb toward life, and no one is safe from being disrespected. Everyone is in a rush to get where they have no clue what is there, and going haphazardly through life is what is giving them all a scare. To make it through a day is a big accomplishment for us. Each day is a challenge to overcome each other's fuss.

We are making life more complicated than it really is, and by doing so we are blinded, and it is God that we miss. So how are we to get out from under all this mayhem? Could it be as simple as thinking of others first whenever you can? What God has taught me is that He alone will meet my every need, and to receive this from Him I must give to others His seed.

It is up to me to be an example of what God desires, and by doing this I will be able to fan someone else's spiritual fire. If others can see that trusting in God is not particularly hard, they may be able to flip over and read the other side of the card. Saving a soul does not have to be a glitzy grand affair. It is as simple as showing love and that someone really does care.

One soul at a time should be your only concern. God will take care of the rest when you teach someone to discern. God does work in mysterious ways with wonders to perform, and to recognize that will allow you to have a lot less scorn. He is the one in control of every facet of your life. He only wants what is best for you, but you are the one causing the strife. Our discontent is our own doing, and that is a fact, and we do this when we think that our life is not exact.

To feel that should tell you that you are not feeling God. Could it be that you would rather hear human applause? Human gratification does not last like we want it to. Only God has the power to give you glory in all that you do. He is consistent and will always remain at your side, and He will be the last one sitting with you on life's roller-coaster ride.

Never doubt for one second that God is with you right now, and if you cannot feel His presence then it is you that will not allow. Find a Bible from somewhere and read Exodus chapter twenty. I will bet for sure that you will find wisdom aplenty. Discern what you read on each line, and one day you too can join in and help save humankind.

Chapter Fourteen — Bestselling Book of All Time

Of all the books that have ever been written, the Holy Bible is one for which few readers are smitten.

Only a few have read every word that it has to say, and yet all of us will have heard about it in some way.

The Bible is looked at as a thing to fear because its teachings are not always clear.

We have based the Bible around the Ten Commandments and teach its true contents only at random.

Unto each of us has been given free will. God gave it to two and each of us has it still.

Two choices were given unto Adam and Eve and of that apple they chose to eat.

A lesson for them was given to the rest of us to understand choices and to trust.

In the Bible there are many firsthand authors; each has some wisdom to be offered.

Jesus Himself has a lot to say about God and why we should follow His way.

The Bible has a beginning and it has an end, and what is in between is from what we transcend.

Basically we hold God's ten rules as true and base our human laws around them for me and you.

In court you must swear on a Bible to guarantee that for what you are about to say you are liable.

We give criminals their day in court because they made the choice from our laws to depart.

We pray on Sunday and then we go shop, not taking the time to believe that God will not be forgot.

We marry someone that we really love and then have an affair with the neighbour that we covet.

We throw God's name around in profanity and ignore that it is not a swear word but His identity.

Our parents we constantly cause grief for the good or bad unto you they did teach.

We try to define God to suit our needs, forgetting we must love Him above all things.

We build many shrines in the name of God even if what we think they represent is odd.

What you just read are God's Ten Commandments. Can you now see what each one represents?

How you view life's commandments is not for me to say; you will reap what you sow every day.

For me the commandments are quite clear: they teach us to love God and each other so dear.

You can read them over a hundred times, and each time you will see that it is you that God defines.

If you take the time to understand you will see that each commandment was written to protect thee.

Not only to protect us from ourselves and each other, but also to teach us to treat each other better.

How you read the Bible is of no concern; the way you interpret it is how you will learn.

The Sun Neither Rises nor Sets

Open it up on any given day to whatever page, and your mind will learn something new for you to say.

In some of my darkest and deepest hours I did not curl up and from life cower.

My Bible I took down from the shelf, flipped it open to any page, and learned about myself.

The answers to life are written throughout this book, yet it barely gets a second look.

Our perception has occurred over time, and we have come to accept how we treat humankind.

We are given free will from the goodness of God's heart to give us the choice to live together or apart.

God's overall plan started when He made night and day; from start to finish He has the last say.

How did God one day just materialize to make heaven, earth, and all our lives?

If God created everything that you see, then who created God for all of eternity?

This is the question that we each find profound and base our belief or unbelief around.

Some of us do not question God's existence as truth, while some need concrete and tangible proof.

We look to each other for the answer to this question, trying to get each other to keep on guessing.

The answer to this question no human will speak; it is the answer that God has chosen to keep.

Sharing the answer with each of us will take away our lesson of learning to trust.

The place from which God does reside is too much to handle in the human mind.

He has the answer to the question you seek, and how you lived is when at the end He will speak.

For no matter what you do, think, or say, God will share the answer on your judgment day.

If you knew this answer, what would you live for? The answer is for God to use to settle the score.

He gives us all the tools that we need; He has even written them in a book that we do not read.

What is taught through the pages of the Bible are there to show that a belief in Him is dependable.

Of our own free will we can believe or not; He gave you free will to hear the answer you sought.

Each moment of your life is designed by His reason, the same way He put thought into each season.

As each season marks a time of year, it is the same in His own eyes that your life does appear.

No two lives will He make the same, and each of us is His own work on which His hand remains.

How you deal with the free will that He gives unto thee will bring into your life what you will reap.

No soul is a lost soul in His eyes, and that is why He gives you so many tries.

He has given you the choice to do good or bad, both of which can leave you either happy or sad.

The Bible was written to show you the right path and give to you the insight you never knew you had.

The Bible is not written to memorize every word; it was written to teach you what you never heard.

The teachings in the Bible are to some profound; to others they are what keeps our hearts sound.

The Sun Neither Rises nor Sets

Living your life is just as hard as reading the Bible; both hold things for which we are liable.

The Bible is not meant to be an easy read; it is meant to in your soul plant a seed.

Whether or not you understand every word, your soul will grasp the meaning of what it heard.

The effort you make to read God's book will perk your soul up to take another look.

The more you read will quench your soul's thirst, for what it knows should always come first.

Each chapter of the Bible gives your soul inner peace, and reading from it lets your faith be released.

The more you read, the more you will believe, and soon your doubts will all be relieved.

The wisdom in the Bible leaves you wanting more, and you will wonder why you never read it before.

Reading the Bible takes an open mind; read the Bible and let your soul decide.

If you think that the Bible is not for you, ask yourself how you are going to get through.

If you shun the Bible as just another book, how are you going to learn what gets you off the hook?

If you will not take the time to discern on God's words, how will you know the whisper you heard?

Reading the Bible from cover to cover will not make you a modern-day scholar.

You can only retain what your soul wants to know, and the messages are there to help it grow.

Keep the Bible on hand, and during a time of need, flip it open to any page and begin to read.

You will be enlightened by the words written there, whether or not they are the answer to your prayer.

Opening your Bible is opening your soul to God, and this act of faith will get His approving nod.

If you need to see God to believe, hold His book in your hands and it's God you will meet.

Open it up to whatever page you want, read a few verses, and know that by Him you've been taught.

The Bible may be an inanimate object, but it is alive with wisdom that is hard to reject.

That is why many of us refuse to open it, for we know it holds the truth we do not want to admit.

To have it spelled out for us makes it harder to sin, and why rock the boat when you have a good thing?

Is your life really all that it is cracked up to be, or is it time to pick up the Bible and read?

Are you struggling to know what life is about? Maybe it's time to read the book that you doubt.

You do not have to read it by starting with the first page; just open it up and read what it has to say.

It was not written with a set plot in mind; it was written to give lessons to humankind.

The storyline will not get lost if you read it out of turn; each chapter has a message to be learned.

Trust that God will give you insight as you need, and believe that in your soul He will plant the seed.

Your faith will start to grow leaps and bounds, and your inner peace will find solid ground.

My own Bible I received at the age of six, and it remains intact with nothing to fix.

The Sun Neither Rises nor Sets

The second page has my name and the date to remind me of how things rest with fate.

My mom died the month before this book came to me, and the irony of that I have come to see.

The final words in the Bible are directed at the human race to offer each other Jesus's grace.

An amen added to make everything be so will allow your soul to learn what it wants to know.

Chapter Fifteen — Bricks, Mortar, Soul, Cornerstone

Church is the place where sinners go to understand all it is that they do not know. It is one hour taken out of every week that we go listen to what God has to teach. We go through the motions of each ritual, forgetting at times their purpose and goal. We gather as one that has the same faith and say all our prayers for God to take. We feel our congregation is where we belong, because they, just like you, have done what is wrong.

The church is a safe place to be because we think that nobody judges you and me. Every soul in that church wants to do God's work and hopes to get insight from His spoken word. We then leave church and shake the pastor's hand, and we step outside thinking that life is grand. We fulfilled one of God's commandments that day by keeping the Sabbath sacred as He would say. We made the effort and put on our Sunday best and went to church just like the rest. We smile, nod, and feel really content to know that we are not the only ones from where sin came and went. We think our fellow parishioners have sinned just like us, so attending church becomes a must.

Attending church is a personal choice, and your reason for doing so only you can voice. Is it something you have done all your life and now you go with your kids, husband, or wife? Is it your meeting place before you go buy lunch and do not speak about what you learned as you munch? Is it where you went when you heard your calling, and you now depend on it to keep you from falling? Do you take what was taught in church that day and go out to find others to follow His way?

We go to church with our money in our envelope, feeling guilty if it is not as much as the church hoped. We give what we can even when times are tough, and fret and worry that it is not enough. We put it in an envelope so that nobody knows how much more or less your love for God goes. We try to volunteer at every function that the church puts on and worry that not doing so is wrong. We want those at church that we consider to be the elite to think that we are good Christians when we meet. We put ourselves out there for readings and choir to help so that the church does not have to hire.

We marvel at those that put up their hand and wonder if we are doing enough to help our church stand. We come every Sunday with our cheque already written. Isn't that enough to show God what we are smitten? A presence in the church should show my support, and four hours a month is what I can afford. I am doing my duty by making my presence known, and in fifty-two hours a year I feel my faith has grown.

What about the other twenty-seven thousand hours in a year when you are loving those you keep near? Do you stretch the fifty-two hours of church time over the twenty-seven thousand hours over which you must climb? Attending church does not settle your life's score. What you do outside of it is what brings you to God's door. No person should be made to feel that they are the worst because they do not attend what we call a church.

Church is simply what you want it to be, and life and reality are everything else that you see. Church is a building that we call God's house, but your soul is where God lives the most. Your soul is an extension of what you learn in church, and your soul is where you discern on God's word. How you choose to believe in God and what He has to say is through the whisper that you hear inside yourself every day.

Your soul already knows what the church wants to teach, and we go to church to confirm where we are weak. Your soul knew that it had free will all along to learn if what God said was right or wrong. His saving grace is not limited to those who pack the pew. His grace is for all who believe He is true. Some of His greatest believers do not attend a church, for they look to their soul to hear God's spoken word. They believe in God without any doubt, and trust that only He knows what it is all about. His followers come in every shape and size, and their commonality is knowing their soul is where God resides.

They are not boastful when trying to teach others God's way. Instead, they teach by example what their soul has to say. We have gotten carried away from what the Sabbath means. We mince words and try to keep God's laws clean. There is no way that every person can attend on Sunday. There are not enough churches to sit them all anyway. What about the sick, the dying, or those who cannot get there? It is not right to choose which is fair or unfair.

The world cannot shut down for one hour in a day so that each person can hear what God has to say. We are naïve to think that for an hour the world must stop so we can sit together and be taught. If you are realistic about our modern world, you would understand why some of us must work. Our technologies need to be managed each day, for we depend on them to run our world this way. Although they are smarter than any human mind, their very existence is dependent on humankind.

We excuse those who keep our world running smooth and pray for them, hoping they are doing the same too. So that covers them off, but what about the rest who put off on Sunday what six other days have not met? You have six other days to go out to eat and shop. Why do it on Sunday and the other six days not? No stores need to be open or restaurants either on the day that God chose for you to have no bother. Sunday is meant as a day of rest and a day to discern if we are doing our best.

Whether or not you go to church to think about this does not matter if the point is missed. You can formally go to church and hear God's word or sit at your kitchen table with the whisper you heard. On Sunday God wants you to take the time to reflect on yourself and what you hear inside. You have six other days of hustle and bustle, why use the seventh to continue the tussle?

Spend Sunday doing what God wants the most. Have your family over and cook a roast. Touch base with a friend that you have not seen in a while. Reaching out on Sundays is what makes God smile. Have a sit-down dinner with your kids, husband, or wife, and take time to pray and catch up with each other's life. Cozy up on the couch with a book you want to read, but just before doing that, tell God your every need. Take a long walk through a beautiful park and pray for God's insight to give you a much-needed spark.

Hug your kids and look them in the eye and tell them you love them for everything that they try. Take a hot bath and close your eyes for a moment and praise God for the bath's relaxing enjoyment. Cuddle up on the couch with the one you love and tell each other you are glad they were sent from above. Gather the family around to play a board game, and when the game is done it is your love that will remain. At the end of the day gather the family around and hug each other as the earth goes round.

You owe it to God, and you owe it to yourself to one day a week take your Bible off the shelf. You do not have to open it and you do not have to read, just hold it in your hands and tell God your need. Take as much time on Sunday as you can to rejuvenate yourself and your fellow man.

Showing love to someone on the Sabbath day will help you do the other six days the same way. If you do not stop and reflect at least one day a week, how do you expect God to help you with all that you seek?

Go to church if you want to hear the answer, but take the time when you get home to hear the whisper. He does not just speak for fifty-two hours out of the year; He speaks every single day, but it is up to you to hear.

Chapter Sixteen — Bound to a Higher Power

In my quest to express what God wants me to say, I read what others write to understand God in their way. Many books have been written with someone's point of view, and they have done their homework to show us how to look at God anew. Whether or not I agree or disagree, there is something fundamentally the same that we all want you to see.

As a human there is no way that any one person can be right. It is all about perception when we examine God's insight. If one were to remove religion and all the history it entails, one would be left with a society that would be doomed to fail. Religion is not about thinking that anyone's God is supreme; it is all about believing in a faith that no one else has seen.

The faith I speak of is the ingrained belief that you have a soul, and it is your soul that gives you insight to reach your goal. A soul does not dictate religion, as it is there to give you hope. Have you not ever wondered how on this earth you can cope? Take away all the controversial religious history that we adore, and you will find that your soul knows more.

We get locked into a religion because our loved ones do the same. Early on we are taught a religion for our family legacy to remain. What is believed is what each religion teaches to its young. We think we have it right to know where we belong. It becomes our mission to make our religion the one, and we lose sight of the fact that we can all see the same sun.

Each day the earth rises and then sets without our thought as we manoeuvre through each day with our purpose forever sought. There are questions that will have no answers that day, and we rest each night where some of us will pray. And without fail, there is the sun to start a new day of light, and what we prayed for gets lost there in the night.

On and on goes this ritual of sleeping only to once again wake, and we do this lifelong habit for however long it takes. Sleep, wake, sleep, wake, it is something we all have in common. Can you see where I am going with this act that we give homage?

While we are awake, we function as others expect that we should, but when we rest at night we sleep as our neighbour would. Only our dreams to remember when we rise the next morn, but our deepest sleep was the same as what others perform. In our sleep we do not have to be a believer in anything, and we cannot control what it is that our sleep will bring.

For a span of time, we sleep and trust that we will wake. Have you figured it out that God is anything but fake? Religion of the soul is knowing that sleep is inevitable and understand while awake you do what makes you capable.

It is not necessary to shrine your God in a ceremony or ritual, for what is at the centre is keeping your soul full. Mindless acts of conformity are not what your soul desires, nor does it want the aggression that religion conspires. Religion pits us against one another as the one who is right, and by doing this battle we have lost what is God's insight.

When I think of my baptismal religion at the Catholic church, I can fully see how we can think that God leaves us in a lurch. Do not get me wrong, I am pleased to have a religion of my own, but what I have come to understand is that I am not alone. You see, my faith is not built around a church made of stone. My faith is my belief that there is salvation in the unknown.

I do not have all the answers that we earnestly seek. The answers to your life can only be for yourself to speak. Religion is a tool that we must use to give our youth direction. After that it is for them to find out their own soul's perfection. Each soul has a purpose of its very own design, and the power that molded each soul can never on this earth be defined.

I know with great conviction that God exists for all of us, and the true meaning of God has been diminished in all this religious fuss. My vision of God may differ from yours and that is not wrong. What is pitiful is how we select to whom God will belong. We teach each other that sin is a sure way to eternal hell and that that is the end all to be all, and there is no more to tell.

Herein lies the conflict that causes far too much strife; there is room for salvation before the end of your life. God is goodness and of that no one can ever raise dispute, for I am sure that it is the good that we all aspire to. There is a marked difference between evil and goodness, and both have been used to get us in today's mess.

We want to test the limits of what God is going to allow and we don't live for the moment and see the here and now. We have been accepting of what we know is not God's way and we think if we partake that God will not hear what we have to say. We are righteous in our religions that we are above the evil, but God is not so easily forgiving of these righteously blind people.

To sit by and watch evil is as bad as committing it. It does no good for your faith thinking you are safe to sit. We have complicated things beyond our own comprehension, and what should be so clear is gone and no longer mentioned. We want to be politically correct, so we diminish our faith. We have become numb to reality and on a hero we continue to wait.

There must be someone who can change what we have done. Someone to fix how we sleep and then arise to see the sun. Is there no one out there who can show us the light? Can anyone help me to find my soul and its delight? Yes, there is, and you look upon them each day. It is that person in the mirror who has so much to say.

Take another look at the reflection that you see in the mirror. Now look a bit closer and see the soul that you fear. Stop for a moment and appreciate all that is you. It matters little of your body's condition to realize what you are due. Take yourself outside of what you may think your reflection is. Can you see the soul there that you have chosen to miss? Look closer and gaze into the eyes God has given to you. Focus on them and see what they are telling you to do.

Speak to your eyes as if you would speak to another. What are your eyes telling you as you share your bother? Are your eyes filled with hurt, anger, and so much pain? Do you see somewhere in there where they want to love again? If you think a happy thought, what do your eyes do? Is there a tiny spark of light somewhere inside you?

Cry to yourself if you must to feel all the hurt, and watch your tears as they drop onto your shirt. Do not be afraid of that person you see looking so sad. Embrace that person with all the love that you ever had. That is the person that deserves all the love that you must give, and staring back at you in the mirror is the person you must forgive.

Forgive yourself for ignoring what has been there all along, the fact that you do have a soul and it's to God that it belongs. If you doubt the existence of a soul then answer me this: how is it possible to feel love when it is someone you kiss? What inside of you melts when a baby gives you a smile? What sparks your anger when a child is defiled? Where does the sense of pride come from for a job well done? What spurns us on to do right by our daughter and son?

How come we help the less fortunate to get back on their feet? Where does the love come from when it is our soul mate that we meet? Who came up with the miracle of conception for babies to be born? A miracle that has withstood time and never seems to become worn. Why do we feel such joy at times that we feel we might burst? How is it possible to heal and get over our worst?

How come when we cut ourselves everybody's blood is red? Why must we all be born only to end our life as dead? How come our body images are different, but we all have a brain and heart? If we were ever turned inside out, would we be able to tell each other apart? Why do we smile when we are happy and frown when we are mad? Why do we lash out in anger and give hugs when we are glad?

How come some people choose to kill another human being? What is inside that person that no one else is seeing? Why do some people only do good while others cause mayhem? What makes some of us aspire while others do not think they can?

Need I continue or are you seeing the point I am trying to make? Some of us know our souls and some of us are fake. We think it's religion that guides humans along the way when it is actually our souls that dictate to us each day. Our soul understands that free will is a way of life. Some of us will choose the goodness and some will choose the strife.

It is a conscious decision we make to believe or not to believe, and all of this is done because we teach religion instead of a soul to perceive. Religion is not humanity; it only gives us a basis for faith, and connecting that with your soul is on what it truly waits. Faith is a state of mind that feeds the hunger of your soul. Can't you understand that your soul knows that God is its goal?

Have I offended your sensibilities with my honest candour? Or have I given you cause to re-evaluate and wonder? We are the same, you and I, even though we have never met. I can guarantee that I know you, for our souls already connect. Your lifestyle is your own and in that we may be different, but our soul's yearning is the same and that is apparent.

All the things I desire, I know you want them too, and that is to be loved, respected, and heard in all that we do. Take away all the prejudices that our society will dictate, and it becomes apparent what will be all our fate. Conceptually I know you agree with what I write here, but your beliefs may not allow you to confront what you fear.

Our many religions have a purpose, that much is true. It would be a boring world if your religion did not understand you. God gave us our differences for us to understand free will. Truly He knew what He was doing when this unto us He did instill. The journey back to God cannot be an easy one for a soul because each has a mission to help us become faithful.

The intricacies of our society work against our soul's mission, and we diminish our soul's worth with our human vision. I have come to understand my soul with each line that I write, and what I have grasped is that my soul has God's insight. Through God's divinity my soul has expressed many things, all of which I have written with only more wisdom to bring.

I listen to society's teachings and then I wait for God to speak, and what I have learned doing this is that as humans we are weak. We prefer to be led rather than listen to our soul's whisper. For some reason we think that another is just that much wiser. We hinge onto their every word, seeking the answers we want when all along our souls had the answers to flaunt. No human can teach us the intricacies of the soul that we have. Only God can inspire the soul's desires that will outlast.

If no one can teach us, how do we find the soul that we seek? Find someone that you trust that knows of the God that I speak. See how this person lives and if they are a good example. Try what they do and bring it into your life as a sample. Because my faith is steadfast, I know that this is correct, for people have been influenced by my life of no regrets.

People have mocked the God that I love and disparaged my faith in what I knew was above. I did not force my faith on them, for I knew that was futile; all I did was live with faith, and they understood after a while. They had so many hurts and grudges of which they could not let go. There was no room in their soul for the God they needed to know.

I would pray for their salvation and urge them to believe, and I would ask God to assist them to switch what they perceive. Never wavering in my faith, I would endure their cruel words, for I knew that God was listening and that all was being heard. Oh, how it hurt my soul to hear God being trashed so bad, and it was more than I could bear to see them so sad.

And then it happened: each of them had their epiphany moment, and I could do nothing except praise God for their comments. They cannot go back now that their soul has been found, for they know that what they have is something very profound. A peace has descended into their soul that is divine, and now it is more important to themselves to be happy and kind.

Grasping that they are not alone any longer gave them a power on their side that feeds their spiritual hunger. Seeing these transformations deepens my faith that much more. I am in awe of God, who has so much more in store. To understand the pull of God and why we should have appreciation, you need to know people will shield themselves with an addiction.

Whether it is alcohol, drugs, or other things used to endure, each leads to discovering that God is the cure. Replacing "crutches" with God's insight gives control to what a soul knows is right. It is a journey to learn one's purpose in life, and finding your soul will get you through the strife.

When I see darkness surrounding a body, I can also see a light shining that helps them to not walk blindly. It amazes me the peace that can be accepted as fact, and there is a great feeling of comfort when we interact. I do not force my faith into what they know, for I understand that I am the example that they are using to grow. They can see in me what it is that their soul desires, and all I can do is lend God's support as they put out their pain's fire.

I can do nothing except praise God's formidable power for the way He patiently waits for each of our appointed hour. In time we each have an opportunity to be saved. God will give each of us a chance to escape from what we are enslaved.

I can remember what it felt like on the other side of that fence. The times I was always angry and on the defence. I struggled along with what I thought was to live life and kept to myself what I thought was my strife. I balked at self-pity for the injustices done to me, meanwhile bemoaning the reasons for what I could be.

For thirty years of my life, I lived in a bad case of denial, keeping my pain to myself and putting others on trial. Seven years after that I was transformed and revived, and I have come to understand what I need to survive. It did not happen overnight, and I would be lying if I said it did. There were many memories for me to let go of in order to live. I had sunk low, and the darkness was too much to bear, and it was then that I asked God to get me the heck out of there.

My path led me to a church that was named for a saint, and I feared what was to come, but I did not hesitate. From this church I learned what my baptism meant. Slowly but surely, I came to see where God had come and went. My son was ten at that time, and I had him baptized at last. After that, the light became brighter, and the insight came fast.

Each day the load became lighter, and I was in awe watching the first miracle I saw. The sluggishness of thirty years was beginning to drop off and the peace felt so good that it would make me spontaneously laugh. The joy I felt at times made my heart want to burst, and I knew to keep it I would have to face my life's worst.

So I picked one thing at a time and I brought it to God, and we would work on it together even though I know that sounds odd. Each experience of my life made sense when God described it, and I learned what they meant and how they all came to fit. My childhood abuse had a purpose in amongst all the pain, and my teen years and twenties brought it all back to me again.

Turning thirty years old was the beginning of the end, and seven years later I understood about whom I must depend. I harbour no grudges for the abuse I was forced to endure, for God has swiped away my pain and shown me the cure.

Religion cannot teach us how to have God's friendship. What it teaches us is to fear Him and how to worship. God is not to be feared, for fear will keep us from Him, but we are to trust in Him that He will lead us from sin. God should be viewed as you would treat your best friend, and give to Him the love to your best friend you would send. The same way you nourish a friendship is what God needs too. It is all about taking time for Him to pull you through.

My best friend in the world comes second in my life, for I know that this friend cannot take away my strife. My friends are the ones that receive the love that God gives me, and it is my friendship with God that allows me to be what I want to be. My friendship with God has its difficulties, it is true, because sometimes I want to disagree with what He wants me to do.

I have learned that it is okay to question what is God's intent for answers received from Him for which I then vent. My humanness will have me doubt that of which I am capable, but my faith remains strong, and God keeps the boat stable. Most importantly, I have learned that God is in complete control, and I am my unhappiest when I do not do what I am told.

God always gives us the answers to choose carefully, and our destiny is written on the soul that He gave so easily. Religion is only a reminder that there is a power out there, but no religion can show you why your life seems unfair. Finding that out is for you and God to make clear, and it cannot be done if it is God that you have been taught to fear.

It is this fear that pushes so many away from God's love, for they have been taught that they are unworthy to go to God above. That unasked-for judgment forces people to live in sin, and what they are really in need of is for someone to show them how to begin. Right now, as you read this, God says you are worthy. He wants you to forget society's judgment and give to Him your worry. He wants you to know that it is other humans judging you, none of whom have this right to do what only God can do.

All souls are worth saving, and that is the gospel truth, and God is the only one that gets to give each soul its final reproof. To sit in judgment of others tarnishes the soul that you have inside, and it is wrong to think that you have God's power to judge and decide. No one knows the reasons for what goes on in another's soul, and our mission is simply to save a soul as our life's common goal.

Religion will not save the world; that will be done by God, and only He can determine on which path you will trod. Salvation does not come by attending a church once a week. You will receive salvation when each day it is to God that you speak. I do not mean by performing religious rituals that are old. I mean that you must listen for God and what you are being told.

God speaks to our souls every day to give them guidance, and His wisdom is not reserved for the one day of our faith's pretense. When you truly have God in your soul, you will know what I mean. You will be guided by a peace that to others can be seen. Surrounding you will be a light that cannot be resisted, and others will want what you have persisted.

Through God's guidance and strength you will be an example, and those that are drawn to you will not be able to resist a sample. Even the most hard-core disbelievers will wonder what it is, this thing that you have that they have chosen to miss. Having this relationship with God does not make you a saint. There will always be temptation calling ever softly and faint.

You will never be without the free will to commit sin, but it is up to you and your humanness to allow sin in. That is what faith is for, and only you can keep it alive. It is that ability to understand that God helps your soul to survive. Faith is hanging in there with God when times are tough, and knowing that no matter what, your faith in Him is enough.

In every trial and tribulation God is teaching a life lesson. We must learn when to react and stay away from where we should not be messing. We need to be that in tune with God that we hear His insight, and our every thought should be of God no matter whether we are wrong or right. The direction we receive in life must be what our soul desires. It must never be about putting out someone else's spiritual fire.

You have every right to disagree with the sin that you see others do, but it is not your place to judge how another soul pulls through. To judge someone leaves you open for God to judge you. Take back your judgment of others and begin anew.

I do believe that our society reflects our judging. This need to pull others down for what we ourselves are grudging. Our jealousness of another's success makes us want them to fail, and then we can feel justified about what our life has entailed. What a sad situation to secretly will someone's demise just so we can live a lie and keep our faith in disguise.

Do not kid yourself for one second if you think that God cannot see, for your own demise will be the spite that you kept secretly. I have felt the wrath of God for thoughts that were impure. He will eventually bring karma and of that you can be sure. It may not be that day, next month, or even in a long year, but God always brings back to us what it is that we most fear.

Just when you have forgotten that transgression from the past you will learn that your memory is short, but that God's can outlast. When you do not make amends with God for a human weakness, in time you will have to endure what are His justices. It only takes a second to help a soul that needs it, and you will get that back too when the time comes for it to fit.

How does one know which of these acts they have performed? Ask yourself if you loved or if you were left feeling scorned. Either way you will reap what you sow, and that is a fact. God does not want pain for us, He only wants our loving acts. Somehow, we feel that causing others to hurt is our given right, but it is because we lack the gumption to share what is God's insight.

We have this perception that we can play God down here, and we react to situations as if we want others to live in fear. Assuming we are in control leads us to act and not think. This assumption is what is pushing us to the brink. We are not in control of anything except choosing right from wrong. The rest is left up to God to decide where we belong.

Every decision has a consequence that must be fulfilled, and every choice has a reward that unto you must be spilled. Religion teaches us to revere God, who is rigid and unbending. If this were the case, would He give us chances that are unending? Day after day God gives us an opportunity to believe in Him. Repeatedly He continues to forgive our sins.

Why does He do this act of love repeatedly each day? Because God will not be content until all souls to Him make their way. The only way this happens is for each of us to believe. We must have faith in the soul that He gave us to receive. We must realize that it is our soul that keeps us alive, and in each of our souls God has instilled what we need to survive.

Our selfish ways must be recognized as our undoing, and this need to surpass others and ignore what is ensuing. It is futile to think that your monetary worth defines you, for there are no stores in heaven to buy what you need to. Does any one person deserve more than what anyone else has? What makes us think we are deserving of what we have amassed? Is it because you have worked for it and therefore it is yours? And because you are blessed you think that will open the doors?

Think again very carefully before you decide to answer me, and first understand that your wealth has little meaning to thee. Imagine for some reason a billionaire lost it all and was left on the street with no one to call. What would this person become without wealth to guide them? Would they somehow have to learn what it is they have within? To start from the bottom again on what would they depend? Would it be on the soul that they have that is now their only friend?

Do you think that they would then understand net worth and know that their soul has all the value on this earth? This example is to show you that our souls are the same. Take everything away and it's your soul that remains. We are all exactly equal and we need to understand that. To elevate one another is a human, not a God act. God does not care about our material things; He has no interest in your gold, silver, or pretty rings.

You cannot put a price tag on a soul, for they are all worth more. They are all priceless to God and cannot be found in any store. You have riches beyond the imagination right inside your body. There are things in there that are nowhere in the world's commodity.

I have come to realize that we have put a price on religion. That we judge each other on the strength of their vision. Those that are weakest we shun as not being worthy of God's love, and we see them as unrighteous and not worthy to go up above. Then there are those that we deem to have their faith right, and yet we have no way of knowing what they do when out of sight.

We blindly follow humans, thinking they have all the answers, and we are disappointed over and over when they do not meet our desires. Therein lies what we must overcome each day to be able to understand that God has the final say. What you are seeking cannot be found unless you know your soul, and a soul cannot guide us unless we accept that God is the goal. Around and around this circle goes with you as its protractor, and God is the motion that we sometimes do not factor.

What never ceases to amaze me about God is how He provides, and I am grateful for the blessings that He decides. Never do I go without, for He always gives to me what I need, and in His own way He always brings to me what I plead. It is not always done in a way that I want or expect, but what He provides I am always grateful to accept.

I take nothing for granted and count my blessings every day. God has given me more than I will ever be able to repay. All that He asks is that I share what was taught to me, and this costs me nothing, as God's wisdom comes with no fee. So I conduct His wishes without a thought for personal gain, for I know that for me He has done the same. God loves unconditionally whether you think that or not. If He did not love this way, then we would cease to be taught.

We are human, after all, and our mistakes He already knows. His only hope is that we learn so that our soul can grow. God will not stop loving you, even when you mess up bad, if you recognize the mistakes that you have had. To do a mistake over and over when you know it is wrong is the times that God leaves you to find out where you belong.

You are still on His radar screen, but He will not force you. God cannot force free will, even though sometimes He really wants to. Your admission to God that you need Him must be done willingly. He Himself knows that forcing faith is an act of futility. Unless we are true to our souls, God cannot work through us, for He can see into the depth of a soul and all its fuss.

Having one shred of doubt will leave you questioning alone. God cannot reveal His wisdom until it is your soul that He owns. Religion does not teach us how to have this intimate relationship. We are taught to keep God at arm's length unless we have a hardship. It is impossible to understand God unless you love Him, and for many of us, we are not sure how to make this love begin.

There is a mental block in place that we cannot love what we cannot see, but I am telling you right now that you can see God fully. All you need do is look at another human being that you love, and how you love that person is how you love God up above. That person is God, for they carry a soul with them, and to love that person is to love your own soul within. Receiving love from another person is as God would love you, and nurturing all this love is how God can shine through.

God is love, and it is a gift that He shares with everyone. You can count on God's love like the predictability of the sun. There will be times when we question God's wisdom and insight, and it is okay to question, but remember that He is always right. For reasons of His own He does things that we disagree with, and we forget that God's karma is real and not a myth.

There must be a balance on earth to ensure that all is fair. What we reap we sow, and we will get back our fair share. You may think an act you did was not really that bad, but what you do not understand is the effect on someone that it had. If another human being lost dignity because of you, you can be sure that God saw what you did not want Him to. If another human being received the love you must give, you can be sure that God saw and a past mistake He will forgive.

This is karma, and it must take place no matter what. All of us must be accountable whether we like it or not. Why do bad things happen to good people and vice versa? It is because at one time we earned what is our karma. Were you a bully in school and then learned the error of this? Could be that today you have to deal with a bully that if they left you would not miss. Did you ever make fun of someone's appearance and then laugh? Is there someone you love today who is experiencing that aftermath?

We must be careful what we say and do to others, because God's karma guarantees that you will reap that bother. Acknowledging to God that you are sorry for your sins will be your salvation in life before His karma begins. It is never too late to make amends for all your wrongs, and doing this will free up space for where your soul will belong.

I wrote this rhyme to shed some light on what we call religion, and it is for you to think about as you discern on your salvation. Religion is only the stepping stone toward a relationship with God. It is not the ending to a long path that we each must trod.

God is not religion; He is a lifestyle that must be lived each day. He must be at the centre of what we do and what we say. Our thoughts, deeds, and actions must be done with Him in mind. God rewards all things, and sometimes He must be cruel to be kind. He must be number one when we have decisions to make, and depending on others before Him is our biggest mistake. When you consider God's feelings before you choose what to do, you can never go wrong, because God is the soul that is you.

Chapter Seventeen — Yeshua

Many things I have written with God as the main point, but there is someone else that we must regard and not disappoint. God has a son whom we must get to know and love. It is through Jesus that you will get to finally meet God up above. God sent His only son to earth as a visual for us to believe. God had His son suffer for our sins to bring us much-needed relief.

Jesus's time on earth causes us humans to debate. We have tried to convince one another that Jesus was not a saint. Our skepticism has us asking one another for some proof when meanwhile our soul carries Jesus's living truth. Jesus was born to humans, raised by humans, and died for humans, and in doing so we have been assured by God of Jesus's second coming.

Jesus's time on earth was kept short, but He taught so much about bringing peace to those we touch. Jesus performed His miracles for us to see God's power. Jesus spoke truths about each of our appointed hour.

Any parent can attest to the anguish they feel when their child is in pain. God too felt this anguish when He brought His son home again. Jesus had a mission, and He obediently did as He was told. All of us have a mission to get back into God's fold. We may not be able to duplicate Jesus's power to heal on demand, but we are given the power to accept and understand.

There are many things here on this earth that we will never know, but don't you find it interesting that God and Jesus are there as you grow? Every person on this earth will hear of God and Jesus in some way. It fascinates me that in any culture God has a say.

Leaders come and go, and history is full of many villains, but God and Jesus are a constant that we teach our children. God and Jesus fit into any era, and they never seem to go out of style. They have yet to leave our society and come back after a while.

Our quest to find answers as to our reasons to be here can only be found with God and Jesus, both of whom we needn't fear. We keep them at arm's length thinking we are safe if we do, but by doing this we are denying Jesus and God, who both live through you. Denial is acceptance that you must turn inside out. Most likely you are waiting for someone to tell you what it is all about.

I love God and Jesus more than I love anything on this earth, and yes, I love God and Jesus more than the son to whom I gave birth. You may wonder how it is possible to have a love that strong. I can love like this because I know where I belong. Nothing compares to the acceptance I feel from God and Jesus. They both have my trust that I know to be saved is a must.

I take nothing for granted and praise them for my blessings. I also mind my own business and refrain from messing. What I have learned is that a mission has been given to each of us, and it is important to seek out the mission without kicking up a fuss. Jesus's own death had a purpose that we do not fully understand. All of us have a purpose, like Jesus, to save our fellow man.

Compassion is what God and Jesus have that we do not always use. We are too wrapped up in our own selves and what has made us bruise. For some reason we think we are owed something for our suffering. I am here to tell you that your pain is God and Jesus's greatest offering. Giving yourself over to them to heal what is causing your pain will allow you to return the same back to humans again.

The pettiness that humans display will pale when you believe, and you begin to understand that all humans need Jesus's relief. Instead of accepting simplicity, we ask for miracles to abound. Is it not miracle enough that you are even around? I have seen many miracles that I know are God and Jesus's doing. Each have been life-changing and an answer to why I have been stewing.

Miracles are performed every day, and they are not always grand. You yourself are a miracle that you must come to understand. You may think you have nothing to offer, but of that I disagree, for every single person has a purpose that they are meant to see. Jesus will not steer you wrong, and He is there no matter what, but it takes you to hear Him calling and be open to be taught.

Through Jesus you will learn what God is all about. Jesus is the starting block to washing away all your doubt. We have had the luxury of Jesus gracing the earth with His presence, but more importantly in each of us is Jesus's divine essence. Some have deemed it as the Holy Spirit that we all carry, but I see it as the soul that was given to us humans to marry.

Your body functions as it's biologically supposed to be, but inside of your body is the soul that makes up you and me. It fascinates me how a body is made of flesh and bone, but without a soul the body cannot function on its own. Take away what it is that allows a body to move about and you will only have a shell of a human without any clout.

Jesus lives in each of us, as does His loving father. We are to depend on each of them to help us overcome our bother. To deny this is to delay what is inevitably to be your fate, and Jesus has all the time in the world on your soul to wait. You, on the other hand, have a timeline to get it right, and Jesus will not force you if you continue to struggle and fight. Acceptance is key to unlocking the door that you ignore. Only then can Jesus give you what your life has in store.

The other day I witnessed an accident in which I was almost involved. Do you realize how many factors had to be in place for that not to evolve? Our life is like that and based around God's perfect timing. For that reason alone, I do not question why God has me rhyming. I write and I write, knowing He will reveal why I do this thing, and what I have written only He knows what it will bring.

We should not question our fate, for it is in exceptionally good hands. All you must do is accept, trust, believe, and then you will understand. If Jesus knocked on your door today, what would you do? Would you invite Him in or ignore the house call paid to you? Would your worry be that your house is not clean enough? Or is it your worry that Jesus will see past all the dust?

My concern would not be material; it would be spiritual. How my home looks is meaningless if my soul is not still. I would invite Jesus in knowing that I am not perfection, and I would accept His reprimand and His appreciation. Jesus is not to be feared, He is to be held in high regard, and He is the one you must turn to when life seems hard.

He will not reject you when you repent with your whole heart. What He does is lead you to your path for you to do your part. At thirty years of age, I reclaimed Jesus when I could no longer see, and over the years, I have gained His wisdom, which is free. My journey to Jesus was anything but an easy ride, but never once have I regretted allowing Jesus to help me to decide.

Many things I had to put into perspective and let go, and it took a few attempts for me to realize who was in control. Now when I look back over the years that I have lived I can understand my fate and the reasons for those that I forgive. I cherish my relationship with God and Jesus, for they are one. Each holds a place in my soul, as does my only son.

I have been given the gift to see others through Jesus's eyes, and what I can see in all humans is their soul waiting to decide. This is not a burden I carry; I accept that I can, and my mission is to reunite souls with their applicable human. I do this by living a life of humbleness and see myself as meek, for to be strong I understand that I also need to be weak.

I take nothing for granted and accept what is my fate, but I do not sit around either and allow my life to be up for debate. What I know is that coincidence is Jesus at work. Coincidence is Jesus trying to show you a quirk. Nothing happens by chance; everything is done by God's hand. Jesus's life and death were both something that God planned.

God's power is mighty, and He will always get His way. He does this despite you and what your humanness has to say. If you choose to struggle along, He will leave you to that, for He has many other souls to lead that accept Him as fact. It hurts God to know that any of His souls are lost, but He realizes that we have free will, which came at a cost.

Our soul knows the difference from right and wrong, and God gave us the ability to accept where we belong. The same way that some souls choose to believe that God does not exist is the only way that other souls can accept God and not resist. Some souls learn early on that God is their saving grace, while other souls refuse to accept that in God they have a place. If God made us all believers, how would His followers be saved? If we did not have souls to help, then our destiny would be delayed.

There are believers and nonbelievers, which is the undisputed truth, and a believer must help a nonbeliever to accept God's reproof. Deep down inside, all souls do believe that God is for real, and we must win back for God all the souls that Satan was able to steal. Therein lies the challenge that all souls must endure: whether to believe that God or Satan is the cure.

I have had my own struggles with this throughout my life, and what I have learned is that God is peace and Satan is strife. The choices I have made that have left me feeling alone I know today were made by Satan to make God groan. Satan makes it easy, where God makes you work hard. There is nothing Satan likes more than when it's God that you disregard.

Satan tempted Jesus Himself to test His faith in God. Jesus rejected Satan and received God's approving nod. Our tests today are similar, and we must be careful, for Satan camouflages his deceptions and he is very spiteful. You can tell which souls have chosen God or Satan to survive, and it is truly light or darkness that keeps them alive.

I have been where it is dark and felt the desperation, and I now live in the light and am guided by God's inspiration. I have carried burdens that at times broke my back, and now I have a lighter load, for God gives me what I lack. I have struggled and fought against letting God in, and I now rest peacefully and ask God what I can do for Him.

My search-and-rescue mission did not happen overnight. It took me a long time to earn God's divine wisdom and insight. Where Satan offers instant gratification when you choose his way, God values Himself enough to wait on you to hear what He has to say. God gives you bite-sized chunks to savour and to swallow. Satan, on the other hand, guarantees the whole portion if it's him you follow. God stays by your side when you decide that He is right. Satan, on the other hand, will flee like a thief in the night.

When Jesus resisted Satan, Satan hung his head in shame. Jesus passed His test, and you too can do the same. We cannot be Jesus; to think you can is to surely fail. Jesus took away our sins when on the cross He was nailed. Jesus is our saviour, and through Him you will find God. Is it God or Satan's path you have chosen to trod? Ask yourself this hard question and your answer is your fate. Which of these two on judgment day does your eternity wait?

-- Christ's Masses --

It is here once again, this season of which we have lost sight. We have become a society that has overlooked what God knows is right. The pressure to impress is compounded into one day, and we want to fulfill wish lists and what they have to say. We revere a man in a red suit and hinge our wishes on him, and meanwhile God, Jesus, the saints, the angels, and the Holy Spirit can see where we sin.

There is controversy these days about Jesus and His birth, and there are those that believe that Jesus's bloodline is still on earth. What purpose can be derived from questioning God's divinity? Do those who spew these conflicts understand what they mean?

This continuous need to cast doubt in our world is what is causing our mayhem, and those who are doing this are trying to destroy our fellow man. Think about it carefully as you determine your own truth, for where God has given much, the disbelievers have no proof.

A book has been written that no other can ever match. It is a book that tells a story that many believe as fact. The Bible has withstood the test of time and is printed often, and it has remained around long after other authors' books are forgotten. Our highest courts use the Bible to ensure the truth is told, and regardless of the trial's outcome, the Bible is there for us to behold. Swearing on the Bible is a contract that God will honour, and doing so lightly will leave you sitting in the corner.

It is purely desperation that is causing so much controversy. Our need for answers has allowed us to take God too lightly. There are those who are trying to force God's hand with their deceit. They want God to reveal Himself so that they can meet. They have yet to figure out that God holds all the power, and He will meet up with all of us at His appointed hour.

God gave us free will to assist Him when it is time, for He knows that there must be punishment for what are our crimes. It is the battle of good and evil that we are witnessing now, and those who are doubters have the most sweat on their brow. Believers do not live in the "what ifs," for we have nothing to lose, and we know that nothing good will come from what the doubters profuse.

Believers do not have to worry that their goodness is in question, and there is no need to prepare for God a list of their confessions. God will readily accept a believer, for their faith is the key that will unlock the door to a place that doubters will never see.

Christmas is a time of year that God judges our actions. Do we honour His son's birthday, or do we continue with our infractions? How long do you think that God will tolerate our absolute disregard? Closing out each year this way will only make the next one hard. Each new year brings to us more of God's warning signs, and slowly but surely, we are going to see what He wrote between the lines.

Christmastime is not about letting the rich get richer. It is a time for us to reflect on what is the bigger picture. Millions and millions we spend to show our love, and by doing so we miss what God sends from above. It is an absolute atrocity to God that we waste time doing this — spending tons of money that is thanked with a hug and kiss.

Can you imagine the changes we could make if we would compromise and give our love to others who would be surprised? We do not appreciate, and we take too much for granted. Has the time not yet come for us to get our seeds of peace planted? Those of us who have been blessed with the comforts of a home need to put ourselves in the place of those who spend Christmas alone.

What about those children who have no one with them on Christmas Day? No one to love them deeply and give them the right words to say. This world we live in should not be a place where children die, and we should not be so nonchalant as they take their last breath with a sigh. What is wrong with our society that we allow this to take place? Not helping our fellow man is to God an absolute disgrace.

God gets blamed for the mayhem that we can see on earth, but He did try once to rectify that when He gave His only son for birth. There was an opportunity back then to accept God's divinity. It was people, not God, who rejected the peace we want to see. A choice was given, and a choice was made to end Jesus's life, and today we live the aftermath for what was back then a point of strife.

Don't you see that it is not God that we are supposed to blame? We have continued the cycle of those who did not want Jesus to remain. Religion too has taken a bad rap for the mess we are in, but it is us people, not religion, which is the place to begin.

Christmastime is not about religion; it is about feeling content. It is about understanding where our humanness came and went. We must get back to the basics of what it means to love, and that starts with us trusting in the God who sees from above. There is so much doubt for an entity that is so pure, and we have lost the will to turn to the one who has the cure.

Our minds are tainted, and our souls are nowhere to be found. We are too consumed with life to look for what is truly profound. We have set ourselves up for failure with our selfishness, but thankfully there's God waiting for us to figure out the mess.

So how do we do it and begin to turn around our mistakes? It must begin by realizing that God is real and not fake. We must understand that God is love and that is what we crave. We each must find our soul and learn to love it for it to be saved. That is the starting point that will change the world, because believing in God, yourself, and others will stop the end at which we are hurled.

"Is it as truly simple as that?" you ask with all your doubt. Yes, I tell you, my friend, that that is what it is all about. One person at a time could change the way they think, and all of us together can pull us back from the brink. You may think we are too far gone, but that is not the case. There is still a chance for us to fix this and save the human race.

All the billions and billions of dollars raised to help those in need will do nothing at all if we do not change our emotional greed. It is not money that is going to change what the world desires. It is a shift in our thinking that will put out the doubting fires. Money is only a Band-Aid, and it will not heal the wound — the wound that began from the time that Jesus left Mary's womb.

Thirty years Jesus lived to bring the glory of God to us, and even back then there were disbelievers who kicked up a fuss. Our saviour was murdered by those who were scared, and no humiliation was left unturned, and no degrading was spared. Jesus was judged, spat on, and whipped until He bled. A crown of thorns and a cross He carried, and to His death place He was led.

Nailed to the cross and stabbed one more time for good measure, His cloak was fought over and taken for someone's pleasure.

Left there to die as if He was a criminal deserving of death, and still He beseeched God's forgiveness for us to His final breath. That was not the end of God's need to bring His son home, for Jesus is back with God, but the Holy Spirit was left behind to roam. A horrific event designed by God to assess our humanness; a moment in time for us to own up and confess.

We are not alone, for God has been with us all along, loving us so deeply and wanting us back where we belong. Can't you see, my friends who have so much doubt? There is a God, and He has proven He has all the clout. We are to realize that fact and stop with our mind games, for without God and His son nothing else will remain.

I am grateful for God's grace, although at times I feel unworthy, but without His greatness, my life would not be a success story. I do consider myself a success for what I have thus far, with a wonderful son, a fulfilling career, loving friends, and so much more. How I have been so blessed is a gift beyond what words can say. They have all come from Jesus, whose birth we celebrate this day.

His birth was a means to save us all from ourselves. A way for us to revere Him and not keep Him on a shelf. Do you have any idea how pleased He is when it is Him that we celebrate? Or the pain He must feel when we remember Him too late? This time of year we are not meant to be on the receiving end. We are to give of ourselves to strangers, family, and friend. Never was this the time for us to give accolades to old St. Nick, and we have lost sight of Jesus in our society's bag of tricks.

I will leave you with this thought about Christmas as I bring this rhyme to a close. Why can't we feel three hundred and sixty-four other days what one day must show? Why do we reserve our compassion for a common day that we share together? Why can't we do this all year to help each other to get better? Christmas is not meant to be about who can give the best gift. It is about God's need to show us how we can overcome our rift.

Chapter Eighteen — Fire & Brimstone

The word hell conjures up images of evil, fire, demons, mayhem, and upheaval.

All the negative emotions that make up you and me are seen in the hell that we can see.

We think hell is somewhere underground, but like heaven, it is nowhere to be found.

There is no evidence of heaven or hell, and believing in either is for God's judgment day to tell.

Hell once sat remarkably close to God, but on God's love hell decided that it would trod.

God could not keep hell in heaven; it had chosen the dark side of free will and had to learn a lesson.

God sent hell to dwell on earth, much to hell's delight and mirth.

God knew what would happen when man saw hell, but in His wisdom, He knew the end would tell.

We live hell on earth every single day, and both God and hell want us to see it their way.

Hell has many names; which one is right is not clear. It goes by Devil, Satan, and Lucifer.

Its image, like God, is what you want it to be, but unlike God it does not care about you or me.

Every day you battle with what God calls free will; it is the choice between good and evil.

God knew what would happen when He sent hell our way, beginning in a garden on a fateful day.

Satan is here until God decides when it is enough; Satan knows it's on a timeline to make our life rough.

Every soul on earth will be tempted by Satan one day, and succumbing to it will only bring us dismay.

God designed your soul with Satan in mind, and He split free will in half, not to be unkind.

Both portions of free will carry the same weight; which one you chose is on what God and Satan wait.

Satan knows the weaknesses of every soul, and it is these that it wants us each to know.

Satan knows that it does not have to play by the rules, and its goal is to make God look like a fool.

It tries to convince us that God's way is too hard, and each soul is tested to see who holds the card.

Even Satan does not know the extent of God's power, but it knows that it has an appointed hour.

It only has a certain amount of time to collect souls for God to decide where each one will go.

Satan does not care about the soul that it gets, and it thrives on souls that are filled with regret.

It wants you to believe that there is an easy way out, and it laughs gleefully when in God you doubt.

It only takes a second to let Satan in, and the hell that we talk about will begin.

Satan's playground has a place in every soul, and it is also whispering, telling you which way to go.

The Sun Neither Rises nor Sets

We are accustomed to Satan's hell on earth, and we battle it each day, searching for our self-worth.

We have temptation put in our path, and when the soul is won Satan leaves it in the aftermath.

Satan will clutter your path while you are coping because it must destroy any sign of hoping.

It must ensure that you never turn to God to lead you from the path that Satan gave you to trod.

Where Satan pushes temptation in your face, God sits quietly and waits for you to accept His grace.

God knows what Satan is putting you through, and He knows that it is what you are choosing to do.

God and Satan know you have decisions to make, and they show you the path they want you to take.

God gave Satan earth to have as its domain, for He needs a place for some souls to remain.

One day God will throw the heavens open wide, and each soul will be standing in line.

That is what we call judgment day, and that is when God will have His final say.

Each soul will be able to see hell down below and know that it's the place that they don't want to go.

Hell is not fire, demons, or mayhem; hell is knowing that you will never feel God's love again.

Hell is being able to see heaven up above and know that you cannot be a part of that love.

Hell will be living with your regrets every day and knowing it could have been a different way.

Hell is seeing those you love since birth enjoying heaven while you are suffering on earth.

Hell is knowing that it is all said and done, and you no longer have God to whom you can run.

Hell is living each day wanting one more chance and knowing God will never give you another glance.

Hell is crying out to God, and He will not listen, for He gave you the time, but you kept on missing.

Hell is knowing that you failed God's test and those you mocked are who He loves the best.

Hell is living every day with people just like you, who only care about themselves and all that they do.

Hell is knowing that free will is all gone and the hope for redemption is all done.

Hell is living life with only negative emotions and looking at heaven and its loving commotion.

If you knew there was a way to not end up in hell, would you not listen to what God must tell?

If you knew that what I have written is true, would you not change what you think, say, or do?

If you were given a glimpse into what could be your fate, would you seek your calling and not wait?

You have free will, and it is up to you to decide, and only you can determine where you will reside.

Neither Satan nor God will give up on your soul; in the end they each want you to live in their home.

God wants you back, knowing you did your best; Satan wants you knowing that you failed God's tests.

God has told us quite clearly what He wants us to do, and that is to see Him in all that is you.

Your mistakes are many and those He will forgive if you have faith and trust in the life that you live.

The Sun Neither Rises nor Sets

Satan's purpose on earth is also clear, and it is to make you live in doubt and in fear.

Your mistakes will be many, and Satan relishes those, using them to bring your faith to a close.

No human can pinpoint God's judgment day; it could be tomorrow or a number too long to say.

God knows the exact moment in time, and He will be there as you are waiting in line.

Heaven or hell, which one do you want? Carefully think, my friend, for you can only have one.

If you still have doubts, remember this line as true: Satan believes in God, so why shouldn't you?

Chapter Nineteen — Salvaging Your Soul

Imagine if you will that a huge ship is floating in the sea, and on that ship is enough money to make everyone on earth wealthy. Let us say that the ship sinks and all the money goes down with it. Would you be part of the salvaging crew if you knew you were going to get a bit of it? To be honest is to say that we would want to be part of that team, for we would all want to have more riches than we had ever seen.

We each have something that God values more than money, and you can believe that coming from a God that makes each day sunny. Your soul is priceless and something that God wants you to save, and inside of your soul is more wealth than you can ever crave.

You are that ship that sank with valuable cargo on board, and you have wealth that you are not supposed to hoard. Salvation comes to those who value God over material things, and doing this in your life has many riches to bring.

We are led to believe that God will only save the righteous, therefore we condemn His saving grace as highly suspicious. It is impossible, we think, to live our life without sin, for too much has happened along the way to know where to begin.

As a sinner, I realize I am not perfection, and I have done things that did not get God's appreciation. Thankfully, God is forgiving and my wrongs I could redeem, and through God my soul has gone to places I would have never been. My soul has been salvaged and I am grateful for that. God in His wisdom has shown my soul where it is supposed to be at.

It is important to God that we understand that we are lost. It is even more important that we salvage our soul at all cost. Salvation is to come back from that which makes us sin and recognize that our most precious treasure is the soul that we have within.

We think that sinning is ignoring the rules that God wrote, but what we do not know is that God gave us rules as a footnote. Before you can abide by His rules and manage your bother, you must love God first and then love another. These two rules are the path to your salvation, for when you follow them you can manage any situation.

God knew His rules would be hard for humans with free will, but on each soul He had to have these rules fully instilled. He then gave each soul its very own whisper to hear. The whispering of the soul is your God that you keep near. What you consider to be unrest is God talking to you. He is quietly trying to guide you to a salvation that is true. Your soul belongs to God, and it is a treasure He wants to save, and He gives you every opportunity to hear Him before you go to your grave.

We are each a shipwreck that has sunk into the depths of sin, but our souls cannot be saved by God unless we believe in Him. Salvage, save, salvation are the steps needed to rescue a soul. Each of us must learn these steps and succumb to a common goal. All souls are worth rescuing, and God does not choose favourites; losing even one soul to sin makes all humans regret.

God has given each of us the ability to save and to salvage, but salvation, on the other hand, is only something that God can judge. It is our God-given duty to hold all souls in high regard. He gave us this option knowing that following it would be hard. All of us cloud our obligation to God with earthly things, and under all that deceit is the salvation that He must bring.

We consider our life to be the most important asset we carry when truly our most valuable commodity is the soul of which we are leery. In a heartbeat all that you value can be taken away, and you could be left with a soul that has nowhere to stay. If you have not salvaged your soul then you have lost all, and when there is nothing left, God is the only soft place to fall. We can acquire more material things, that much is true, but there is no replacement for the soul that is you.

We marvel at human nature that can overcome defeat. Each time that occurs is when God and your soul meet. He is telling you that all souls are worth taking into account. He is telling you that there is victory behind all your doubt. Trials and tribulations are true tests of our character, and each is designed to help us write our life's next chapter.

We are faced with challenges that we must see as a test. A challenge is given to show you where your soul has unrest. God cannot make it easy, because that would defeat our purpose, and we must learn that God has a mission for each of us. You can have salvation when you repent your wrongs, and when you have cleansed your soul God will show you where you belong.

Each day that God gives me is another chance to get it right. I am truly blessed each day to have God's wisdom and insight. To have God in my life means to have peace in my soul, and it is only through God that I will learn what is my life's goal. God is the only one that truly has your best interests at heart, and He patiently waits for you to finally do your part.

We think we must give up so much to have God in our life, and we continue to put up with what is not always our strife. God gives us a test and we reject it as too hard, and God gives blessings to those who hold His tests in high regard. Saving yourself will give you the power to save others, and we all have this ability to lessen someone else's bother.

In our life we have free will to select right or wrong choices, and choosing one must be done by listening to our inner voices. Each day we are faced with a moment to hear each of them, and how you deal with each one determines your soul within.

I know there are those who will doubt what I have to say, and it is for those people specifically that God helps me to write this way. I know what I know, and God has more wisdom to share. He has given me the ability to show what is fair and unfair.

I have saved my soul and now I must keep it afloat, and the only way to do this is by getting others onto His boat. To ignore your calling is to think that you are in control. You need to let go and salvage yours and another's soul.

Chapter Twenty — What Goes around Comes Around

Karma is a word that I use at least once a day, whether to myself or to another the word I will say. I believe in karma and abide by its defined power. To sway from karma's truth is to earn yourself a light or dark hour. Holding karma close as God's powerful unwritten rule will be the key to help you to be the victor or a fool. Karma is all-encompassing, and it has no bounds. In its simplest form it is "what goes around comes around."

You may have heard this said, but do you understand that there is payback for every woman, child, and man? Karma is based around the choices that we must make, and payback comes whether we are being real or fake. For every action there is an opposite or an equal reaction. God rewards all deeds and punishes our every infraction.

When you receive good, it is for a deed that was well done, and when you receive bad, it is for your own compassion that was gone. A decision made by you sets off a chain of events, and that decision will gain God's approval or force Him to vent. Some decisions will reveal an immediate response, and other decisions will not be known until God gives His nod. Your decisions do not affect just you, for they involve others, and karma comes to those that you think your decision will not bother.

A sure way to know that karma will be coming your way is to knowingly partake in something good or bad on any given day. When you do good, you get good, and when you do bad, you get bad. Knowingly doing these things will make you happy or sad. Karma knows no prejudice, and it applies to everyone. Men, women, and children will all have karma to come.

Taking life for granted and thinking there is no consequence will ensure a time in our life when karma came and went. Take this for an example if you do not understand karma fully: a child that knows it is wrong but continues in life to bully. That child will grow up one day and have kids of their own, and one of their kids will be haunted by the unknown. The child will fall victim to a bully's wrath, even though they themselves did not choose that path.

The adult, now a parent, that knowingly bullied others as a child has brought a karma into their home that is anything but mild. The child must endure what their parent sowed to keep balance of the wrongs of which we each know. For every action there is an opposite or an equal reaction, and God rewards all deeds and punishes our every infraction.

Your decisions do not just affect you; they involve others, and karma comes to those whom you think your decision will not bother. God's timing is precise, and He has selected the right time. Only He knows when to reward a deed or punish a crime. A crime to God is to knowingly disregard another person's soul, and His golden rule is written to cause you less burden to toil.

The rule says to do unto others as you would have them do unto you. God tracks very carefully how you abide by this rule. The rule sounds simple enough, but it can be hard, because the rule is designed to hold yourself in high regard. Everyone has a soul that they must acknowledge as true, and God judges every single soul for what they say and do.

It is only God's judgment that we should want or fear, and accepting that your fate is in God's hands should make it clear. Karma is God's law, and it makes complete sense to Him. Getting karma from God is based on what you take or give.

A coincidence is God's way of giving a reminder. A miracle is to show that He is kinder. Nothing happens by chance; everything happens for a reason. God's karma is immediate, or it can take several seasons. All your choices and decisions will receive God's feedback. Karma comes to show what your soul has and what it lacks.

God speaks to us each day with what He puts in our path, and how you deal with it will determine the aftermath. You only have a split second to react in a certain way, and that reaction will be given back to you someday.

What are your prejudices and for what do you judge others? Do you have patience or does your anger make others run for cover? Have you any compassion, and is it always sincere? Are you true to yourself or are you someone to fear? Is it always about you or do others truly matter? Do you tolerate others or is it their soul that you shatter?

The way you treat others is about how you see yourself, and you are the mirror to what is on your own life's shelf. We busily pass judgments based on what we do not know. Passing judgment on others should show us where we need to grow. Judging others becomes a train that is out of control, and when the train will jump the track is dependent on your soul.

Do you wreak havoc or search for peace? Is your conviction sure or do you hide when you are weak? Each soul God created is not the same, but humans are known to play mind games. The mind games you play are not with another person. Your mind games earn you peace or can make your life worsen.

God is always one step ahead, for He can see what you cannot. His power is immense and cannot be understood by man. It is God that rules the world and decides each outcome, and His reasoning makes sense to Him, but not to everyone. You cannot know the history of each soul as God does, and that is why we question when a judgment comes from above.

Bad things happen to good people, and the reverse happens too. God's karma is correct in His rewards or punishment for all that you do. The clock that God uses is not set on human's time, and karma can come at any moment as a reminder and a sign. God's karma is used to keep order, and it is precise and exact. Karma is God's way of showing that He is real and a fact.

Denouncing karma as untrue is a sure way to have it come your way, but acknowledging karma will ensure you watch what you do and say. Karma is not limited to acts; it also applies to what you think, and your mind is the beginning of the karma into which you sink. Karma affects the innocent even if they are not wrong, and sometimes karma comes where we do not think it belongs.

Those are the times that we question God's wisdom as unfair. What we do not know are the events that brought karma over there. Our decisions in life are like a pebble thrown on a pond, and the ripples from that decision continue even when we think they are gone. We walk away from the decision thinking it is sound, but what we reap from that decision will always bring karma around.

Karma has its own history, and it can take generations to come. Your karma may be waiting to affect your granddaughter or grandson. What you do today may never bring karma your way, but someone will feel the affects of your karma someday. That is why it is crucial to accept karma as God's law and to understand that He knows what you think no one saw. Your karma is not reserved for strangers; it is for those that you hold dear. Karma's payback will affect those that we keep near.

When you question God's karma, you should question yourself and look at what you have done and kept on your life's shelf. If you look deep enough, karma's reasons will come through. Karma always must pay back everything that we do. That is the balance of life whether you like it or not. Karma must take place whether it is what you brought. It seems unfair that someone else's karma becomes yours, but that must be the way until we acknowledge our soul's door. When you understand karma is when the door opens, and you will accept all souls and how they are coping.

When you accept that disregarding souls is to your demise, you will take off the mask you wear as a disguise. You cannot hide what every single human knows. Who you are is exactly what in every human grows. All humans are the same, no matter their status in life. No human is safe from karma's peace or its strife.

When you set your goals in life, karma should be at the top of the list, because centring your goals around karma will help you to hit or to miss. Keeping your focus on God and what His karma can bring will allow Him to show His divinity to you in everything. Understanding that God's way is the only way to go will lead you down a path of redemption that you did not know.

It is never too late to ask God to forgive our every sin. Doing this will allow God to bring good karma in. Acknowledgement of God is to acknowledge your soul inside, and acceptance of your soul is what helps God to decide.

The Sun Neither Rises nor Sets

When you accept your soul for real it is impossible to turn back, for your soul is the vessel that God uses to show what you lack.

Rejection is what we fear from the humans we see around, but God does not reject, and His acceptance knows no bounds. He has no prejudice; He accepts every human for who they are. It is us humans that carry our prejudices too far. That is why there is karma to show who is really in control, and until that is understood, all souls will struggle and toil.

To try and play God by making up your own rules and excuses will only bring back to you what you are adamantly producing. No human has the right to cause someone else pain, yet we all have the right to help someone else to gain. We bring others down because we think it puts us ahead, not realizing that karma has a place in what we did or said.

It is futile to think that karma does not apply to you, that denial itself will ensure that karma comes through. God in His wisdom gave all humans the right to choose, and He knew this would help Him to determine who would win and who would lose. God's ultimate reward for abiding by karma is a seat at His table, of which we humans have debated.

For those that trust God, there is no room for them to doubt, and it is distrusting souls that continue to bring karma about. God is quite clear that karma descends from all time, and it is understanding this truth over which all souls must climb. No generation is safe from what the prior one has done, and it is imperative that we do not tarnish the next generations to come.

The answer to peace and how to achieve it down here is to regard every soul, especially the one you hold dear. For every negative you believe about someone there is a positive, and taking time to recognize that will allow your soul to open. Knowing yourself will give you compassion for others, for what makes you happy or sad makes someone else smile or suffer.

Every soul is connected because God wanted it that way. He wants every soul back in heaven with Him someday. To disregard a soul during your time here on earth will determine your entrance to heaven and your worth. Reservations in heaven are for those who follow God's law, and there is no room in heaven for those who insist on carrying this flaw.

If you cannot get it right in all the time that God has given to you, you will not get to visit the place where all is made new. God has firm rules for His house and who He lets in. There is no room in God's house for those who habitually sin. God's house is a haven for those who acknowledge their soul, and in God's house there is not space for burden or toil.

You must earn your place with God; it is handed to no one. God gives you every opportunity with the appearance of the sun. Each day is a fresh start to find your soul inside, and no day passes without giving you a chance to decide. Each day every single second counts, and what you do during that time gives God His clout. Nothing goes unnoticed and God catches every detail. Karma comes to all of us to show us a pass or fail.

Acceptance and acknowledgement are what God wants most, and that is done by regarding others through the soul He gave you to host. You are tested every day whether you realize it or not. God is always giving lessons so that His law can be taught. Something insignificant to you could be a test, it is true, for God to pass judgment on all that you say, think, or do. Keeping that in the forefront of your mind each day will have you welcoming karma or trying to keep it at bay.

Chapter Twenty-One — Spiritual Apprehension

To have faith is to trust without doubt, and having faith in God is what this next chapter is about. Being faithful is not reserved for the person you wed. Faithfulness is not something that we should come to dread. Marrying someone cannot guarantee that they will be faithful. Having blind faith in a human will not help you at all.

No human is perfection; we have our faults to own. You will never fully appreciate another human and what they know. You will only know what they want to share with you, and it is impossible to know another soul through and through. There are things we keep to ourselves and tell no one, for sharing everything with someone may make them turn and run.

We all have secrets, and none of us bares our entire soul, and that is why to humans we cannot be faithful. We do not trust each other fully, and that causes strife. Look at how many times you fight with your husband or wife. You fight because you do not think the other has it right. You distrust their decisions and want to share your insight. You do not have faith in them as a person and you become a nag, and the vows you said on your wedding day begin to sag.

Humans are fickle and they change from day to day, and you will never fully understand what they do, think, or say. It is on purpose that God created humans like this. He did it so that having faith in Him would not be missed. God is the only one that your faith should rest on. He is always the one remaining when everyone else is gone. God is the only one that has faith in you beyond any doubt, and He is the only one your faith should be built on and about.

God gave you life and knows you outside and in. He is the only one that knows all your honorable deeds and sins. God's faith in you knows no earthly bounds, and He is the one that your faith should be built around. God does not disappoint; He is fair in all that He does. He is the only one who knows why your soul kicks up a fuss. To lack faith in God is the root of all your mishaps, and to have faith in God brings goodness dropped into your lap.

Having faith in God means giving up what you cannot control, and faith will determine if your cup is half empty or half full. God's will that we battle is what brings us such discord. Following God's way will bring you peace and so much more. Putting your life into God's hands is His ultimate test, and trusting in Him above everything will show Him your best.

Humans will disappoint you and will let you down, but having faith in God is what will keep your soul sound. God has a plan for everyone, of that you can be sure. He is the only truthful answer and will always be the cure. For thirty years of my life, I walked around in a fog. I knew God was there, but by too many things I was bogged. I knew all my life that He was the way for me to go, but like everyone else I wanted to control what I did not know.

It was that time in my life that I threw myself at God's feet, and it was then that my soul and I got to meet. Finding peace with my soul did not happen overnight. First, I had to give up control to receive God's insight. Giving up control meant having faith in that what I could not see. Having faith meant I trusted in what God had in store for me.

What a relief it was to give back what was not really mine. I gave up the control and my life has been nothing but fine. I lack for nothing, and I have everything that I need. More importantly, God has given me all these pages that you read. A wisdom comes to those who blindly have faith in God, for He knows you are sincere about where you have trod.

I do not question God's wisdom, for I have seen it at work. I know what can happen when from His faith someone shirks. My faith in God is an example that I set each day, and I have helped non-believers hear what God has to say. I do not preach, I do not judge, and I never belittle anyone, for I understand that every soul has a song that is unsung.

I see everyone as I was on my thirtieth birthday, not being sure about life and how it got to be this way. I know God has given me a gift to be shared with others. It is the gift of faith, and by believing you will have no bother. Sure, there's life to live and none of it can be perfected, but it is much easier to take if faith is not being rejected.

When I am faced with something to make me want to defend, I seek God's wisdom to see what about myself I must mend. Earning God's wisdom is a daily task for each one of us. To hear God's wisdom, having trust and faith is a must. God knows what is best and it is against this that we fight. It is our humanness that makes us want to always be right.

What is lost on us is that God's karma rules all, and ignoring this truth is what makes us take a fall. If something is done to me that I know is wrong, I give the control of the outcome to God, where it belongs. To meddle in what I do not know is coming down the pike will make things worse and give me karma that I do not like. In His own time God will always give everyone their due, and God has a way of letting you know when His karma has come through.

I have witnessed God's payback to those who hurt me by having faith that their karma was what I got to see. I never wish ill onto others because I do not have to. I know God will ensure payback for all that they do. Knowing this keeps me following God's way with care, because His karma will also be done to me to be fair.

I try to see everyone through God's eyes, it is true, and I include myself in that in all that I do. My humanness lets me question God from time to time when He has done something that I think is a crime. It is fair to do that because that is what makes our faith stronger, and not understanding God's way will only make your path go longer.

Having faith is a state of being, not a state of mind, and surrounding yourself with faith leaves you open to be kind. Faith is believing that God will always come through. Faith is knowing that God has His best interests in you. Faith is acceptance that God knows what you do not. Faith is understanding that God makes amends if you will not. Faith is trusting that God only knows what is for the best. Faith is accepting that God gave you a soul as a test.

When I am put in a position where I must ask why, my thoughts go immediately to my God in the sky. The very fact that I ask why should help me to see that God is at work with reasons that are unknown to me. In time He will share the answer to my question to Him. The answer is for my good deed or for a way that I sinned. A good deed or a sin are not always cut and dry, and each has its place whether you do or decide not to try.

It matters not to God what you think is right or wrong. He has His own plan to put your soul where it belongs. God has all the wisdom, and His mind cannot be changed. Your life is in His hands, and He already has it arranged. Having faith in Him and accepting this as the truth will give you a peace that is endless and has little reproof. When your eyes are on God you can see a better place, for your soul is the space in which God houses your faith.

Accepting your soul is what God wants for each of us, and when you accept your soul, life becomes less of a fuss. To have faith is giving up control and letting God run the show. It is your faith that unleashes the soul you must know. Every second of your life is a chance for you to find faith, and until then, God will patiently tend to your soul upon whom He waits.

Chapter Twenty-Two — Driven by Desire

In life we are given what God calls free will, and it is the ability to choose to go up or down hill.

Each way will be a struggle no matter what, and each decision is made by what we have been taught.

We make decisions that are influenced by others, so we aren't responsible for our own bother.

We decide even though we hesitate, but we want instant gratification, so we decide not to wait.

Temptation comes when we least expect, and our soul tries to tell us what it knows we will regret.

That's when free will comes into the picture and the doubting side of your soul decides quicker.

Once you experience temptation that beckons you, you get another opportunity to decide what to do.

That second chance will decide the path you take, and it is then that you lie in the bed that you make.

For you were given the chance, not once but twice, to make the decision your soul knew was right.

Temptation makes you think that you have all the control as it continues to wreak havoc on your soul.

So consumed do you get by this outside source that you eventually veer from your life's course.

Suddenly before you know what has happened, your soul was replaced, and temptation is clapping.

Temptation knows that you aren't as perfect as God, and it enjoys the fact that on your soul it can trod.

Temptation knows that God has given you free will; it knew it back then and it knows it still.

God designed free will to be that way so that we would listen to what our soul has to say.

If you are a fast learner, you will understand fate; if you are not, it is on you that your soul will wait.

Inside each body a soul will reside, and in that soul is where God will decide.

Each decision your soul will have to make is based on whether you are being real or being fake.

Being real lets you hear the whisper inside; being fake allows you to deny what your soul sighs.

You can choose to embrace temptation, and if you do or do not, you owe your soul the explanation.

"Why did I choose to take this path in life knowing full well that it's from my soul that I took flight?"

"It's an annoying thing this soul we have, anyway, telling me what's best and to do things its way."

"I don't have to listen, I can do what I want … look at that woman, I want what she flaunts."

"I don't have to listen, I can do what I want … one more drink, barkeep, even though I can't walk."

"I don't have to listen, I can do what I want … I've switched to cocaine from smoking pot."

The Sun Neither Rises nor Sets

"I don't have to listen, I can do what I want … I need money because I'm unhappy with what I've got."

"I don't have to listen, I can do what I want … God help me, please, because I'm really lost."

Those are the words He has been waiting to hear as you continue with temptation out of fear.

Admitting to Him that you were wrong will get you back to your soul to which you belong.

Each temptation that you decide to take can be overcome by the right decision you make.

You were the one who invited it in, and now you must make the decision to start all over again.

That decision is hard because we admit we were wrong and must face up to what we knew all along.

Your soul stays with you no matter what you do; it tolerates your temptation if that is what you choose.

It becomes for you your guiding light; trust in it, even in your longest, darkest night.

When you arrive in your greatest despair, look inside at your guiding light that is always there.

The anguish that you feel is the temptation as it dies and screams in frustration that you dare to defy.

It will con you, lie to you, and try to tempt you to come back, and that should show you where it is at.

It is vicious and forces you to doubt, because it does not want you to know what God is all about.

It tells you that God's way is much too hard and wants you to think that you hold all the cards.

It wants you to believe that it is your only hope and then abandons you when you cannot cope.

Once it has done to you what it came to do, it moves on to another to bring them the same doom.

You are left standing with your world falling down, not knowing your soul or where it can be found.

Remember that you are down, but you are not out; you must grow faith the same way you grow doubt.

Each day you squander to please temptation is the number of days you will need to get redemption.

You were willing to let temptation decide, you owe the same time to hear the whisper inside.

You need to replace the temptation with your trust and understand that believing in God is a must.

You made a mistake and for that you must pay; how long your road back is, only God can say.

Giving in to temptation always has a consequence; it is a reminder to us of where our soul went.

You must be willing to accept the error of your ways and know that God will forgive you that day.

His forgiveness is instant, and you will have His grace, but it is a long road to Him that you will face.

He knows the strengths and weaknesses of your soul, and He will dare you to make Him your goal.

You will be tempted time and time again, and what your soul wants the most will finally win.

Temptation does not want your soul to know self-love, because to love yourself is to love God above.

To accept your soul as God's work of art will finally make temptation turn and depart.

When it is God's love that you seek, you will realize that it makes you feel strong, not weak.

The Sun Neither Rises nor Sets

Each day of believing gets you that much stronger, and your temptation in life will not linger.

Temptation knows when you hear God's will, and it is then that it will vacate and let your soul be still.

Temptation knows that free will works both ways and will leave you alone to come back another day.

It will appear in your life from time to time to assess your faith that you continue to climb.

It can do nothing to a soul that is pure; it can do nothing to a soul that knows that God is the cure.

That is why it is a must to hear the whisper inside and trust in the good that your soul wants to decide.

The peace that comes with a rested soul will come when you accept your self-love and all that it holds.

No temptation on earth can replace this peace, so love yourself and make your temptations release.

Chapter Twenty-Three – Irresistible Power

The most asked question in life has to be "Where is my life going?" and we ponder this at times to understand how things are flowing. The routine for us remains the same; we are born to die and leave behind a name.

Two complete strangers met one day, and love becomes theirs. They start a new life together knowing that each other cares. Eventually they start a family to which you were born, and now you have a mom and dad between whom you are torn. These two people you call parents are strangers to you, the same way that they had been strangers at a certain time too.

But now you are considered a family because of a thing called DNA: a child conceived by two people who happened to just meet up one day. Was it fate or was it destiny that started the chain reaction? Can you say which one of these things played a role to your satisfaction? How wonderfully odd it is to ask a question without an answer and to think hard about what happened to make you a person.

Your life started because two strangers decided to have a child, and they raised you to adulthood with mayhem, or maybe it was mild. Years down the road you meet the person of your dreams. They are the one for you and no one else will do, it seems. Another two strangers meet one day, and love becomes theirs. They start a new life together knowing that each other cares.

What must take place for this blip in time to transpire? How many things must align perfectly to give you your heart's desire? Is it destiny or is it fate that ensures that life will continue? Which one of these two things shapes what is to become of you?

The Sun Neither Rises nor Sets

I believe in fate and destiny, for God controls each one the same way He controls the moon and the guarantee of the sun. Your life was designed by God with the purest intent, and He gives you the opportunity to discover its contents. He has His reasons for two strangers to meet and love one another. From them He may give you a sister and a brother. It was fate that brought you together to be a family, and what happens to you before your life ends will be your destiny.

We are not simply born to live a life without a purpose. Each of us has a reason for what is to be our life's course. There are certain things in your life that must take place. It is futile to fight them or think they are to you a disgrace. You cannot change your destiny, but you can shape your life. God gave us the capabilities to live in peace or in strife.

These two things are up to you, but your destiny is His. You may not get yours, but God will never miss. There are two sure things in life, and they are birth and death. You will have to do both to have your first and last breath. What happens in between is nothing short of a miracle. It is fascinating to me the life that we get that makes us the same people.

We eat, we sleep, we breathe, we fight, we love, and we all live, and watching over this is God, who is there to always forgive. We are not perfection, us humans, which makes life interesting, and our struggles are made as we try and figure out our destiny. We awake each day never truly knowing what the day will hold, yet we go out and face the world as if we were truly that bold. Sometimes we have situations that will assess our humanness, and other times our life will be quiet and without any mess.

Day after day we live in a world that we think has gone mad, just trying to get by and searching for what will make us glad. We question our life's purpose and try to fulfill our needs, but for some reason we cannot seem to grow our destiny's seed. Our frustration with this takes away from what we are to do, and we keep striving for that one thing to pull us through.

It is this drive to question the unknown that stifles us; this innate fear we have that we will get lost in all the fuss. If we are not out there impressing others, what would be the sense? If we do not leave our mark here, who will remember our presence? What we fail to understand is that our destiny is not always grand. Could be that your destiny was simply to one day take a stand. Maybe you are here to give birth to a future leader, or perhaps you are an unknown author who is to be an accomplished writer.

My own destiny I ponder occasionally too, wondering why I write so much and yet it is always new. What is the obsession I have to write so many rhymes? Everything that is written is something different all the time. Where do these words come from that flow like a river, and why do they at times up and down my spine send a shiver? Is it my destiny to write something that will somehow seem profound? How is that I can write God's words without hearing a sound?

What is this connection with God that I have? Am I truly a channel for Him to share His spiritual salve? Day after day I write, yet I know I have not said enough. It takes little effort to write, and the rhymes are not tough. "Why the rhyming?" I ask God to explain to me, and I understand now that it is His way of teaching us another way to see.

Typically, we read to gain knowledge from a book, and the way I write is also to have you take another look. In the lines are meaning that are not always clear at first, so you must read and reread to understand each verse. To read a book from cover to cover would to some be boring, but a rhyme is itself a splendid story.

"What am I to do with all of these rhymes that I have written?" I ask this very carefully to God, with whom I am smitten. "What is the point of writing rhymes which no one can read?" He assured me that they will be used when there becomes a need. I have come to understand that what I write is God's insight, and early on in life I knew that I had something that I was to write. I remember a lot of times trying to put on paper what I knew, but it never seemed right what I wanted to share with you.

Our destiny is a nagging feeling that will not go away. It is this sensation that pulls us and leads us through our day. Little by little your destiny is revealed by circumstance, and you cannot delay destiny, for it is not left up to chance. Each detail has been crafted with a result. Some of the details bring delight and some you think are an insult.

It is an absolute miracle to me how life continues to unfold. How in every millisecond that passes your destiny to you is being told. Every moment throughout your day has significance to it, and all things must be put into place for your destiny to fit. We say sometimes, "But for the grace of God there goes me," and we continue our day not understanding our destiny.

You are right to be glad that another's destiny is not yours, but have you ever wondered what God has in store? If we each have a destiny, how will we know this? Your destiny is given to you in signs that you cannot miss. Our destiny cannot be denied, but we override what we know because we think we are in control.

We make decisions and choices that are based on our humanness, and then we curse God for getting us into the mess. God understands this weakness that as humans we display, and He sends you another sign to show you how to make your way. God's signs are subtle for you to discern carefully, and until you understand that you will overlook your destiny.

It is a massive game of chess that God plays with each soul. Each move is calculated and to checkmate your destiny is your goal. Sometimes you make a move not realizing what you have done, and God's next move finds you losing one of your pawns.

Life is not meant to be lived with a haphazard point of view. We are not supposed to let even a minute pass and not know what to do. There are no excuses that God will accept to justify our ignorance when we have all had the chance to overcome our circumstance. There have been many opportunities to accept God's divinity, and if we cannot see it in our own lives then we have plenty of others lives to see.

What would it take for me to show you that destiny exists? Would you believe me if I could give to your soul what it cannot resist? If I could wave a magic wand and give you what you desire, would that put out your spiritual longing that is on fire? I am afraid it would not, for destiny is not obtained so easily. Destiny is revealed to you when you believe in God freely.

Denial of destiny is a slow death for those that will defy, and acceptance of destiny is a life of contentment for those who will try. We all have a destiny, and it is up to us to seek it out, but destiny cannot be understood when it is overshadowed by doubt. Each day is a brand-new gift to be opened with anticipation, and the beauty of life is to be surprised by God's explanation.

Good fortune or bad fortune, in each there is a lesson, and both are there to teach you what is your life's mission. Nothing in life should be taken for granted, know this as true, for God has a way of changing what you thought defined you. A person's life can change in an instant for good or for bad, and what we must understand is that our life is God's to be had.

God keeps us on our toes to ensure we understand His intent, and we must never get too comfortable with what makes us content. We are to seek our destiny daily and watch for the signs and remember that God sometimes must be cruel to be kind. What we think is tragic has a meaning yet to be seen, and what we see as a miracle makes tragedy seem less mean.

One person's destiny is a teaching tool for someone else, and all of us can help each other to seek the destiny that we shelf. Can a person change their destiny to be that which they want? Unfortunately. we cannot manipulate the destiny that God flaunts. Destiny's journey is designed to give us moments in which to decide. You can accept that it is inevitable or your can opt out of the ride.

We all have the capabilities to allow life to take its course, and we also have the capabilities to make the outcome the worst. This is done with a conscious decision to keep what you think is control, and by doing this you allow the mishaps to take their toil. You cannot fight your destiny no matter how hard you try, and to not recognize that early on allows your destiny to with you die.

If you are adamant that you know what your life entails, you are destined to live a life that you have chosen to fail. If you are adamant that your life's destiny is out of your hands, you are destined to live a life that has no room for reprimand. Destiny is not about chance or the whims of luck, it is all about God being the key and your soul the lock.

God reveals all things in His own time for us to see, and I can attest to that, for He has done it enough times for me. It is not like I sit around and wait for my destiny to appear. What I do is live my life knowing that God will make it clear. The beauty of destiny is that you never know when to expect, but whatever God gives to you is for you to willingly accept.

Good or bad, there are reasons for what He gives to you, and inside of each experience is the strength you need to pull through. I have heard a saying that into my life I have made fit, and the saying is "If God leads you to it, He will pull you through it." No matter what, you must believe that God is there, and He does not go far when you are faced with what is fair and unfair. The things that God brings to you are His way of giving a test. You must decide for yourself: do you want your destiny or unrest?

Each day is a brand-new gift to be opened with anticipation, and the beauty of life is to be surprised by God's explanation.

Chapter Twenty-Four — Second Glances

Each day we allow our perceptions to guide our way and we make snap decisions based on what others have to say. Our naivety allows us to not go below the surface to understand that for each of us God has a purpose. We are locked into a society that makes decisions too fast, and our first impressions are not made to be the last.

Think carefully about what I am about to share with you, this thing we call perception to help us pull through. There are three sides to every story when you are looking for reproof, and they are yours, the other person's, and the actual truth. Perception designs how you and someone else can see the same thing, but what is unknown to either is what the truth will bring.

You meet someone for the first time and your perception is clear, and you judge them not for who they are, but for what you fear. Our humanness searches for a flaw to assure imperfection. This, my friend, is how humans use perception. What we see as true can be construed in a different light, and it is against this fact that we are in a constant fight.

You have heard the expression, "I'm a good judge of character." The key word there is "judge," and that is what is the matter. It is impossible to judge someone based on your opinion, for your opinion matters little in God's kingdom.

A perception is based around what us humans think is true, but it is simply a way of not allowing the truth to come through. We hide behind perceptions because it is the easiest way to believe this holds us unaccountable for what we do, think, and say. There is accountability to God, and He will make sure of that, and thinking that is untrue is why we are where we are at.

We disregard each other's souls when an opinion is formed. You do not know the soul and the reason it was born. The soul's mission is unknown, yet you choose to judge. That soul may have come to show you what you begrudge. Each soul is significant to God in His ultimate plan, and how we perceive someone is not the same as God can.

What I have come to realize is that every soul is a test, and how I accept that soul shows my weaknesses and my best. Every single person has something to teach someone else. It is not academic, but it does pertain to what is on your life shelf. What makes us believe we are experts to think our opinion is right and to judge another soul that was made by God's glorious insight?

Each soul has a story that you will never know, and their story is their own about a life they have tried to grow. To use your human perception to pass judgment on them should show you your own story and where you have been. How you perceive yourself is not always what others see, and their opinion is their perception, which means little to me.

I have concluded that it is God that I must impress, and He is the only one that can show me what I must address. His judgment is not clouded by perception, for He sees only the truth. I fear no human's opinion, but I do fear God's reproof.

When God brings someone into my life, I hold all perceptions in check, for this person has come to show me what I need to fix next. God has entrusted me with the ability to see through His eyes and accepting that has helped me to see each soul in disguise. The exterior we wear is not an indication of what is within, and each soul that I see has been where I have been.

All souls want acceptance, not human rejection, and thinking that another human can fulfill us is the number-one misperception. That is why we continuously seek approval from others with this unstable desire to give others our bothers. What I have come to understand is that everyone's plate is full, and they have no more room to take on what you must toil.

To believe that any human has the answer to your prayer is to perceive that they have a power that is just not there. Another person cannot define you because they are in the same boat, and what they must contend with does not rely on your vote. Why we continue on this path is our humanness at work; this unfounded perception used to pick apart each other's quirk.

When I think of some comments that I have heard about me, I smile to myself and try not to take it too literally. I have been told many things of how others think I am and what their perception is of me I cannot and will not defend. How a human views me is the least of my worries, as they have no understanding of me and all my stories. What they see is not actually what they will get, and their perception of me will not let them win their bet.

The rules that I follow are the ones written on my soul. God wrote them there and for that I am forever grateful. I have accepted His permission that He has bestowed on everyone; the permission to accept that no soul's journey is ever done. What you think you know today can be changed tomorrow, and for that reason alone I choose not to cause others sorrow.

To unbend your perceptions is what life is all about, and staying steadfast to perception is what fills us with doubt. Every soul can change if it is given half a chance, and your perception of a soul cannot be done in one glance.

Chapter Twenty-Five — Values Are Cliché

Have you ever taken the time to ask yourself what it is that you value? Would it surprise you to know that others want the same things too? When I reflect on the many rhymes that I have written, it has occurred to me that they are values of which God is smitten. Rhyme after rhyme has flowed from many a blue pen, and each rhyme has the potential to show you how to begin.

They have all accumulated to what I know is a lesson about the lack of values that in this world we are missing. Our disregard for one another has a reason for me now. It is all because we do not cherish anything that we vow. We teach and we preach, but there is so much more lacking. You cannot keep values without God's backing.

It seems so obvious to me now as I start this rhyme that what I have been wanting to capture has been there the whole time. As with everything I write, God is now guiding my words and He has waited until now for the rhymes to be heard. All the things that we value are hinged on the word "respect," and your life will have no purpose unless this you are able to accept.

Respect for oneself leads to respecting our many differences, and the lack of respect is the reason for our mayhem and occurrences. The simplicity of our purpose is too good to be true, and it can all be summed up in one word for me and you. To not respect that we can be different is to our own detriment, and this lack of respect is what has led to our disappointment.

We as humans have crossed the line with all our judging, and somewhere we have gotten lost in all that we are grudging. For some reason we have concluded that we must be right with our assumptions about life that do not have God's insight. We argue and we fight about whose views are right and wrong and we pull each other down to where we do not belong.

It may shock you to know that everyone's opinion counts. We are humans seeking our soul to see to what it amounts. It comes down to the salvation that we do or do not want, and our need for respect is why our values we continue to flaunt. Can I ask you for your reasoning as to why cultures disagree? Is it for the past that they want some accountability? What do you believe should occur to change what is the past? How can we rectify it and put it to rest at last?

For how long must we suffer for what was human error? When are we going to realize that souls look the same in God's mirror? There is no culture that is mightier than another down here, and letting go of that fact will gain the respect that we all fear. For us to accept that everyone is equal across the board is to view our souls as the same, and then we can share the respect that we hoard.

Think about it carefully before you take offense to what I have to say, for each and every one of us is only human at the end of the day. Our cultural differences are unique and do not need to change, as they have a purpose to show us God's magnificent range. To believe one is above another diminishes God's purpose for us, because understanding that we are a human is a God-given must.

We ourselves have set each other up to fail God's test, and it has become a mission of ours to give each other unrest. What would happen one day if our skin colour suddenly turned blue? Say that everyone on earth was the same colour as me and you? Add to that a hair colour that everyone saw as pink and add facial features with eyes of green that did not blink. Imagine after that that we all thought the same way. What then would you talk about? What then would you say? Would it be the perfect world that you believe to be right when we all walk around with the exact same insight?

Thankfully this is not the case, and we can be different. So the question becomes: Where has the respect come and went? When did it become okay to disrespect who we are? My fellow humans, I think we have pushed the envelope too far. We have become caught up in a society that is lost, yet we want to be the one left standing at all costs.

Our battles have become an almost automatic reflex where we have conditioned ourselves not to give each other respect. We no longer understand why we feel the need to rebel, and the basis for our discontent is the stories we continue to tell. Over time we have come to lose respect and that is a crime. What you should value is the purpose of this rhyme.

If you were to write down your values for others to see, you may also be surprised at another's list that you read. Fundamentally we all want the same things in life, and overlooking that fact is what continues to cause us more strife. In amongst all our values is the need to be respected for who we are. Aren't you tired of carrying around someone else's emotional scar?

Do you want to be free to do what you know is right? Don't you want to have peace and to give up the big fight? Are we really that lost that our souls cannot be found? Is there hope for us yet to seek that which is truly profound? God has yet to give up on us to learn the values we desire, and by doing so, He will allow us to look that much higher.

Do you not realize that respect is the answer that we seek? Disrespecting one another is what is making us weak. Respect is a value that God holds in high regard, and respecting Him and others is what we have made so hard. We have put all these conditions in place that do not make sense, like limiting ourselves to who gets to be in God's presence.

All of us will be judged by God, who isn't always revered, and His judgment will come whether you do or do not hear. Think about that when you seek the purpose of your life. There must be justification for all that has been our strife. God's purpose for our existence is rolled up tightly in respect. Learn to do that with each other and you will begin to accept.

Respecting our differences is one of God's greatest tests, and on this you will be judged as having done your best. To concentrate solely on your judgment of others will not leave you open to rectify your bother. There are no boundaries that God has put into place. We ourselves have built those around each other's race. In God's eyes we look the same to Him, and He knows that it is from our souls that we must begin.

Our souls reflect God, and He knows this. It is us as humans who have let this go amiss. Our exterior is not a duplicate of the soul that God gave you. Your soul is God that is trying to pull you through. How can I say that with conviction to you doubters out there? Well, take away the exterior and to what do you stare? Would you be able to guess who we are without skin as a cover? I am guessing not, and therefore you have now discerned on what could possibly be your bother.

Let us take it a step further as to what we think keeps us alive. Can we truly pinpoint that to your heart or your mind? They are the same for everyone who has them, and their function in all of us meets the same end. Now let us go a little deeper to find the truth: that there is something in us to give us the ultimate reproof. We call it our personality, and God calls it your soul. It is that part of you that has God as its goal.

You want the answers to life, yet you had them all along. Underneath it all, there is only one place that we belong. Recognizing each other's soul allows respect to happen, and when you can see another soul the angels will be clapping. Do you know that it can be is as simple as that, to respect that each soul is exactly where you are at? Remove all the facades and outer masks that we wear and what you will find is another soul kept in there.

It is a soul that is experiencing life the same as you are and seeking to find acceptance under each scar. Each soul has a mission that was lovingly given by God and was sent down to earth to assist where others have trod. All souls have wisdom much deeper than a brain can comprehend, and recognizing this wisdom is the beginning to your end.

Tuning into your soul allows your mission to begin, and to disregard your soul will never allow God to come in. In each soul God instilled what He calls free will. He gave it to Adam and Eve and it's ours to discern still. It would defeat God's purpose to not allow us to have a choice, and besides, God's whisper is another beckoning voice. It is that age-old battle of good versus evil that we must endure, and succumbing to evil is to keep respect out of the cure.

In life there are only two sides on which you can choose to be. You either want to hurt others or you care what others will see. There is no in between, and you must be one or the other. Do you assist others easily or do you want to give them more bother?

What do you value in life? I have asked you from the start. Do you respect other souls, or do you want to tear them apart? Is it in you to recognize what is out of your normal scope? Can you see that there is salvation and room left to hope? Deciding today what it is that you value will find God not letting your soul be skewed.

Chapter Twenty-Six — Teach, Don't Preach

We all receive our calling from God at some time in our lives. Sometimes we hear it and sometimes it gets lost in all the strife. Some callings seem large where others are small, but to God they are worthy, and He has designed them all.

I have heard my calling, but it seems out of my reach. I know my calling from God is to practise what I teach. Hours I have spent writing and putting my thoughts to paper, trying to explain God's way to help all souls to be better. It is an itch that I cannot scratch, this calling I have received, for I know that God wants me to shed new light on what we perceive.

His divinity guides my pen across the many pages I have written as I search to find the words about a God of whom I am smitten. For reasons of His own He has chosen me to say His words, and across many pages I have written that which I heard. I always felt that I had something profound to say, but never did I imagine that the words would come out this way.

My inspiration is not my own, for it is God that drives my pen as I write what He shares with me every now and then. I accept that God has a plan for the many words I have written here. I have written out of love and no rebuke do I fear. My intimate moments with God that produced these pages assures me that I can manage any skeptic that rages. For sure there are those who will think I have lost my mind to believe that my writing is done by someone so divine.

I accept that as fact and I do not fear their backlash, for their fear is simply about the knowledge that they lack. Could I be right, this woman who is an average person? Do I have the inside track on a world that continues to worsen? I know that God could not have a nonbeliever write so much, for all the words that I have written my soul too has touched.

Everything I say is how my life goes, and I practise what I preach because my soul already knows. What I realize about this life is that nothing goes unnoticed. By humans, yes, but not by the God that made us. My every action, every deed, every sin is given a grade, each of them given to me for a decision to be made.

Do I heed God's wisdom and carefully decide my fate, or do I do what I want and on His karma decide to wait? I have felt God's wrath when I did not listen to Him speak. His wrath came to me to show me where I am weak. I have also felt God's approval when I passed one of His tests. His reward for doing so is to know I did my best.

I am not a scholar, and I cannot quote any scripture, but my teachings come from a much bigger picture. What God gives as His insight is for me to do my best and comes to me not to contest. I have no one to answer to, for God tells me what to say, and I do not question why He has chosen me to write this way. All that I say comes from a wisdom that I do not fully know, and it is a wisdom designed to help me and others to grow.

I am in awe that God has given me this gift to help others to cope with what they think is a rift. When I think back to all that I have endured, I realize God wants me to share what I have learned. I have been hurt beyond words but have loved just as hard. To this day I hold every human as God wants me to regard. I do not judge another soul for what they think, say, or do. What I try to discern is what has been pulling them through.

Our bodies are a mirror to the soul we keep inside, and our body's actions will display what our soul decides. We sort personalities on what we think we know, but how can we know when we don't truly see a soul? We want to think someone is a certain way to make it easy, and we ignore what God gives to each of us so freely. We all know it's wrong to knowingly hurt someone else, yet we do this act constantly to others and to ourself.

What is this drive by humans to keep each other down? That is what causes God to have a frown. I am as guilty as anyone for feeling worried and insecure, and there have been times when I have acted out against what I fear. I have been in that place where jealousy rules the mind, and I chose to hurt someone instead of trying to be kind.

It was important what humans thought about me, and I sank down deep into what humans think is reality. What a vicious cycle that is to be judging others so harsh because you fear that your own soul needs a good wash. Freedom came to me when I realized it is not my place to judge. Peace followed that when I forgave and released what I begrudged.

I unloaded burdens that were not mine to carry anyway, and I gave ownership back to others for what they think, do, or say. When I did all that, I could clearly see what I missed. Suddenly there was just me and an unfinished to-do list. The list was long, and I did not know where to start, for what I thought was in my control began to fall apart.

There was darkness, there was mayhem, and I sank low. Purging myself was hard and the process was painfully slow. At times I wanted to give up and take the easy way out and go back to that world of disregard and self-doubt; that world of denial that allows humans to sin and is a place reserved for evil that will not let goodness in.

God kept me on track by showing me where humans have gone wrong. He showed me how we meddle where we do not belong. He shared His insight of how we are all the same and it is us humans, not God, who changed the rules of the game. God has been consistent about His expectations of us, but we are the ones that balk at it and kick up a fuss.

Denying that we are not at fault for what we see today is exactly why we refuse to see things God's way. We have free will; God gave it to us for a reason. What we have forgotten is who free will should be pleasing. Free will is not designed for yours or another's gratification. God's concept for free will is His own form of education.

Free will is not totally free, and there is a price to pay for it. God's answer to your free will is always a perfect fit. Wisely using free will is truly for you one of God's hardest tasks. To abuse free will is to bring what you may not have asked. How do you know if you are using free will all right? Simply ask yourself if you are using your own or God's insight.

No one has the wisdom that God achieves, for they could not oversee all that God knows and sees. The tiny portion that God allows us to know is a pittance compared to what He manages and controls. Every human has a role to play in God's ultimate plan, and how you accept your role will determine where you have ran. Will you run toward God believing that He is correct, or will you go it on your own thinking you are perfect?

As humans, we do not want to acknowledge where we are weak, for we become easy prey to those who have only revenge to seek. There are those who live in misery and cause others pain. They are the ones who are out for their own personal gain. We fear them, for they do not care who it is that they bring down, and we seek to please them even though they make us frown.

These are the souls that I feel most sorry for, having to live life always trying to settle a score. What a burden to carry, no wonder they have no peace trying to keep track of all the mayhem that they reap. I have carried such a burden at one time in my life, thinking it was okay to cause other people strife. Juggling those deceptions caused me more bad than good. I did not get that I was not doing all that I could. Focusing on others' ills kept my soul far away, and little did I know what my soul had to say.

Today I avoid unnecessary burden at all costs now that I have found my soul that I never want to get lost. I refuse to play human mind games, and upon God I choose to look, for to partake in humans' trivialness would diminish my book. What I write are the words that God wants me to preach, and every single line has a meaning and something to teach.

It is not good enough that I just write the words here, but I must be a living example of the God that I hold near. All that I do must be centred around God's way, for I know that God has the final say. Not acknowledging that as fact will be to my own demise. That is why I am real and choose not to wear a disguise.

Honesty is truly the best policy to live your life by. It is a much easier way to go, and I suggest giving it a try. To be honest means sticking to what you know is a fact, and it certainly does not mean pointing out what you think others lack. To be dishonest to yourself means you judge another's flaws, and an unacceptance of human weaknesses breaks all of God's laws.

To prey on the weak to build yourself up is all wrong, and eventually that comes back to you, where it belongs. To denounce the strong will show that you are weak, and realizing that should make you feel meek. So where is the middle ground in all this complicated mess? How does one go from mayhem to a place of peacefulness?

God created humans to be equal in His eyes, and the statuses that we have created makes God sigh. He shakes His head when He sees the classes that we have created, each one decided by us and never to be openly debated. Upper class, middle class, and lower class is how we define, and once you are in a category you cannot seem to cross the line.

Disabled, demented, and criminals are titles that we wear, each one given by a society that is known not to be fair. God recognizes none of that, and it is that we need to fear. God sees us all as equal, and of that He is quite clear. In God's world there is no division, and everyone will be the same. Accepting that gets you there, and not doing so means on earth you will remain.

We live hell on earth so that God can decide for all of eternity with whom He wishes to reside. Who you may think is unworthy may already have a place at His table, for they were someone that did all that they were able. You see, where we pass judgment and do not sway from it is not the final judgment God uses to make everything fit.

While you are so busily passing judgment here and there, God is doing His own thing to ensure that all is kept fair. Your worry should not be about what others choose to do. Your focus should be on what God's opinion is of you. When you realize what matters is only what God thinks, it somehow becomes less important to push others to the brink.

A person's opinion matters little when all is said and done. What matters is being true to God and where you came from. To be able to rest peacefully each night should be your goal, and you should not have to worry about what you gave others to toil. It is imperative that you keep your own doorstep clean, and by doing this God can work and His way will be seen. It is a much better place that God has ready for you. His intentions are the right ones to pull you through.

Being an example of God is His expectation of us, and when you accept that as right there can be no more fuss. Allow God to work through you for the betterment of man. He will not disappoint, and He will teach you all that He can. What you learn from God should be shared and not preached. A good steward of God will always practise what they teach.

Chapter Twenty-Seven — Natural Selection

How man has evolved is a question to ponder. "Why are we here today?" makes many sit and wonder. Going back over time gives us many eras to be seen. All of them are complicated and not understood entirely. We call it history, but God calls it His Story, for each amazing period of the past is a chapter of God's writing. He wrote each era with each generation in His mind. What He gave to us is entertainment as we figure out humankind.

God used His imagination to make His Story profound. Life certainly would be boring without all His insight around. Try as you might, you will never fully understand His Story, for God's infinite wisdom is impossible to conceive fully.

We have had so many different eras that we know little about. Why they happened leaves us with something to doubt. It is simplicity when you realize that God designed all things, and that each era has its place in the wonders that He has yet to bring. We make it complicated when we try to reason the past and go over each era and why it could not last.

Take the past for what it is and do not over-analyze it too much. God has His reasons for why He designed it to be as such. Search the world we live in today for the answers you want to find, but what you see before you today is what will define humankind.

I too am held in awe when I think of all that God has done. Many fascinating things have taken place and then were gone. It is too mind boggling to think of everything that has taken place, but to keep it in perspective is to know it happened by God's grace. The happenings of the past should show you God's power; take peace in knowing that He is with you every hour.

The Sun Neither Rises nor Sets

Who would not want such a wonderment in their corner, this God of ours that makes each era that much bolder? For Him to have created that which we question is His way of ensuring He remains a part of the equation. No one has all the answers for what takes place here. Only God knows and will not share because He knows that is what we fear.

He cannot tell us because He knows we will not understand. He is reserving that time for when He sets foot on our land. All things will be made clear when He has no more to write. Then and only then will we have all of God's insight. The past is a distraction for those to avoid the here and now. We need to focus on the present and stop questioning the how.

Everything that God wants you to know can be found in yourself. God's biggest achievements are not found on any library shelf. Each soul designed by God has a bigger place in His Story, and discovering your soul, not the past, should be your only worry.

The common denominator in all eras are the souls that were there. Each soul had a mission, and God left nothing to spare. Our era is simply another chapter in God's storybook, another opportunity for us to give our souls another look. Each day is only one of millions that God has put together, and your life has its own plot that is unlike any other.

His reasons for giving you life are to be found by you. You are part of His Story, and you need to see that as true. The past is for amusement; no answers are found there. The answers are in the living, whether or not you think that is fair. Connecting the dots of your life makes the most sense for you to discover where your soul came and went.

Our era has a different wrapping, but the soul's purposes are the same. Each soul has a purpose, and no soul is ever lame. To find the meaning of life is to look within yourself. Your soul has more wisdom that any book on any shelf. The greatest discovery of all time is a soul that is found, for within each soul is His Story waiting to be profound.

God answers all questions when your soul rests with Him. He cannot share this with you if it is in the past that you live. He has given us many choices in which to believe, and finding Him as the right answer is what you must achieve. The journey for all souls is not an easy road to travel, and your purpose in life is for you and your soul to unravel.

To do this is to accept that God oversees all things, and it is God, not humans, who has the wisdom to bring. God doles out His wisdom little bits at a time. His wisdom is shared to let you know that you are doing fine. Every second of your life is a wonderment to be revered. Your soul is to be cherished and to never be feared.

Ignoring our soul leaves us searching for answers. Acknowledging our soul allows the answer to come faster. It is within each soul that God has bestowed the truth. You have the answers, for you are His living proof. A human, by far, is the number-one wonder of the world. Each one is unique with its own His Story to be unfurled.

We should fascinate each other more than we think, for inside each human is the answers that we seek. Each soul has a place in His Story and that is a fact. If you want to find the answers to life then find the soul that you lack.

Chapter Twenty-Eight – You Are Not a Superior Being

We discriminate when we judge the colour of one's face and it is important to us to ensure that everyone is in their place. Discrimination comes from ignorance and fear of the unknown. Years and years have been invested for discrimination to be grown.

It is a fact that we are different, and that is the way it is supposed to be. One of God's greatest tests is for humans to live in harmony. Each race has a gift that they are here to share, and we judge each race thinking that our own has been treated unfair.

I am Caucasian, and to the world I am white. Some think that is a good thing, and others do not think that it is all right. The colour of one's skin should not determine their worth, but what shapes our humanness is what we should be taught from birth.

All children are blind to colour and play with each other until someone mentions why another colour has been a bother. Prejudices are not inbred; they are taught, and the answers to cease this ignorance are what needs to be sought. To those that discriminate I have to say, "You don't get it; what you think you know, in God's world doesn't fit."

It is this drive for control that forces us to point fingers, and we have allowed the ignorance from the past to fester and linger. I am here to tell you that without skin we would look the same. Skin is just the glue that holds together your inner frame.

When we wrap presents, there are no two that look alike, and we wrap them differently so that they are pretty to our sight. That was God's plan when He created each race, and how we have come to judge each other He thinks is a disgrace. If for one minute you admired each race for its attributes, I am sure you would begin to see what is behind the dispute.

As with all humans, no race has what it needs for perfection, and all races must work together to uncover that deception. Each race has a culture for which they should be proud, and to judge another race for who they are keeps our head out of the clouds. We should respect each race for what it has to offer, but instead we denounce and think each race is a bother.

We are all created equal with something that we are to teach, and no race is above another no matter what we preach. It is futile to think that one race is superior to the next, and to go on thinking this is to continue with the human trainwreck. God will not allow this disdain to take place in heaven, and it is important for us to stop trying to keep things even.

God is the only scorekeeper, and He will have the final say. He is the ultimate referee in the game of life that we play. We should accept our penalties before the game is done, because God's penalty box is huge and in it there is no fun. It is never too late to rethink and change your mind, but it must be done before God has to be cruel to be kind.

The chances to start fresh come with each new day, and we must learn to love one another before the chances go away. If you were taught that other races are not equal to you, it is time you rethink what each race is here to do. No race can be fully understood, and that is fine. The key is to accept and stop trying to read each other's mind.

Respecting a race for what they have endured over the years will bring you understanding of what it is that you fear. His Story teaches us that the past has a place in our present, but we keep alive what it is that causes us to resent. Human ignorance has shaped the society in which we live, and we are so far down that we think there is no more to give. It is up to us to forgive what we have done to each other, and the time is fast approaching for us to give up our bother.

We must stop thinking that humans owe us anything and focus on God, who has His own judgments to bring. No human dead or alive can give the payback that God will reap, and it is futile to expect a human to know what God must keep. We are trying to impose on each other our point of view when really it is only God's opinion that should matter to you.

In the whole scheme of things our pettiness amounts to zero, and overcoming that pettiness will make each of us God's hero. When you find yourself being closed, stop and think for one second: should you be open to reality or what it is that you reckon? The beauty of humans is that we can change what we think, and it is up to us to stop discrimination in the eyes that we blink.

Viewing each other as equals is the challenge that God gives, and accepting our uniqueness will bring understanding to how we live. God's purpose for our diversities is for us to become one. Doing this will eliminate losing, and we will be the ones to have won. Our humanness wants to complicate and therefore we flounder, and no one wants to give in to make our world that much sounder.

We begrudge each other, believing that we are owed a sorry when truly the pain we carry only compounds the worry. Equality was handed down by God, who does not differentiate, and trying to refute this with Him will find you losing the debate. "You're equal and you're equal" is what you will hear from Him, and to think anything else is against Him sin.

When you put it into perspective, the overall picture is scary, and God has no time for what it is we choose to see unclearly. To understand this is the shift that is needed by all, because we are setting ourselves up for a painful fall.

The end to discrimination can only come when humans change. It is the ability to accept that which we derange. When we can look at one another the same way God looks at us, it will be the beginning of the end of all this discrimination fuss. Souls do not have a colour because God designed it that way. Our souls, not our skin colour, will be back with God one day.

-- Bullying --

A bull is an animal that is one of God's many creatures. He has horns on his head as one of his identifying features. The horns are used to make other cows and bulls fear him, and they ensure he remains dominant in the pen that he is in.

There are humans who also have a bull's horns and they wear them like a painful thorn. The thorns are what prompt them to harm others, and what put their horns there becomes all our bother. At some point in our lives, we bullied or were victim to a bully. Why this must happen in our society, I do not understand fully.

Our species prefers to let the fittest survive, but bullying someone will always keep a soul from being alive. I have been on both sides of this fence. I have been bullied and I have pushed down someone who had no defence. Being a child is not excuse enough to hurt another soul to show that we are tough.

It is true that bullying is done by someone who is a coward. What they fear cannot be seen, for their fear is inward. Bullying is not exclusive to where our children play, and I can see bullying going on amongst adults every day. As children we bullied others right out in plain sight, but an adult uses mind games to encourage a verbal fight. Bullying is not limited to an act that is physical. It is also a mental tool used to make our life unlivable.

Today we are horrified at the violence we see in our schools, yet we all use bullying as one of life's coping tools. There is at least one person in your life whom you try to dominate, thinking you are ahead of the game by deciding their fate. You may not physically do this person any harm, but bullying can still be done by putting on deceitful charm. This subtle bullying done by adults is the worst, for it is brushed off as another of life's many hurts.

There is a consequence for physically bringing someone down, so why is there no consequence for the bullying with no sound? We as human have no laws that punish mind games, but God in His wisdom has His own all the same. You may think no one notices the game you play, the game where you think no one else should have a say.

God sees everything and He keeps close track, and when you least expect it, He will always give payback. It may be an infraction that you have forgotten about, but God's memory is long, and He carries a lot of clout. No one is safe from karma, which is God's law, and at some point we all learn what God is made of. God rewards or punishes for all that you do, and believing that is the truth is what should pull you through.

God is patient and for the right moment He awaits to give back what you did, whether it was done in love or hate. What is the intent of what is inside your heart and mind? Are you open or closed? Are you going to be cruel or kind?

Our society has lost sight of what is the living truth, and our actions decide the fairness and degree of God's reproof. All deeds, good or bad, are noticed by someone you cannot see. Each one is a reward or a punishment for you and me. When a child is a bully, we punish and condemn them as wrong, but we put up with the adult bullying that has gone on for too long.

To diminish another soul is bullying at its finest, and we do this all the time when we are not giving our best. Bullying a soul is like a blow to God who created it. God made a soul for everyone, and each one is a perfect fit. When you recognize God in every person that you see, there can be no excuses for any physical or verbal profanity. When you know that God is judging every move that you make, there can be no excuses for allowing yourself to be fake.

When you accept that it is God that doles out the payback, there can be no excuses for hurting others for what you lack. When you understand that a soul's peace rests with God, there can be no excuses when on a soul you decide to trod.

It is this disregard for others that has us seeing mayhem. God's payback comes in time to all women, children, and men. We continuously question our world with all its violence without realizing that it is God keeping everything in balance. Trying to make sense or reason for the way things are will only confuse you as to why God has brought it this far.

No human mind could manage all that God knows. Only God can determine what we each need to grow. What we view as wrong is what God in His wisdom is making right. A human would go mad if they had all of God's insight. God holds us accountable for every decision we make, and that is why we learn right from wrong at such an early age.

Babies fascinate me with all the wisdom that they hold; a wisdom that God gave to them while they were in the womb. A child is smarter than those we consider to be adults. A child does not judge what we consider are others' faults. We as adults instill prejudice and judgment in our children. We are the ones that sway them away to commit sin.

You may take this hard, but believe it as true, our children are better adults than either me or you. We want to protect our children, so we fill them with fear, and they become confused about the God that they hold near. We teach them early on to be careful about who they should trust and leave out God when children know trusting Him is a must.

We do not assure them that God is with them all the time and that He will ensure payback for yours and my crimes. A child bullies not because they are mean or demented. A child bullies because of the society that we as adults have invented.

Chapter Twenty-Nine – You Are Never Alone

When you are all by yourself, what is it that you fear that makes you want to have someone else near?

What is it about your own company that makes you think that you are so boring?

Why do we wrap our hearts up tight with another and when they depart think we won't recover?

In life if you do not know your own identity, you will attach yourself to what you don't want to be.

In time you will live a life that is not yours and think to yourself, *What am I with this person for?*

They're not filling this gap I have inside me, but I'll stay with them anyway so that I'm not lonely.

We fear facing life's challenges alone and therefore we stay with what it is that we bemoan.

If that person decides to go away, they take themselves with them and with yourself you stay.

How you manage the pain of this separation should give you insight and a clear indication.

There is no human that can fill your empty space; that can only be done by God's grace.

Rushing from one relationship into the next will not help you to amend what was wrecked.

It is unfair of you to love with a broken heart; doing that keeps you and your soul apart.

Loving someone half-heartedly is only hurting the person in the mirror that you see.

Not loving yourself before you love another is what is causing your loneliness and all its bother.

When you dig deep and look hard at your inside you will see where the real love resides.

If you look in the mirror and do not like what you see, are you then telling the world how to treat thee?

If your soul is lost and never to be found, do you really think someone else's will make you sound?

You miss someone when they leave for a while, but when they leave for good you see your junk pile.

When you remove all the stuff that is them and not you, your own true self will come shining through.

The sadness that comes with losing someone is one of the worst pains from which a lot of us run.

Instead of embracing it, we choose to deny and bring into our life that which we are trying to defy.

What we forget is that in life we are never alone; God has been with you since the day you were born.

He is always just a prayer away to see you through your darkest days.

He will not erase the pain you are going through, but what He will do is help you find you.

He wants you to trust and have faith in Him that through the pain you will love again.

The Sun Neither Rises nor Sets

We want the pain to go away fast, yet it seems to last and last.

Every day is an effort just to get out of bed, and some of us think we would be better off dead.

The darkness consumes our every waking hour and behind our grief we continue to cower.

We want someone to say the right thing to take away the pain and let our heart sing.

The urge to do something crazy is so strong, and we do not care anymore if we do anything wrong.

Sometimes we want to hurt the one that caused us pain, and the need for revenge makes us insane.

We want them to suffer the same way we are, and there are those who will take it too far.

When there seems to be no end in sight, you need to stop depending on yourself and look for the light.

Your time with grief you can do nothing about, but trusting in God will soothe away your doubt.

When you cry your tears of sadness and pain, remember that you cry them to love again.

Trust in your soul that this too shall pass, and believe that God is there if you would only ask.

Understand that He will not force His faith on you; He can only come in when you allow Him to.

Your sadness and pain are not lost on Him; He is waiting patiently for you to let Him in.

Reach for the hand that God has extended to you, and He will hold yours as He guides you through.

God won't leave you to struggle on your own, for He has been with you since the day you were born.

You are never alone even if you think you are; God is in you, and He has brought you this far.

Take that step and embrace God's love and you will find no end to the support from above.

Chapter Thirty — Choose Compassion over Cynicism

It is amazing the amount of people who in your life will tread, some briefly and some stay as a friend.

Not everyone we meet will be dear to our heart; a few we will hold close, and the rest we keep apart.

For reasons we do not know why, a stranger becomes a friend that we keep by our side.

You met and for some reason your souls clicked, and you became fast friends as the clock ticked.

You were different, but you found common ground and knew that the friendship was sound.

Your secrets are shared with this person to whom you turn when you are really hurting.

All the things that make you smile in a day are shared with this person who can see things your way.

This person is ranked high on your priority list, and you try to ensure they are included and not missed.

This person knows when you need a hug, and they sense when about something you are bugged.

They always have the right words to say and give hope to you when your life is in disarray.

They don't judge who you are, and if they do you feel okay telling them that they have gone too far.

Our friends we treat with the utmost care, because without them you would only be half of a pair.

Some friends we love more and call them our best, and they mean more to us than the rest.

We try to connect with them at least once a day, not wanting to miss anything that comes their way.

Our friends' opinions we hold in high regard, and we ask for their advice when times are good or hard.

Whether we do what they lovingly suggest never changes the fact that we consider them our best.

Peace is yours when you sit with a friend, and you can talk without the conversation coming to an end.

We feel blessed if we have more friends than others and have many more that we do not bother.

We have an opinion of what a loyal friend is; summed up, it is that person that your soul would miss.

The friendship with which you should take the most care is the person in the mirror that you stare.

Treating yourself like the friend that you love so much takes your own understanding and loving touch.

Imagine that your soul could talk with you: what do you think it would say to get you through?

Would it say all the things that your friend does when you turn to them seeking some love?

As humans we need to hear words spoken aloud to assure each other about why we are around.

We need a friend to always be honest and true, and even if they are not, we still accept what they do.

The Sun Neither Rises nor Sets

A friend is the same as others in your life; they are not always wrong, and they are not always right.

To regard them higher than you regard your soul is to take away from you and the life that you toil.

We think a friend is truly a Godsend, because we figure they will be with us to the end.

What we forget is that our one and only faithful friend is yourself, who will be with you to the end.

The comfort and wisdom a friend has to offer can be found in yourself every minute of every hour.

We do not want to talk to ourselves because we will look crazy and what is heard sounds hazy.

"That is why I have friends in my life to walk me through my achievements and my strife."

"I need my friends to assure me that I'm on the right track even though they also lack."

"But that's okay, because they know best; I'll listen to the one I agree with and forget the rest."

Your friends can share with you what they know, but it is your opinion of yourself that lets you grow.

Our friends are exactly as we want them to be — someone to lean on and to help us to see.

We burden a friend and seek their insight without searching our soul for what is wrong or right.

We want our friend to point us in the right direction, and we think their answer is perfection.

We forget sometimes that our friend also has a soul, and it is to their soul that you bring your life's toil.

Their soul has a mission in life, and it could be to help you to get your soul right.

They do not have the answer to your every prayer, as they have sent a few of their own up there.

Your friend cannot hear what your soul whispers; it is unfair to expect them to know the whole picture.

It is you who can hear your calling, and expecting a friend to make sense of it is your falling.

Your friend is just as confused as you are, and depending on each other's opinions will not get you far.

When you conclude that you are your own best friend, you will understand where your soul ends.

When you allow your soul to be the way it is supposed to be, the light goes on and you can see.

You believe that you can stand on your own feet, and it is you doing it, not the friends you meet.

Accepting that your friend does not know your inside helps you see it is their life they need to decide.

Being responsible for what we make our friends talk about will force us to look inward without doubt.

Having your friend value all your insecurities is forcing their soul to speak about what they can't see.

Your friend's soul cannot begin to guess what your own soul whispers as it tells you your life's test.

You truly are your own best friend, because no one else knows where your soul has been.

There is no human who knows you inside and out, and none that can understand your self-doubt.

There is no person who knows exactly what to say to coach your soul and send it on its way.

Your soul knows what they can never fathom and cringes when you follow their advice at random.

Asking your friend about something should never be asked so that a decision is forthcoming.

The weight of your world should not be given to a friend; they have their own burdens to attend.

Your friend should be second to what your soul decides; your soul has dibs on what it knows inside.

Sharing with your friend what is the truth lets them off the hook when their advice you reproof.

Your friend should be there as a companion only, whose soul you accept and regard fondly.

Your friend is there when you need a human touch and is someone you should love very much.

Your friend should not be judged for what they are called to do and what they know to get through.

Instead, give back to them the question they bring and ask them what their own soul must think.

They say, "I don't know," and that is untrue, so you encourage them to see what their soul wants to do.

A loyal friend will not waver or bend when showing you that you are your own best friend.

That is the greatest gift they give to you and me: to let you love yourself and the soul they cannot see.

Directing you to discern with your own soul is what is needed in a friendship role.

Showing them it is on their own soul they should depend will teach them to be their own best friend.

Some friendships will end because they are all wrong, and for unknown reasons you no longer belong.

You can either stop talking or own up to the fact that your friendship is no longer where it is at.

It is painful to be the one to end a friendship, but it is big of you to take ownership of it.

The lesson given when you let a friendship go is that one day you will be the receiver and know.

You will remember the time you said goodbye to a friend and know you are feeling what they did then.

They will also wonder if what they did was right, to send someone away from their sight.

We are as good a friend as we are to our self; friendships are as different as the books on your shelf.

Each has something to say and was sent to show us something along the way.

Whether the friendship was brief or a long time, what you learned should be cherished inside.

No one should feel that their friendship was not good enough, even if it was rocky and tough.

Judging a friend for what we think they are not is to judge yourself for the friendship that you sought.

They aren't able to live up to your expectations because being a friend to yourself has no explanation.

If you can't deal with the person you are, your friendships in life will only take you so far.

Accepting that you are your own best friend will give you understanding before a friendship you end.

When you realize your friend and you are imperfect, you get the wisdom unto yourself to reflect.

Did you love unconditionally and give it your best? Was it you or them that was your hardest test?

If you gave it your all without any doubt, then you know what being your own friend is all about.

The Sun Neither Rises nor Sets

Ousting a friend should be considered carefully; are your motives quite clear or sort of murky?

Is the friend in the way or is there something else you want, like a new friend that you want to flaunt?

Have you lost touch because you got busy elsewhere? Is losing a friendship from your neglect fair?

Are their traits things you do not like much, and you use that as your excuse to remain out of touch?

Friends tolerate you the same as you tolerate them; you too have traits that they wish you would end.

But they choose to accept you for the friend you are, whether you are closest to them or apart.

They don't want your friendship taken away and count themselves lucky to know you another day.

Our friendships we should treat like we treat ourselves; by doing that, our judgments can then be felt.

For you to judge a friend for the way they happen to be leaves the door open for them to judge thee.

Accepting faults will help you accept your own, and doing this together will help each other to grow.

Snuffing out a friendship like you would a candle should show you in yourself what you cannot handle.

We disregard souls who fail to meet our standards, and do not stop to think that that soul is a reminder.

Into our life are brought people that are a test to show us, and God, if we are really doing our best.

No soul wants to be turned away for not measuring up; we all have a chip on our half-full cup.

If you really want to end a friendship for all time, take one more look at the mountain you must climb.

What is before you is also what your friend must defeat, and they will need you when they are weak.

They should know that even if you do not talk for days that they have your help to find their way.

One of the greatest gifts you can give to a friend is letting them know that you are there until the end.

When you can't talk every day, somehow ensure your friends know that you think of them anyway.

Some friends will know our everyday thoughts; some go away and bring back what they were taught.

If a friend does not attend your friendship, you should consider their woes and hardships.

A friend is to us the only way they know how; they may live in the past and not the here and now.

Maybe your friend needs your guiding light to help them find the love they have tucked out of sight.

Could be your friend's love is bursting to come out, but they hold back from you because of self-doubt.

Turning away a friend because of their trappings will solidify in them all that they are lacking.

Stop with the "she can't, I can't, he does, and I don't" and give your friendship some hope.

You would want another chance with the soul in you; for you are your best friend through and through.

Chapter Thirty-One — Relationship Musings

One day in your life love will appear and you will embrace that feeling and keep it near. Every moment of every day will be filled with thoughts of this person whose love you forever sought. The yearning to be with them will not go away, and you cannot stop the urge to connect with them every day. They have something that no one else has, and you are astounded with the love that you have amassed.

One day you did not know them and the next you are in love, and you thank the heavens and God above. The love may only last days, or it may last years, and it could bring you joy, or it could bring you tears. How is it that we could love a stranger? We can count them on each finger. Into our lives they came and went, and we thought each one was heaven sent. We cling to the ones that do us the most harm and take for granted the one with whom we walk arm in arm.

In our fear of not wanting to be alone we sometimes stay where no more love can be grown. Love brings out every emotion to man: passion, hate, contentment, fear, happy, and sad. If you have been in love, you know of what I speak, that loving someone more than yourself will make you weak. When you meet your love, you come as you are, and each lesson in your life you carry on your soul like a scar. The person will never know what your life brought you; they only see you as the answer to pull them through.

What you willingly give to this person may not be enough, and they get needy and start to make your life rough. In their eyes you can do nothing that is right, and they hold you in contempt, going on their own insight.

They judge the way you love as right or wrong, not realizing it is themselves they have not loved all along.

There are many differences for a man and a woman, and how they choose to love is all ingrown. We view these differences as a hindrance when we should see them as part of life's dance. It is not for you to say how this person should love, the one that you thought was sent from above. They are who they are, and they will not change by you demanding what is out of their range.

How to make a person be something they are not is what so many failed loves have sought. We know these differences off by heart and sometimes find the irony in what keeps us apart. We fight this battle each day, wanting the other to see it our way. "He said, she said, he did, she will" now begin the sentences about the life that we bemoan. It is easy to judge the one that causes us unrest, not realizing that they are also living life's test.

We get caught in the trap of judging what we each do that we think is helping ourselves to get through. Onto each other we put the blame for what is in our own heart before along they came. Loving someone else should never be a burden, and loving yourself should never be about hurting. When you see a relationship you think is perfection, do you yearn for what you see to be your own reflection? Do you wonder if their social life is the same as their private? Are they happy or is it you that they covet?

When you are single you want to be with someone else, and when you are with them you want to be by yourself. Why is it that we can feel like we are all alone even when the one we love waits for us at home? Books have been written about why we feel these things and how to deal with what your life must bring. Some teach us things that we did not know, and a few will be from what our wisdom grows. Each book written will carry a lesson about everything in life that we keep guessing. We read and read, wanting to hear the answers, and fail to hear what our own soul whispers.

Look to yourself to find true love, and it is then that you will understand what is up above. Accepting who you are is an extremely challenging thing to do, because you refuse to understand why you are you. We get caught up in a role that we think we should play and seeking ourselves gets delayed. In life you may wear many different hats, and eventually you forget where you came and went.

Where did the real you get lost in the mix to end up in a relationship that you cannot fix? You were oh so happy with this person at one time. Why now do you feel like you committed a crime? You take and they take, you give and they give, and you wonder: Is this really for what I live? When did this person become a bore? How did they become someone you no longer adore?

If you feel this way, then yourself you should ask, "Do I love myself first or do I love myself last? If I cannot appreciate what I see in the mirror, how can I expect anyone else to hold me dear? If I do and say things to cause others pain, then I have no right to judge when they give me the same."

If you treat your loved one less than you would treat your friend, it is obvious that your love will end. Why do we act one way behind our home door yet put on another face when we are out at the store? Our loved ones will always suffer our wrath, because we think we have the right to treat them that bad.

There is no way you would treat your boss at work like you do your loved one for their every little quirk. Willingly or not, you respect the one that signs your cheque, and those at home you want to wring their neck. What puts these two people on a different scale? Why succeed for your boss and for your loved ones you fail? What is this drive to be something we are not and to impress others and forget what we got?

We think someone else will quench our discontent and expect this from our loved one on whom we vent. Your dreams are shattered when you think they are not the one, and it is then that you ask, "Should I stay or run?" From what are you running, is it them or you? If you loved yourself, don't you think that you would get through? When you know you and have faith in your heart, you will begin to understand from where you got your start.

Taking the time you need to find who you are is truly the only thing that will take you far. Denying yourself the will to live your life will only breed discontent and cause you strife. Think next time before you speak, and remember that we are all weak. Molding someone else into what you want them to see is you molding you into what you want to be. Insisting that someone do this or do that will be ignored and get lost in the vat.

Forcing the issue will only push them away, and eventually they hear nothing you have to say. The person who has been sent to you is also there to teach you a thing or two. When you move past what frustrates you about them, your heart will be opened for what you yen. We have no control over what our loved ones do or say, and all we can do is figure out why we act in a certain way.

Are you holding a grudge that should be dead? Do you need to get or give forgiveness for something you dread? Are you carrying around the weight of the world for words of regret at a loved one you hurled? Are you sitting on a time bomb of anger and pain that is ready to explode at your loved one again? Are you judgmental and find fault with all and cannot see that your own faults are just as tall? Are you quick to disagree with another's thoughts, forgetting that your opinion is not what they sought? Are you consumed with the fact that life is unfair, not realizing that you are the one that keeps you there?

Are you immersed in a loved one's identity, thinking that who they are will set you free? Are you so wrapped up in your loved one's life that you could not cut free even if you had a knife? Are you and your loved one now one and the same to think that you are on the same page? Are you strong enough to take that first step to discover what is to come in your life yet? Are you so muddled up in what you cannot control that you have set aside the contentment of your soul? Are you too proud to say "I do not know what to do" that you will not give God the control back to help you through? Are you filled with doubt that God's love is genuine and choose to instead about your life to whine?

When you accept the fact that no human can answer what your heart and soul have whispered, you will see the light and know that it's you who chose wrong or right. It does not matter who you surround yourself with; it is always with yourself that you have the biggest rift. Accepting yourself as the human you are will release your trapped soul and let it soar. It is true that the truth will set you free and that truth comes from faith and the will to believe.

When you understand the importance of you is when God will give to you what is due. There is nothing He can do when your sights are elsewhere, but He will wait for you to decide that His way is fair. Turning to Him will not change the relationship that you are in, but what it will do is cleanse you and help you to begin. Accepting God's way will help you to stop and think about any words you are about to speak. Whether the words be of wisdom or to cause hurt, He gives them to you to help you to learn.

Of course, as a human your emotions run wild, but in time they will not compare to your soul when it is mild. The trials and tribulations heaped on you each day are much easier when you choose to follow His way. Understand that even if you are, you are never alone, and you always have God and your precious soul. You may think that neither of these listen to you as you try to control what you think will get you through. Of course you will ignore them as does everyone else, as you continue to clean off everyone else's shelf.

You think that you alone can make everyone right, but only God can do that when we each have insight. He knows that believing in Him is done by free will, for He started it that way and it is that way still. He will never force you to believe in Him — that is for you to decide as a precious human. Loving yourself comes from a relationship with God that will guide you where He wants you to trod.

If you are honest with yourself, you know that it is true that a relationship will not work unless you start to love you. Now go and look at the loved one you hold so dear; is it them or yourself that you truly fear? Do you still see them as the reason for your discontent, or do you now see it is your own halo that is bent? An inner peace comes from knowing the truth: that loving others comes from your own reproof. It is that moment in time when you come to accept that how you treat yourself is what you will expect.

When you choose to live your life and what is going on in it, you will open the door to God's long-awaited visit. Do not ask Him for a miracle to make everything right; ask Him only for His wisdom and His insight. He cannot change the path of your destiny; He leaves that up to you with the choices He brings. Taking responsibility for how you treat others will help you deal with the guilt that has you smothered. Own up to the fact that your destiny you choose by denying or accepting your own inner truth.

Remember that when you give others your blame, they cannot accept it, as theirs is the same. Each of us has our own sins to redeem, and we do not need others to give us more than what we have seen. Our own life's tribulations are for us to deal with, and thinking someone else will fix them is a myth. Who you are is not for someone else to fathom. You are you to deal with now and not at random. If your relationship has been all about coping, stop living your own lie and start right now by hoping. Take this very second, this moment in time, and start to live your own rhyme.

-- Family --

Family is a small word to which we give a lot of clout. We think it is important to know them and have them about. We do not get to choose our family; they are chosen for us. Some families can get along and for others there is always a fuss.

My own family has dysfunction, and we rarely ever talk. It is easier that way than to go back over where we have walked. I never knew my mom, and my father has never been one. He acts like it is our fault what he did to his daughter and son. What he wants to forget is what my brother and I live each day. He thinks we have forgotten his actions and what he had to say.

I have never forgotten, but what I did was forgive. To not let it go would never give me my own life to live. I have no animosity for my father, this is true, and I am living proof that your family does not define you. My brother, on the other hand, holds his anger inside, and when he will let it go to heal is for him to decide.

I used to wonder all the time how my father got off scot-free thinking there is no justification for what he did to my mom, brother, and me. How does he get to act like nothing had taken place? Why does he not want to apologize and look at my face?

Many years have passed since I was a broken-down child. I carried so much hurt that I rarely smiled. As an adult today I can understand many things, most of all that family is what you must bring. They are there no matter what, and the past is the past. What is important is to heal the hurt that you have amassed. There comes a point when you must leave the past behind to concentrate on the present and to yourself be kind.

I choose to not have a father, not because of what he did; we do not talk because to him I am still a little kid. He is the one that cannot deal with his parental sins, and I refuse to carry his burdens and go to where he has been. Would a sorry do at this point you may wonder. I'm unsure, as I do not have trust left for him in a relationship that has gone asunder.

He is old-school and for him to not acknowledge is to forget. To own up would show him where his parenting came and went. It is easier for him to act like I do not exist so he can live easier and forget what he missed. It is true that no one is perfection, and I can readily admit that, but there comes a time where you must admit where you are at.

I feel sorry for my father as he ages each day, acting like he is righteous and has nothing to say. He who left wounds and scars on a defenceless child. Does he not know that God will be anything but mild? That is where I am at, and I truly hope he repents, for God will speak loudly where I could never vent. What my father has done is between him and God now. God takes care of all things and that is His solemn vow.

On the other hand, I have a family that I love endlessly. They include my brother, my sister, and my son, who reflects me. These three people love me as much as I adore them. Each one has a place in my heart where no one has been.

My brother and I had only known dysfunction growing up, and where my cup is half full, my brother has a half-empty cup. His anger about his childhood is immense to this day, where I have forgiven and put the memories away. Our sister was not raised with us and does not know our pain. She is the one who knows love and how to give it again and again.

We all have the same father, but our moms are our own. My sister knew her mom, but to me and my brother our mom is unknown. My brother and I lost our mom when we were young. She died in a plane crash before her song was sung. My sister's mom died when my sister was a teen, and the love that they shared is something my brother and I never seen. Both moms gone and we are left with a father who did not care. There is no justice in that, and it still seems unfair.

Our triangle became a square when my son was born, and he has become the common thread in three lives that were torn. My siblings love my son beyond words. No negative, only positive words has he ever heard. Both my sister and brother marvel at the job that I have done raising my child to be a well-adjusted and happy son.

How was that possible after the way that I was raised? I was simply mild with the discipline and always poured on the praise. My son has never doubted that he is loved and cherished. Our relationship is strong, and it has no reason to perish. I broke the cycle of dysfunction that my father gave to me, and my son has been given the life that I always wanted to see.

My father has no place in my life and that was his choosing. He thinks avoidance is winning, but it is actually losing. His fourth wife's kids are what his world revolves around, for none of them have the memories that three of us carry around. He chooses silence, so we leave him with his thoughts while the three of us try to find that which we have always sought.

Family is not necessarily blood, for I have many good friends, and each friend fills a void where family love has never been. I use the term family very loosely when it's mine that I describe. You may hold a certain title, but it's not always who you are inside. I have a man that I call father, but that is about it. Sperm does not in itself make a father a perfect fit.

Family should be an example of what you want to aspire to, and there should be unconditional love for all that you do. Let the world judge you; your family should never do this. Family are the people that when they are gone you will miss.

My father's choices in life are not there for me to judge, and the victory for me is to forgive and not hold a grudge. As with all things in life, karma always comes around, and I trust fully in God that His justice will know no bounds. I leave my father to live with what he knows he did. God never leaves unpunished a crime done unto a kid. Your family does not define you and thank heaven for that. Who you are to yourself is where your family is at.

Chapter Thirty-Two — Lived Happily Ever After

Today it is too easy to get married and divorced; we do each of these thinking there is no recourse.

We marry someone thinking they are the one and decide we want a divorce when it is no longer fun.

We think if we get married we can trap the love we have and then it won't stray from our other half.

We think that having a ring on our finger will help us to love ourselves where no love seems to linger.

You are not meant to marry the first one you love; if that was the case, you would be married at five.

There are many people whom you will love along the way, and each was supposed to be met that day.

Loving someone else is how we learn to grow, and we need to love others for us to know.

God understands our need to be loved and gave us the commandment not to covet.

To want what someone else already has is what is setting us up for the failures that we amass.

God knew His commandments we would break but gave them with free will to see what we'd take.

He laid out all the rules of life's game and knew we would not play the same.

He knew we would make up rules as we went along, but that didn't change what was right or wrong.

He knew that sex would be equated to love as we try to find the one that He sent from above.

We think our true love is somewhere out there, so we love and leave like we really do not care.

We think the emotions we feel when we fall in love must surely mean this is the one sent from above.

Love is an emotion that is defined in many ways, unlike anger, sadness, and joy that make up our day.

We know what can spark these emotions, but we aren't sure of love and all its commotion.

It is foreign to think that you love what you hate; you loved the person you divorced on a certain date.

We think it is the other emotions that get in the way, but it was you who chose for the love not to stay.

When you still love someone you cannot get, the love you feel for them is this thing called regret.

Each person on each side of a divorce thinks it was the other that made the marriage worse.

The reasons behind why you both want to quit should be questioned with: "Why did you get in it?"

Were your reasons for marrying the right ones or did you marry hoping they'd show you love?

If you are marrying because it is the only love you want, your marriage will become gaunt.

If you believe that the other person defines you, do not get married, because it is already through.

You should not get married until you know who you are; doing this will take you both far.

If you truly know what you want from life, you won't get lost in the title of husband or wife.

God gave a life for you to get through, and you should not marry someone who will not accept you.

Marry someone who complements your soul and not the one that thinks compliments are a goal.

How you learn the difference between the two will only come when with yourself you are true.

You cannot love another until you love yourself, and it is futile to think that they can be your shelf.

If there wasn't such a thing as a divorce, would you tread more carefully in love's obstacle course?

If you knew getting married meant there was no way out, wouldn't you want to do it without doubt?

If you knew the choice you made was for life, would you want to be the best husband or wife?

We want to love a soul before we love ours first and cannot understand why we are constantly hurt.

Our soul is giving us its own insight, but we shush it because we think we are doing what is right.

If your soul is telling you what it already knows, why do you ignore it and insist that love will grow?

If someone is making your soul feel discontent, it is not them, but from you that love came and went.

Today, for some, marriage has become a big joke, and they take for granted the vows that they spoke.

The vows are said to one another on a special day and then they are forgotten and tucked away.

Thought goes into what vows should be said, but is the same thought put into the years ahead?

We think a wedding reflects us as a couple and think if it is not grand enough our marriage will topple.

We put on a grand event for our family and friends, never wanting the love we have to ever end.

We are grateful for who we see there, and the thought of the day ending is more than we can bear.

But end it does, and then the real work begins, and you start to realize what you got yourself in.

You vowed to love this person for all time and that seems like forever now in your eyes.

Just this person now for the rest of your life; you are forever now a husband or a wife.

For some that will not seem like such a bother, but some will wish they were with another.

Why will some regret the decision they made to profess their love so openly on their wedding day?

We said it aloud for all to hear that we would hold this person by our side very dear.

Why do some of us want to take that back when we think it is their love that we lack?

If you knew you had to do it all over again, would you take them as a lover or leave them as a friend?

A marriage is not all about fifty-fifty, it is about the hundred per cent that you give to thee.

To deny who you are for someone else's benefit will be your soul's discontent when on them you vent.

It becomes all their fault and none of your own when the love you have can no longer be grown.

The love is forgotten that you felt on your wedding day, and the vows you spoke you no longer say.

The Sun Neither Rises nor Sets

Our society today allows us to say "Oh well" and lets us divorce and move on to someone else.

We soothe ourselves that there is no consequence for freeing ourselves from a love that came and went.

We do not consider the children born out of our love that have lost the only foundation they know of.

We teach them that love is not sacred, and divorcing is the way out when you can no longer fake it.

They become cynics and if they choose to marry, they know a divorce is the burden they will carry.

Permission is given to not be serious and to divorce if with someone else they become curious.

They are okay to simply live with someone to avoid the complications when things are all done.

We have taken away the yearning of every soul to have peace in the souls that begin in our home.

God knew our society would take the easy way out when our souls became filled with self-doubt.

He can see the outcome of this path that we tread and the results of whereby our choices we are led.

There are two commandments, to not commit adultery or covet what our neighbour holds dear.

Cheating on someone has been accepted as okay, and we desire what others have at least once a day.

We have taken free will a step too far and it is time to re-evaluate the people that we are.

We need to take blame for the decisions we make and get real about the world that has become fake.

We need to look back from which we all got our start and build back up what has been torn apart.

We have dismantled each other's will to have hope and left each other on our own to cope.

We disregard that we each have a soul and no longer believe in God's overall goal.

You are to love God first and then each other, but somehow that has gotten lost in all the bother.

There is too much going on to cherish a husband or wife, and we become bitter and full of strife.

"Why tie myself down to only one person? Isn't it after all only myself that I am hurting?"

You are mistaken if you think that is the case; having no faith is what is destroying the human race.

We are setting ourselves up to fail by ignoring the cross to which Jesus is nailed.

Believing that Jesus died for all our sins will help you to understand where we all must begin.

He knew we would go down before we looked up and decided that we had had about enough.

He knew we would question this society we made and eventually come around to doing it His way.

He knew everything that we would have to face and that eventually we would seek out His grace.

He knew we would seek the soul on our inside and turn to that to help us to decide.

Marrying to divorce is a sure sign that we are nearing rock bottom in this world we have designed.

We are not put here to judge each other's mistakes, and doing that makes us become fake.

We have lost track of all the important things in life: yourself, family, kids, and your husband or wife.

The Sun Neither Rises nor Sets

Losing track of these means losing track of God's love as we defy His teachings sent from up above.

God knows that to love Him above you is what it will take to get you through.

God's love is less complicated than you think; it is our own human doubt to it that we bring.

Having faith in God will calm all your fears, and His true intent for you will start to become clear.

For it is God, not you, that has all the control, and when you accept that, your life will be less of a toil.

Looking at our views on marriage is a start to finding out why our family's foundation is falling apart.

Are you teaching others, and have you been taught, that there is more to life than what you have got?

Have you decided that giving up is okay? Do you follow your own rules or what God has to say?

Do you excuse the choices you make, thinking no one is tracking the love that you fake?

We need to rethink the path down which we are led and accept that life is not over when you are dead.

Even if you do not believe that heaven or hell are true, think for one second like both really do.

Is what you saw where you want to be? Was your soul locked in chains or was it set free?

What does heaven or hell have to do with it anyway? The vows you say in life have the same sway.

The promises you vow when you marry are the same you should make to the soul that you carry.

"In the name of God, I take you, my soul, from this day forward to have and to hold."

"For better or worse, for richer or poorer, in sickness and health, to love and to cherish."

"Until we are parted by death, this is my solemn vow to not let anyone put asunder now."

What you vow to yourself and to another shouldn't come before what is your own bother.

Your soul should come first on this earth; God should come before your soul to see your self-worth.

The vows you say on your wedding day should be the same vows that to yourself you say.

Once you have committed yourself to your soul, loving someone else the same will be your goal.

Loving yourself is one of the greatest gifts you can give to the person that you want to be forever with.

Love God first, your soul second, them third, and the whisper of your soul will always be heard.

Loving yourself second is the greatest test you will live and will determine the love that you must give.

Loving God first lets your love grow to more, and loving others third will let your soul's desires soar.

When you understand why God is one and you are two then you will see God's love in all that you do.

Once your priorities are in line and God's intent is clear, you will begin to love the soul you hold near.

For better or worse, for richer or poorer, it is God and your soul that will be there tomorrow.

God and your soul should be told that you take them from this day forward to have and to hold.

Until we are parted by death, this is my solemn vow: to not let anyone put asunder now.

-- Adultery --

God knew what we would do with His seventh commandment and that we would knowingly unravel our moral fabric. He knew that through the pleasures of the flesh that's where lonely souls would be met. He gave us the ultimate emotion that we call sex, and it is truly one of God's greater tests. To cheat on someone that you profess to love is not lost on God, to whom you think nothing of. He knows what drives your lonely soul when you seek out another when you are not alone. We equate love and sex to be the same emotion, not realizing that each one creates its own commotion.

To love someone as much as you love yourself will help you to understand the commitment that you shelf. To disregard love for the pleasures of the flesh is what is behind your lonely soul's unrest. The intent of sex was to never cause hurt, and it has turned into an emotion that we pervert. We are enraged when a child is sexually abused and forget all the adult souls that we have used. We are mortified when a child's innocence is taken away, yet we assault adults in the same way. We have sunk to a bad low by accepting what we do not want our children to know.

When you ignore adultery, you are setting our children up for what you do not want them to see. Not holding each other accountable for this act is teaching our children that they must live with this fact. By excusing someone for making this mistake, we are showing our children that love is fake. No judgment on earth will be as harsh as God's when it is into adultery that you decide to trod. He warned us not to do this selfish thing, for He knew the mass destruction to our souls it would bring.

All God's commandments are morally correct, and some we ignore and others we believe we have met. If we are honest with ourselves, each commandment we have broken by our actions, our deeds, or the words we have spoken.

We should love God before anyone, and we have each worshipped money over God. We have lost the true meaning of Sunday and we have condemned our parents in some way. We have wished at some time that someone was dead, and we have cheated on our spouse in another's bed. We have kept money given to us by mistake and we have told a lie or two knowing that it was fake. We've each used God's name in the form of a swear and we at one time wanted to be our neighbour over there.

Commandments are broken because we do not stop to think of the consequences our defiance will bring. We think if God did not strike us down than we can continue to toss His commandments around. We think to ourselves that we got away with it and then question the world and the mess that it is in. We trivialize our actions as not that bad and then see the overall picture as something sad. We think "there is no hope for me, as I have sinned," and the fact that you say that is what allows you in. God knew that as humans His commandments we would break, and He gave them to us to decide our own fate. To disregard His commandments as the living truth will be our undoing when we come under His reproof.

No one on earth is made to perfection, and God wrote each commandment knowing there would be objection. His intentions for the commandments are clear; to keep what He has taught close and very dear. When you make the conscious effort to follow His way, His commandments take on new meaning in your day. Following God does not free you from any guilt, but following God is on what your redemption is built. When you make the conscious decision not to live in sin, God teaches you to love and to forgive. You need to forgive yourself for all your mistakes and not repeat them, no matter what it takes. You need to take responsibility for all you say and do and what has prompted you to break God's ten rules.

Once all ten of His commandments are ingrained on your soul, you will have a peace like you have never known.

You cannot live His Ten Commandments to perfection because you live each day with some temptation. Regardless of that, it is your conscious effort to discern on what you know to be right and proper. When you understand that it is your soul that you compromise, you will think twice about walking on sin's side. You have no dark burdens when you walk with God, for His light is shining on the path that you trod. He is there to pick you up when you stumble and fall, and He understands that you are only human after all. He wants you to acknowledge Him in all that you say and do and wants your best effort in the life He gave you. He does not want your half-hearted faith, what He wants is an honest effort and it is on that that He waits.

Unlike the rest of us, only God knows what is in your soul, and it is between you and Him which way you decide to go. His judgment will be swift, and it will be sure whether He judges you down here or up there. He gave us His warning with the Ten Commandments, and He gave us free will to them to commit. To shun His commandments as too hard to keep is what has you up at night without any sleep. No soul is at unrest when it believes in God, for it knows that it has His approving nod. You cannot believe in God and continue to sin, for your soul is your conscience you have within. Once your soul has had a taste of God's good grace, you know it will walk you through every sin you face. You will be tempted, believe that much to be true, but trusting in God will always pull you through.

When you are weak God will be your strength, no matter the challenge or its unending length. You will be tested time and time again, not only by God, but also by His competitor we call Satan. I have already told you what hell is about, and it is for you to believe it or still to have doubt. God gave you His commandments to help you get through, and it's Satan's job to ensure that you never do. God does not want you to live your life in fear, He wants you to trust in His commandments and hold them dear.

He gave you free will and now it is up to you to decide. Is it in heaven or hell that you want to reside? There is no third choice, it is cut and dried, and when all is done will you know that you really tried? To cheat on someone that you profess to love is cheating on yourself and God up above. The pain you create when you cheat could all have been prevented with a commandment you should keep. The grass that you decided to mow over there is not as good as the grass that you decided not to bear. You can be told that fact a hundred times, but it is up to you to read between God's insightful lines.

Chapter Thirty-Three – It Is All About Me

Each day someone new may come along for us to meet, and how you interact with them shows the degree of your conceit. Is their status below you or do you wish you were them? Are you full of yourself or can your beliefs bend? Our society forces us to try and be better than others, and by doing this we forego what are truly our bothers. Our reasons for advancement should always be our own and not built on a foundation of which little is known.

To believe you are above others will only ever end in defeat, and in God's world no soul will get by with human conceit. To think you have it right where everyone has it wrong will surely cause you to mourn for what it is that you long. Conceit is an overinflated ego with something to hide, and putting yourself above others is a long and lonely ride.

It is naïve to believe that you are above everyone, because in a blink of an eye God can give you nowhere to run. To hold yourself in high regard is to bring karma around, and unlike you, God will take you down without a sound. God does not put up with conceit as we do, and He has a way of ensuring that conceit gets its due. Those who are conceited are the ones who are insecure. They bolster themselves up because they are unsure.

Conceited people have so many secrets to hide, and what they cannot see is that we know they have lied. They lie to themselves each time they look in a mirror and they cannot see themselves, for it is their own selves that they fear. Their energy is wasted trying to win us over, and when we see them coming, we should run for cover. We do not want to hear them going on and on about themselves. Can't they see us zoning out and thinking to ourselves?

To be into yourself will take your eyes off God, and no good will come to you when you think others are odd. Believing you are all that can only ever end in disaster, because God's wrath against conceit is what you did not factor.

When I see conceited people, I wonder why they are sad. What has happened in their life to make them so mad? Conceited people are not happy; they are lonely inside, and what they display to the world is an unfulfilled ride. They are lacking something, and arrogance is their defence to try and prove to us that their life makes sense.

No one has it all together and to think that is naïve. Every single soul is defenceless against what God perceives. We are all weak, and strength is an air we put on, and we think we have something to prove before our life is all gone. Look at me, world, and give me my pat on my back, and I will continue to ignore what it is that I lack. We should all feel compassion for conceited souls because they are lost, and showing them another way is our duty at all costs.

Do not judge them, for it is not our place to judge souls, but nudging them toward God should be our common goal. When a human understands that their outer counts for nothing is the light-bulb moment to accept what God must bring. Conceit is a coping mechanism used by the defeated. They have lost all hope and defend this by being conceited.

To be meek before God allows you to see more clearly and allows you to remove all the facades that you have held so dearly. When you give up control to God, more bounty will you receive, and focusing on God before yourself will help you to achieve. Always remember that no human has what it takes, and it is up to us to discern that and point out what is fake.

We do not think we should because we do not want to offend, but just remember that there is a soul in there that you must defend. Pointing out the errors of others should be done with love, and God will give you the right words if you ask from above. Whether or not someone takes your advice to heart, you can rest easier knowing that you gave them a good start. No one wants to hear that we are onto the game that they play. Nonetheless, through you, God must always have His say. Done properly, a soul will accept your reprimand, for all souls need from another a helping hand.

All souls have a mission, and that is to save one another. No soul wants to be considered by humans to be a bother. Our humanness, not our souls, puts on a good front, but sadly enough it is our souls that take the brunt. Leading all souls back to God is what we must do, and to push down a soul to be noticed will not help you to get through.

Every soul must see each other as exactly equal. Conceit is detrimental and to your soul it is fatal. Honesty about yourself is a step in the right direction, and no matter what you think, no human is perfection. Being full of oneself leaves little room for inner peace. Do not doubt for one second that conceit is deceit.

Chapter Thirty-Four — Difficult to Move

We have all been called stubborn or know someone with this trait. We think to be stubborn is to want to win every debate. Stubbornness can be good, depending on the situation. Spiritual stubbornness is wrong and is a deception. To be stubborn sometimes might be for your own health, but ignoring your soul takes away your spiritual wealth.

Some have called me stubborn because I will not sway in my faith, and they want to convince me that there is no God on which I wait. It is not stubbornness I have; it is called having a belief, and the fact that God is in my life gives me spiritual relief. I am not stubborn when it comes to God because I know I am right, and it is also your prerogative to pick apart what God and I write.

My writings would have no purpose if we all believed in God. I have put to paper where God has led me to trod. It is not my place to defend what I am told to say. What I write I write to show that there is another way. God Himself is not stubborn, but He does have rules for us to follow, and it is these rules that the stubborn cannot seem to swallow.

I hear it all the time that they want a miracle to occur, for that is the only way that they will relent and concur. Our miracles have been many if you would just look around. You too can perform your own miracle when it is your soul that you have found. God performs miracles all the time that we choose not to see. Accepting your soul will help you see that His miracles are aplenty.

Our society dictates that success is based around material things, and we are closed-minded to what our life must bring. We depend on human knowledge and then get locked in. It becomes too hard to break free, and as for God, well, we ignore Him. God will not fight stubbornness, for He gave us free will. Coming to Him is by choice and it is that way to this day still.

Those of us who understand God have a duty to perform, and we must be open to reciprocate what others will scorn. It is not my place to judge those who choose not to trust, but keeping God in the spotlight is for me a spiritual must.

If you are rigid in your belief that God does not exist, explain to me why it is His air that you cannot resist. We breathe air each second to stay alive. Have you never wondered why we require air to survive? Each breath you take is from God's mouth to yours. Do you believe that without God you would be more? You are the greatest miracle that God must display, and accepting that as fact will take your stubbornness away.

Doubting God's plan for you makes you feel torn. *Why can't I seem to get out from this place that I have been hurled?* Our humanness balks at admitting where we have been wrong, and we'd rather live in misery and think we do not belong. We think it is a weakness to be vulnerable to each other, so instead we impart what we feel is our bother.

Speaking from experience, I too wanted an answer to believe. I would always ask, "How was it that God was conceived?" I thought if someone told me how it was that God got here, then and only then would I believe in Him without fear. How silly I feel today questioning God's existence, and what I know today takes away all the pretenses.

God cannot share with humans the scope of His insight; for Him to do this would cause us undo fright. Our humanness cannot manage the wonders of heaven, but I am glad He has left it open to let us find Him. For Him to tell all would take away His glory and to know all would cause humans to truly worry. God gives us bite-sized pieces of His insight to chew, and the more you have faith the bigger bites He gives to you.

My faith in God is a topic on which I cannot bend, for He has changed my ways, and on only Him do I depend. His tests for me are not always for me to understand, but to receive His wisdom means I cannot be stubborn. I must be open to rebuke for the things that I write, knowing full well that it comes

The Sun Neither Rises nor Sets

from His insight. I am not here to convince; I am here to teach another way, knowing that God will always be there to give me the words to say.

My experiences with God have convinced me to trust, and I know to have faith in Him is always a must. To think I know better than God is to my own detriment. He has always been there, and His gifts are heaven-sent. It is impossible to stop God once you have let Him in, and the fear of this is what keeps us living in sin. We do not want God to point out what we need to change, and it is much easier to think that we are all on the same page.

Opening your soul to God leads you down your own path, but giving your soul to God will save you in the aftermath. Remove your stubborn thoughts and allow God to work, and He will reveal to you what has been your every quirk. Open your eyes and see the world through God's sight. The peace He has waiting for you will not keep you up at night. Stubbornness is for those who have spiritually shut down, but peace of mind is for those that chose not to keep stubborn around.

Chapter Thirty-Five — Pay It No Mind

There is an act that is done every day as we judge one another by what we choose to say. We try to appease our own insecurities, not realizing that it is ourselves of whom we speak. We want to show others how someone is less by pointing out how they are not doing their best. For some reason, pulling someone else down gives us a sense that we are wearing the crown.

Of others we do constantly complain and out of our mouths does criticism rain. What would we talk about if not for everyone else? Is your life dull compared to what is on their shelf? You may not think so, but others talk about you the same way as you do. Speaking ill about each other is a taught trend that we all do from the beginning to the end. Instead of giving credit where credit is due, we constantly criticize to get ourselves through.

"Everybody does it, so why shouldn't I? It is what is helping me to get by." If what you say about someone else is true, why don't you say it to them and give them their due? It is an unwritten rule that gossip is to be kept from the one to whom our disdain has leapt. Instead of respecting that person on the spot, we go and complain to others as we have been taught. We do not say a word to them out of doubt and fear, and doing so then points the finger at you, my dear.

We do not confront someone who has offended us, and we would rather go to others and kick up a fuss. What would happen if to someone you did say, "What you just said to me has offended me in this way"? Are you worried that you would hurt their feelings for something they said that sent you reeling? Some people are oblivious to what they say and do and sometimes they do not realize that they have offended you.

Judging them for that is not the way to go, but if they have offended you, then they need to know. Telling them that on the spot makes it true, and telling the offence to others makes it overdue. By letting the moment of truth slip away you have forfeited your right to have anything to say. Why take the time to harbour a grudge and take it to others to help you judge? All that is accomplished is a festering sore to which we keep adding on more.

Had you seized the moment and had your say, you would have one less thing to worry about in your day. Telling someone that they have offended you is hard, because we know what is written on our own life's card. We choose not to say a word to our offender, because by doing so our own faults we can remember. What you say about others reflects thee, and it is all about the person in the mirror that you see.

Blasphemy of others leaves the door wide open for each of us to judge in life what others have been coping. Your thoughts on others are your own opinion, and taking them to others is also your decision. When you want to spout what may or may not be true, go look in the mirror at what is looking back at you. Take your finger and point it at the image that is there and at the answers to life's choices you will stare. When you judge others by the words that you speak shows you your own flaws and where you are weak.

It is always the ones that whisper the hardest whose lives are unhappy and filled with darkness. If they could only understand their own pain, it would help them to stop judging others once again. There are those of us who take the no-nonsense approach and speak wisely to the one who in anger just spoke. We say unto them with the utmost care, "Is it at them that you are angry or at yourself that you stare? They are the same as you and me, trying to figure out why they are living."

What you think of others matters not a lot, even though that is what you have always been taught. When you see them for the human that they are, you will realize that you have taken their offence too far. For every one thing that you judge another for can also be found behind your own door. We as humans do not want to face our mistakes and see that judging others is our dignity that we take. Announcing to the world that someone else is not perfect shows what you think of your own self-respect. Keeping yourself equal to those around you gives you the insight that they are also just trying to get through.

To none will perfection ever amass, and who you are does not put you first or put you last. When you whisper something you know nothing about, remember that it is spoken from your own self-doubt. Picking someone else apart for what they do or say will not give you insight on who they are today. Their own crosses in life they too must bear, and you do not know the reason for life that they despair. Judging them for an infraction for all time does not in that second this person define.

Brushing aside that they have a soul too keeps us from realizing that they are the same as me and you. They have every right to be the person they choose to be, the same way you are you and I am me. It is not our place to cause others to hurt because we have chosen not to see our own self-worth. It is not their issue, nor is it mine, if you cannot see what is going on in your own inside. Lashing out at others and pointing your finger should show you where your discontent lingers. Your unhappiness is at the centre when someone else's name you choose to splatter.

Judging others for not doing their best leaves your heart and soul with a feeling of unrest. It is a reminder to yourself every time that for what you judge others you have inside. It is easier to get ourselves lost in the mix instead of looking at ourselves and what we need to fix. Not looking at others and at yourself first is going to show you who needs help the worst. When you learn to be comfortable in your own skin is when you will stop judging and your life will begin.

-- Boasting --

Have you had a painful conversation with someone who boasts? It is painful because they talk about themselves the most. No matter the topic, they can turn it toward their life, and according to them they have felt all the peace and the strife. They belittle your input with their own, which is that much grander, and you begin to wonder if they can walk on water.

When you try to get a word in, they talk over you, because they know it all, unlike you. A person such as this could test the patience of a saint, and their self-centredness makes the realities of life so very faint.

"I, me, my" are the words that are a constant annoying sound, and eventually you wonder how they can keep anyone around. They believe that we want to hear their life story and what they share they think will take away our worry.

It has occurred to me that those that boast are the most insecure, and they are the loudest so they can avoid what they fear. To have someone give their own accolades in every conversation tells me that it's themselves that needs the persuasion.

A person who compliments themselves fears what others think, and they must sell themselves with every eye blink. Someone who boasts is not confident in their own skin and therefore they boast to ignore what is within. A person who boasts has yet to experience life to that point. If they had they would realize that it is not themselves they should anoint.

They have no life experiences that they can share, so they centre the conversation on their self-centred love affair. We accept this trait in humans and then feel sorry for them because they cannot truly see how annoying they have been. They leave the conversation feeling like they have contributed when really what they did was on others' opinions disputed.

One who boasts mostly spews out propaganda they have seen, and half the time they are not even sure what it all means. It is our nature to want to put a boaster in their place, and we want to show them that their actions are a disgrace. Experience teaches that silence is the best tool and not to interrupt, as we all know is a courteous rule.

When it is others' turn to share, they will seek the same respect, knowing full well that they will be ignored as they are waiting to go next. A boastful person wants to do battle with their words, and it is important to them that what they said is heard. Sadly enough, they see a conversation as a one-way street, and all points of the conversation must land at their feet.

Boasting is a means for someone to share what they know, but unfortunately being self-centred does not help others to grow. To concentrate on oneself eventually forces others to tune out, and the one boasting is left feeling more insecure doubt. Then they must try harder to impress their family and peers, and not having their acceptance is something they truly fear.

It is good to keep in mind why people boast; you are a means for them to try and give themselves the most. Their lives have been cut short and they are stuck in a spot, and all they know to that point is how hard they have fought. It is important to them that others know what they have endured, and what they boast about most is what in them has not been cured.

Someone who boasts shares the symptoms but no solutions. They are not equipped to learn from others the resolution. As with anything, changing this behaviour will take time, and dealing with someone who boasts takes you to be the one that's kind. As much as you want to put this person in their proverbial place, succumbing to their level will leave you feeling disgrace.

Faced with an adult that boasts is like dealing with a hurt child. You would not belittle a child with a hurt that they felt was not mild. It is all about teaching someone a new way to view things and eventually they will see the wisdom in what you will bring.

Subtly reprimand with the phrase "Have you thought about this?" Someone that boasts is looking for something that they have missed. They give opinions not realizing that they are seeking advice, so give them something to think about in a way that is nice. We all have a light-bulb moment when we least expect; could be that you are to show someone to see a better fit.

For those who boast and see themselves in these words, remember that all opinions are meant to be heard. You are not always right and that is your downfall. No one on earth ever gets to know it all. We are all nurturing humans and it's our nature to teach, and always remember that fact when we are gearing up to preach. As humans, acceptance is what we all strive for, and acceptance comes easier when you are not demanding more.

Let others learn about you by the things you do. By doing so you will learn about the soul that you never knew. You should never have to sell yourself to gain another's respect, and in time you will be able to understand what others accept. More than anything else, remember that you are an important person, but remember too that what you say can make things worsen.

Think before you speak, for your words are powerful tools, and to boast too much will only make yourself look like a fool. A boaster cannot be taken seriously after a time, for they think they have accomplished all with no more mountains to climb. What they believe they know is not actually the end of the road. There is far too much on this earth for any one person to know.

One who boasts has come to a stalemate in their life, and for some reason they have halted and cannot get over their strife. The world continues but they are stuck in their past, and staying in that place allows them to always remain last. When they see themselves there is when the boasting starts, for they know that they have missed an important part. They will try to hide behind what they think no one sees and will hand out their opinions, which to us may seem too mean.

The reason for the meanness is the anger that they hold near. The anger comes from not accepting the soul that they fear. Content people do not push their thoughts onto others, for they understand what is all our bother. To force others to accept you is to show where you are insecure. You get more respect with a smile than with a sneer.

Boastfulness is not a characteristic held on to by those who are meek. A soul that is settled knows that to boast is to be weak. Those that we hold in the highest regard do not sell themselves, and why we respect them is written in books we keep on our shelves. Through perseverance and subtlety our own greatness will shine, and we must always remember that it's not about I, me, or mine.

-- No! --

A two-letter word can be said that can bring you down. No one on earth likes to hear a "no's" negative sound. At least once a day we are told no in some way, and we do not always appreciate what the no has to say. A no to me means that I must find another route, and saying no to me will not bring a pout. Receiving a no means that someone is not ready to see. Hearing a no is a positive, not a negative, to me.

In every negative situation there is a positive too, but after hearing a no some of us do not know what to do. What I have learned is that no is a test word. When you receive a no, there is more than that to be heard. A no is a yes that someone has turned inside out, and how you deal with a no will help you see your doubt.

I've yet to meet anyone that wants to be told no, but there are a lot of people who will use the no to grow. There are those of us who refuse to give up on a dream, because we honestly believe we have something to be seen. It is true that a closed door means a window is left open, but the trick is to see the window before you give up hoping.

Nothing worth having will ever be handed to you, but if it means that much, you will be able to pull it through. God Himself says no to us and we take that hard, and receiving a no from God is about the only one that I do not want to disregard. A no from God means that He knows what you do not. His no is not being mean; it is His way for you to be taught. Take the no as a lesson to try again in another way. Could be that your need was not meant to come that day.

Some of our greatest inventors and authors were scoffed at. They were told that no one was going to want to know that. Had they succumbed to these things that we humans fear we would never know their greatness that we hold so dear.

Receiving a no from someone means they do not understand you. They are but one person and were not ready for what you knew. Take what you know and move on to another person. Sitting dejected is when your rejection will worsen. What I know is that other humans cannot define me, and it is this mentality that allows souls to be free.

If we allow others to bring us down with their negativity, eventually we give up on what God gave to us as productivity. Every person has something to accomplish in this life. It is humans, not God, who can stab our dreams with a knife. I have seen it too often — this need we have to bring other humans down with the power we feel when we tell someone no with a frown.

Do not get me wrong, there are times when a no is the right thing. Like the times when without a no there is only bad karma to bring. In those incidences, of course, a no is the only way to go. God would never want us to be harmed or to harm another soul. I am not talking about overriding a no to cause harm. This rhyme is written for you to find out what is your charm.

When you have found what it is that you know is correct, you must make it your mission to help others to accept. This cannot be done by taking no as the final say, and with God guiding you it is impossible to go the wrong way. When you believe in something that God does not approve, giving up on it will not make yourself and others lose.

Think back to a time when a no was said to you and how it hurt. Did you give up on yourself because the no was too curt? Was the door closed in your face and you did not see the window? Is the chance still there for you to give your dream a go? It is never too late to make a dream of yours come true. If you trust in God, He will always pull you through. You know in your heart when you are on the right track. Seize the opportunity to succeed and do not look back. Do whatever it is that you feel is something good to do, and God will be there to guide you and help you feel anew.

If you feel strongly about something that needs to be shared, be ready to take the lumps and bumps, but never be scared. It is not an easy path when the outcome is for the good, but you do not want to live a life wondering if you ever could. Perseverance and patience are two things that we must endure. In God's own time, what you desire will be brought near.

Many variables must be put into place for your dreams to transpire, and remember that God is with you down to the wire. If you give up too soon it shows God where you are weak, and He will wait until He hears the wisdom you need to speak. Sometimes a no is for the best when you are not yet ready to receive. God can always see past what it is that we perceive.

It is not His intent to ever steer His children wrong, but we as humans override His intent to get where we belong. By not listening for God's wisdom we fall flat on our face, for sometimes He must pull the carpet out to show us our place. We grudge Him for that because we think we knew what was best, and meanwhile we missed the point of His well-meaning test.

Many times I have received a no from God that I did not fully understand, but in time He always showed me why He gave me His reprimand. In the end I am always thankful that He knew what I did not, and I am forever grateful for the lessons that He has taught. Life is all about that, and it is up to us not to stress; for every single no that is given we have something that we must address.

A no is not a go-ahead to give up on something you desire. It is simply a means for you to look that much higher. To give up on your dreams leaves you without a reason to hope, but God will bring you your dreams if you use Him to cope. There can be no instant gratification for a dream you have within. The only way to get there is to hear your soul and then begin.

Lean heavily on God to lead you and you will not get lost, and when no one else hears you, it is in God that you must trust. The next time someone says no to you, look inside. A no is not the end, but the beginning of another ride.

-- Revenge --

Revenge: this emotion brings up feelings of unfairness, wanting someone to pay for something that they have done to us. It is a surge of anger that strangely enough feels right, and we proceed with a plan for revenge that keeps us up at night. We want to ensure that the pain we feel is justified and that the one who gave us pain must feel why it is that we cried.

It becomes all-consuming, this plan to pay back what is due, and eventually you become what this person is to you. Revenge is not for us to seek no matter the situation, and to belittle yourself to that level will bring no satisfaction. The twisted pleasure you feel when revenge is acted out is short-lived and then karma for this will have to come about.

The repercussions are many for taking matters into your own hands. God's karma is something that we must all come to understand. Revenge is Satan-driven, and his pleasure comes from our pain. Satan urges us to act quickly so that pain will not come to us again. Patience is not a virtue that Satan wants us to feel, and he convinces us that God's karma is not for real. Satan assures us that seeking revenge is the right thing, and he clouds our judgment to what revenge will bring.

God, on the other hand, urges us to patiently wait for Him, and what we fail to see is God getting ready to begin. God's karma is mightier that any human act can perform, and He has a plan of fairness for the one that gave you scorn. To take matters into your own hands forces God to step aside, for He will not partake in what you and Satan decide. What He will do is give you karma for what you have done. You will reap God's wrath, and Satan will be the happy one.

The Sun Neither Rises nor Sets

Two wrongs do not make a right, of that you can be sure, and thinking they do will bring you God's karma to endure. A true test of your character is to trust God's intent. It is only a matter of time before God will have to vent. He does not allow our hurts to go unpunished for very long. God always delivers karma to where it must belong.

I know of what I speak, for I have seen God's karma at work when I have been hurt by people who on their face was a smirk. How badly I wanted to wipe that smirk off their face. Boy, it would have felt good to put them in their place. Just for a moment I allowed myself to imagine their fall and how I couldn't ignore them like they did not matter at all.

It is in that moment that I realize what they are doing to me. I am allowing them and Satan to clap their hands in glee. Instead I do nothing, as I know God just made a note, and eventually we all get back what it is that we tote. Had I acted on what I know was to my soul's detriment, I would not have been able to witness God's karma as it came and went.

What you must understand is that those that do us harm are watching you and waiting for you to set off their alarm. God will blindside them with karma when they least expect, and for doing nothing you have earned God's respect. Revenge is never sweet, and we should not wait on it for spite. It should be good enough for you to know that God will make it right.

Never say "I told you so" when God's karma is done. Be content that God gave you that round to be won. God's karma is for everyone, and you must remember that. To be too full of yourself is for God to show you where you are at. In time, God will eventually have His say, and the challenge for us is to ignore what Satan must display. Absolutely no good can come from the desire to return pain. To do this is God's loss and allows Satan to gain.

The best kind of revenge is to reciprocate with love and rest easy knowing that karma is coming from above. What you as a human could do, God can do ten-fold. It is in your best interest on God to embrace and to hold. He has a way of making things right, and on this you can depend. Allowing God to dole out karma will make you the winner in the end.

There is a person somewhere that you should forgive the same as someone has forgiven you so their own life they could live. Forgiveness is not an option; it is something we must do, for when you forgive, space is freed up in you. To forgive others does not mean a relationship has to be kept. It means to release what caused you or someone else to vent.

Forgiving someone is the hardest task you will ever endure, and accepting forgiveness from someone will allow two people to have a cure. Harbouring a grudge takes energy to continuously feel the pain, and holding on to your hurts leaves you with nothing much to gain. There are many reasons we should forgive a wrong decision. The most important is to give yourself a clearer vision.

If your way is clouded with a fog of discontent, you will not be able to in your life see where God came and went. If someone has done you wrong, forgive them for that. If you have wronged someone, forgive yourself for the spat. It is not always necessary for forgiveness to be known. What is important is the freedom in your soul that is grown.

Whether you repent to God or ask to be forgiven by the one you hurt, either way you must do it humbly and not be overly curt. If the shoe's on the other foot and you are waiting for a sorry, forgive them to God and let Him take care of the worry.

We are fascinated by people who forgive the worst things, and we wonder what this act could bring. Forgiveness is freedom; it means you are no longer shackled. It is to release the pain that we have allowed on us to be heckled.

For many years I allowed people to take my power away. I was the victim waiting to hear what they had to say. Meanwhile my own hurts I was distributing around: their hurts, my hurts, and none of us feeling very sound. I had to dig deep to grasp that the power is all mine. I had to forgive and be forgiven for what I knew was unkind. I started with myself and accepted where I had gone wrong, and only then was I able to return the hurt to where it belonged.

We all have enough on our plates to give us some bother. It is crucial to clean your own plate before picking at another's. What I have learned is that fate plays a role in life and eventually we pay for causing someone else strife. If you repent and truly desire forgiveness for your deeds, God will take care of the rest to fulfill your needs. If you choose to hold on to what you think is owed to you, your soul will not heal and will remain black and blue.

My wounds have healed, but I still carry the scars. Each one is a memento to remind me when I or others have gone too far. I have forgiven enough hurts to know that peace is a better way. Forgiveness is the only way that your soul can have a say. To allow a hurt to fester will lead to spiritual infection, and it clouds your compassion for others' souls and their imperfections.

Never should we judge others, for we are just as guilty of harbouring resentment and staying wrapped up in self-pity. Only when you remove the pettiness that you hold is when God will take over and your soul will become bold. We must always remember that it is only God that can judge, and you too will be penalized if you choose to hold a grudge.

What I understand today is that God will wipe your tears, but only if you succumb to Him and give Him all your fears. You may think its not in you to forgive your greatest hurt, but at the same time you know that there is also someone that you have burnt. To forgive someone else opens your eyes to see where you are weak, and you can forgive someone even if to them the words you never speak.

Holding on to hurt and pain means you want to control the situation when truly you are out of control and your rigidity is the indication. If you are that hard to not forgive, how can your soul be set free? Forgiveness brings peace and harmony to the soul you cannot see. We have all been on both sides, to forgive and be forgiven. Both will determine your happiness and how you are living.

There is only one person in my life where forgiving them was quite hard. This person, I believed, always held on to my life's trump card. This person's cruelty to me went beyond human endurance, and I suffered many abuses due to this person's selfish arrogance. My memories of this person's neglect are too many to count. Love was a long way off and hate was about all they could amount.

The only way for me to get to the place that I am today was to forgive this person and from them take my power away. I had to have compassion to understand that this person is weak, and forgiving this person showed God that I was able to be meek. No words have I spoken to this person because I do not need to. God has heard my words and will do what He needs to.

It is a wonderful feeling when you know God is on your side, and it is easier to live life when you allow Him to help you to decide. In time God takes care of what has hurt one of His souls, and when He has done this, He will ensure you are told.

There is a balance that God must keep to ensure fairness, and it is up to us to choose carefully so we don't have to second guess. Forgive yourself for the hurt that you have given to others and then forgive those who have hurt you and release the bother. God will step in when you do either of these two things, and His forgiveness of you will many blessings bring.

Chapter Thirty-Six – Freedom from Disturbance

How do we get the peace we seek; how do we stop the mayhem that is going on every week?

How do we end senseless killings that are going on; how do we end abuse that has gone on too long?

How do we stop the neglect done to our children; how do we stop this obsession with gambling?

How do we go about saving our animal friends; how do we bring drinking and driving to an end?

How do we cure diseases that we have seen so far; how do we stop wars and ensure there are no more?

How do we stop technology from turning us into machines; how do we ensure water will stay clean?

How do we fix the doubts surrounding the church; how do we build a plane in which no one gets hurt?

How do we teach that all religions are equal; how do we stop child pornography from having a sequel?

How do we stop the destruction after the big game; how do we help politicians to keep things sane?

How do we get back the self-respect that we have lost; how do we understand that love has no cost?

How do we overcome the distrust we feel; how do we ensure that everyone has a meal?

How do we help others to have a home of their own; how to we re-seed love that no longer grows?

How do we ensure an education is given to everyone; how do we stop just anyone from having a gun?

How do we stop a bully's abuse; how do we help everyone to understand that they have a use?

How do we stop high, middle, lower class; how do we stop the discriminations we have amassed?

How do we look beyond the colour of one's skin; how do we instead look at what is within?

How do we stop judging each other's soul; how do we make loving each other our common goal?

How do we stop valuing our material things; how do we learn that self-worth they will not bring?

How do we go about accepting our time on this earth; how do we deal with all our inner hurts?

How do we understand that you get back what you give; how do we slow down and learn how to live?

How do we learn that peace is within our reach; how do we believe in what God has to teach?

How do we put what we think we know aside; how do we understand that it's God that will decide?

How do we learn that there is power in prayer; how do we go from down here to up there?

How do we accept that each of us has a soul; how do we have faith in the life at which we toil?

How do we regard souls as we regard our own; how do we build peace that has never been known?

The Sun Neither Rises nor Sets

How do we make the changes in the way we think; how do we trust in God and all that He will bring?

How do we stop thinking we have all the answers; how do we start coping with our spiritual cancer?

How do we cure the lack of hope in our lives; how do we realize that it is not cut out by God's knife?

How do we have faith that God is there; how do we know that believing in Him will bring His care?

How do we believe that His salvation is near; how do we trust in His way and live without fear?

How do we understand that it is peace that our soul lacks; how do we accept and start to take it back?

How do we know we are the answer to our prayers; how do we get our step on heaven's stairs?

How do we begin to see that peace is up to us; how do we have faith that it's in God we must trust?

How do we own the choices we make; how do we accept that it's our peace that we fake?

How do we fix what has been broken all along; how do we get back to God where we belong?

How do we get strength for life's mountains we must climb? It is done by you and your life's holy rhyme.

Chapter Thirty-Seven — Do Not Take My Word for It

How do you define this thing called love that flies through the world on the wings of a dove? What do you mean when "I love you," you say, or "I love chocolate cake" or a new day? You do not love a human like you love a car, because loving metal over flesh will not get you far. There is family love, friend love, and lovers love too, and each one from time to time covet them we do.

In life, receiving love is a high priority, and in life, giving love is another story. Finding that perfect person to love us the best is certainly what is making our soul have unrest. The love you are seeking will not come from another, as it starts with you and how you manage your bother. If you cannot start from within, then the true meaning of love will elude you time and again.

There are a lot of books written on how to love, yet the answers are all in one book sent from above. The book of which I speak is not an easy read, but within it is planted love's precious seed. The words in this book are printed one way and they have never been changed to what we want them to say. Millions of copies have been printed, and its meaning hasn't changed since the time it was written. This book has been around for the ages and was written to help you through life's stages. We want a quick fix, so that book we ignore and read others that leave us wanting more.

Love is all about facing the fact that receiving love is about how you act. Love is all about seeing the truth that giving love to yourself is the hidden proof. To love yourself is not a selfish thing; loving yourself is how more love you will bring.

It is a sad thing to see in this world of ours how high we have set love's imaginary bar. Our human standards make achieving it impossible and yet God's way makes it very achievable. We have set ourselves up to be filled with self-doubt and believe what others say about us has some clout. He said, she said, so it must be true, this opinion they have of me and you.

How is by giving no respect that you think you should be given the love that you expect? Love is not handed out on a silver platter, but it can be found as you climb your own personal ladder. Every step you take brings you that much closer to beginning anew and giving the old some closure. Love is not to be handed out discriminately, yet it is meant to be handed out to everyone that you see.

Of course, the love you feel when you are with your lover is not the same as you feel for a sister or brother. How you love a friend is how you should love yourself, and you are the key to love when you have no doubt. It is not all about first impressions that we do when we have not learned life's lessons. Judging someone we meet for the very first time is done by seeing the outside and not what is inside. If their outside cover is not what we are taught to expect then we disregard them and give them no respect.

What you see is not always a reflection of the inside, and by doing this to each other we've been having a bumpy ride. For every one person who is judging you brings the total of judging up to two. You are not only judging them, but you are also judging yourself thinking you are the better one and they need the help. It is a game that is played every single day. Who do I love and from whom do I stay away?

It is enough to make heaven's angels cry to see an unloved soul slowly die. The love that the soul so earnestly seeks is the love we carry for ourselves so deep. It is buried beneath all the hurt and pain when our choices brought us hate again. It is not unto others that we should blame our unrest; we should own up to the fact that we are not doing our best.

We think that because someone chooses to overeat it makes them a weakling underneath. We assume that they have no worldly worth because they carry around so much girth. We reason that they use food as a substitute and if they do not stop it, they will be destitute. It is unfair to judge others this way, by what we consider to be the right weight. There are those who will naturally be smaller, as genetics have to factor into the picture. There are those for whom food has become an obsession, and these are the ones that have each of us guessing.

What is the reason behind all that outer weight? What burden is on the inside that they cannot take? Is it as simple as the fact that they do not love themselves that pushes them toward their fridge's shelf? Had they been taught to love themselves from the first day would their lives have gone a unique way? Had they been driven to find their own self-worth would their burdens be less, along with their girth? Had they been taught that loving yourself first would help to alleviate life's pain and hurts? Had they been taught that to carry around burden and grief could be covered up by what they were given to eat?

There is something happening in this world, you see, and that is that we are judging others by what we think they should be. Instead of loving each other for the people we are, we are pushing the envelope too far. It is this for which each of us is at fault, judging others for their decisions made as adults. We make snap judgments by the outer cover and use that to determine if we are better than each other. Surely we set ourselves up to fail by allowing others to determine what our life will entail.

Failure is not determined by the size of your girth; it comes from doubting your own self-worth. Surrounding each of us is our own girdle of truth from which can only come our own reproof. Picking apart another's girdle of truth is not up to me nor is it up to you. When you stop basing your existence around what others think, you will start finding the answers that you seek. How you see yourself is what matters the most, and until you love yourself, down a rocky road you will coast.

You are given the choice to believe what others say about you the same way you can believe what is true. There are those in our lives that we will know intimately, and they are the ones to which our heart we will lead. Even with them we will hold something back to ensure that we do not lack. Loving and accepting who you really are will not be given to you by someone you admire. Their flaws and faults count the same as yours, and their skills and attributes count for so much more.

They are exactly as they are supposed to be, learning about love the same as you and me. How you love someone cannot be right or wrong if you love yourself all along. Loving yourself will not guarantee another's love; what it does is pull you through when it is tested from above. Losing a love from our life leaves us feeling distraught, and the pain we suffer is not easily forgot. We rant and rave that we cannot live without this person who was at one time in our life a stranger.

It is in those times that you are truly tested to love who you are, even though it was rejected. Loving yourself will not lessen the hurt, but it does assure you of your own self-worth. The pain you feel when you lose someone dear is not to be belittled or to be shunned in fear. Believe that the pain that you are going through is the same pain that they are feeling too. Even if they proceed like you do not matter, do not let that perception make you feel sadder. The same way that you think of them each day is the same role in their life that you play.

You have not been forgotten in their mind, and you will be remembered by them for all time. Each day of their life there will always be a reminder because you have become a page in their mind's binder. Yes, even when you each go on and find a new love sent to you from the angels above. You will always remember the love that you lost and know the lesson you learned from it has no cost. Love is given to you to give away, it is free, it is plentiful, and it is in each day. Love is not reserved for that special someone, and you cannot run out by giving it to everyone.

It is possible to love someone that you do not know by knowing who you are and letting it show. Doing this, you teach love by example and show others that love is ample. Getting and losing love does not drain the well, for you have more love inside than you could ever tell. We choose to build a wall around our hearts with each love that comes and departs. We believe that that person took all that we had to give and think they were our reason to live.

They are but a small fraction of your life, whether it was to give you happiness or strife. The common denominator in your life is you, and everything else is a part of how you get through. The world does not revolve around you or I, and the sun will always appear in the sky. How you choose to embrace each new day will define how you give your love away. To fake love for your own personal gain is sure to cause you much undo pain. Faking love is a clear and vivid sign of who you are and what is on your inside.

Loving who you are takes away all the fake, and believing in who you are does a true love make. Unless your own perception of yourself is straight then into your life your own image will you bait. We gravitate to what we think is true by faking love each time to help us get through. Seeing someone else as our own saving grace, we try to escape in life what we need to face.

The perfect relationship we want to find because we think that ourselves it will define. We think another human is the answer to our prayers and will solve all our problems of which we are scared. So we try to be something we know that we are not, hoping not to lose the love that we had sought. Eventually over time you will begin to see that only yourself holds the desired key.

I have been on both sides of the fence, hating myself, loving myself, and wondering where life went. "If I only knew then what I know today," those of us with our eyes open can be heard to say. Why didn't someone tell me what I did not know? Maybe they did, but you chose not to grow.

Loving who you are is a personal choice and will not happen until you squelch the negative voice. Deny it if you will, but it speaks to you each day and helps you to decide to see yourself in another way. That voice shouts out loudly what it thinks you know and drowns out the whispering of your soul. *You are fat, you are dumb, you will not amount to anything; you are ugly, you are stupid, you have nothing to bring.*

Is this what you hear as your inner voice shouts without stopping to realize that it is you that gives it clout? *You are beautiful, you are smart, you can do anything; you are human, you are exactly right, you have much to bring.* Is this what you are not hearing when your soul whispers without stopping to realize that your ego begs to differ? What happened to you to taint your view of love, and was it done by human hand or what you think is above?

Are you thinking that God did this to you when really it was done by someone else trying to get through? Your brain as a baby had a clean slate, and for the teachings of life it did patiently wait. Slowly but surely along your life's way, someone taught you to be the person you are today. Whether it was a kind

The Sun Neither Rises nor Sets

word or something said in jest, what they said to you was their own life's test. They did not always have the perfect thing to say, and they said what they said because they had seen it that way.

Over time we begin to hear their voice as our own and cannot hear the whispering of our own soul. Your soul is exactly as it should be, and it is your soul that knows you better than anybody. Therefore within us we are always in conflict, and we hear the roaring voice and the whisper we miss it. It is that nagging feeling that you have inside, this battle of the voice and the whisper in you where they reside. It is this battle that fills you with self-doubt and keeps you guessing about what life's all about.

Which one do I hear, how do I proceed and learn how to love all that there is about me? You need to take ownership of your life today and retrain yourself to hear what your soul has to say. For every negative thing that you have ever heard, look for the good in it and replace it with that word. Sounds simple enough, you may think, but it is not that easy to come back from the brink. You need to evaluate who you know you are and get real about each of your emotional scars.

How it got there is for you to forgive, whether you did it yourself or by how others chose to live. Stop right now and listen for a second: is it the voice or the whisper that you hear beckon? Does the voice cry out that you will never do it, or can you hear the whisper saying you can do it? The voice would prefer that you curl up and die and the whisper yearns quietly for you to just try.

You see, the whisper is God speaking to you, and the voice is what someone has taught you is true. God is not forceful and will not throw His weight around, and He talks in a whisper so you will stop and hear the sound. He holds your soul close to His heart and He has had it there right from your start. He does not want to see bad come unto you, and He knows that as humans that is what we will choose to do.

You must choose to love the person that you are and believe you can overcome what has happened so far. Open yourself up at first and purge what you think makes you the worst. What others have decided is best for you should never be what is getting you through. Always, always listen for the whisper, and it is then that you will hear what it is you pray for.

There is no textbook written that can define you and what you have done to get through. For if there was such a book, we would each have our own and it would be about the only life you have ever known. There are no patented answers to get you through life; the answers are for you to find on the inside. Following step-by-step programs is not fair if you are not with it and your soul is not there. You set yourself up for failure even before you start if you lie to yourself about who you are in your heart.

Honestly admitting about yourself what is true or false is your stepping stone to figuring out who is at fault. When you accept that it is in your choices that you have a say then you will never go back to thinking the old way.

When you let go of all your many excuses, you will learn to hear the whisper and all that it professes. Loving yourself is also loving God, and this you need to see, for He is inside both you and me.

Dwelling on what we think are our imperfections takes away from the whisper that continues to beckon. Never doubt for a moment that you can be what God knows you to be if you believe in your own reality. By having you want more from life, He is assured that you will overcome your own strife. Love, we think, is a complicated thing and conveniently forget that it is our choices that good or bad bring. Love God first, yourself second, and all else third, and you will hear the whisper of your soul's every word.

When I finished writing these rhymes, my soul let out a sigh, and we are both content with the experience of God's and my rhymes. My humanness says that I have nothing more to say, but my soul is whispering what I will write another day. To sum up what through these pages you have read: it is all about you in all that I have said. If you still have doubts about your self-worth, please start to work on why it is that you hurt.

Do not waste another day on what you cannot control, and accept that your life will be full of toil. Understand that you will never struggle alone and that you have never been alone since the day you were born. Find all the blessings in what God gave to you and have faith in everything that He wants you to do. Your humanness will never know what God has in store to help you to grow.

Do not let others' opinions of you get you down, because it is only in God that your salvation will be found. Our purpose in life is one and the same, and that is to help each other to find love again. Purge the darkness from your life when to God you pray, and always listen to what your soul has to say. Never do anything that will compromise your soul, and make loving God first and yourself second a common goal.

To love the soul that God gave to you on your inside is to love God; in whom each of us He resides. Accept that you are to not judge another's faults, for every one of theirs you have your own to count. Perfection is something you will never see, but that is okay because your soul is exactly how God wants you to be. Look into yourself to find what your life means, and do not be afraid to partake in what is given to you to see. Trust, faith, love, tolerance, belief, and hope, honesty, integrity, peace, prayer, patience, and cope.

Peace is what God's intention is for each soul. Our doubts about Him stop us from attaining this farthermost goal. The sun neither rises nor sets. Believing this allows you to be open to finding the soul you never met.

The Beginning.

Epilogue

I was thirty-six in 2004 when I wrote what I called at that time *Life's Holy Rhymes*. Everything was handwritten to paper and the typed version was done about six years later. For eighteen years the binders sat dormant in my closet. I trusted that at some point that the words written there would find their way into the literary world. As was taught to me and shared in the previous rhymes with you, I was to wait patiently for the universe to contrive the book's path to being published.

Fast forward to 2022. An urgency like what I felt in 2004 started to poke at me, and I knew it was my whisper telling me that the time had come to publish the book. The title for the book came to me in a dream, and I trusted my intuitive self emphatically to know that I was to take the offering.

My humanness questioned whether the world was ready for this book, but my spiritual self knew that all things happen as they are supposed to. We do not need to understand why. We just need to listen and trust the process.

In the past eighteen years my son and I have gone through a lot together. He graduated high school in 2006, started university in 2007, attended college in 2010, and from there slid into the world of substance use, which he struggled to overcome for twelve years. I spent five of those twelve years advocating municipally, provincially, and federally for services to be improved to assist people on their path to recovery.

Of all the things I have had to endure in my life, watching my son struggle with a substance-use disorder has been by far the hardest. My first words to God when I learned of my son's disease was to make it about myself and say, *"I haven't been through enough already?!"*

After I came to terms with that pity party, I quickly realized that as per usual all things in life happen exactly as they are supposed to happen. Why shouldn't my son have a substance-use disorder? Why should he not be given this path to walk? His soul's journey is not for me to determine. My role is to love him while he struggles with this or anything in his life. He does not need my judgment; he needs my love in order for his path to remain lit.

Instead of succumbing to the harshness that comes with loving someone who has a substance-use disorder, I took the voice that God grew in me, and I used it for good. I honestly believe that everything that I have had to endure in my life was purposefully given for me to understand the depths of human despair. To know this despair is to be able to have empathy for how fragile souls are. All souls are weak. The only way for a soul to gain strength is to believe in something much bigger than a human mind could ever understand. The journey to that understanding is by trusting in yourself. You cannot trust the brokenness of other humans to be your answer to how your journey to your soul must happen.

Denial that you are your answer is something our humanness grapples with. We have been conditioned to believe that we need others to tell us what we should and should not being doing on this planet. Our soul gets tamped down because we believe that others know what is best for us. That is the ache that is felt and is what stifles our soul's purpose.

You can meet your soul when you become aware that you are not the noise in your head. Your soul is the watcher, of the noise in your head. When you have come to that understanding, there is nothing you will not do to protect your soul after that.

No human will ever be able to deter your life's journey once you have recognized your soul. Find your soul. You owe it to yourself.

About the Author

Kim Longstreet volunteers for and advocates for many causes in her community, currently giving her time to the RJ Streetz Foundation and establishing services for people struggling with substance-use disorders. She enjoys being in nature and believes in the healing power of meditation, yoga, and prayer. She lives with her dog, Max, in Brandon, Manitoba.

CPSIA information can be obtained
at www.ICGtesting.com
Printed in the USA
BVHW040726090723
666950BV00001B/12